LOKMANYA TILAK

THE ARCHITECT OF AATMANIRBHARA BHARAT

ADWAIT BHUSHAN ATHAWALE

INDIA • SINGAPORE • MALAYSIA

ISBN 979-8-88883-639-2

In memory of
Rashtrakesari Lokmanya Tilak
Krantikesari Sri Aurobindo
Vedantakesari Swami Vivekananda

Contents

Preface

For the past two years, there has been a serious discussion on self-reliance. But there is a serious lack of scholarly literature on self-reliance. This book attempts to fill this lacuna. It provides a theoretical foundation for the concept of self-reliance and traces its historical origin in the 'Tilak school of thought'.

The first chapter builds a theoretical edifice of self-reliance. It establishes self-reliance as an invariance principle that upholds and sustains the political, economic, linguistic, cultural and educational sovereignty of a nation. In the same chapter, there is an analysis of coloniality and its manifestations in five dimensions.

The second chapter gives a brief biography of Tilak. It is written in a particular way to extract basic themes in Tilak's life and his times. Five keywords are used to name these basic themes. The themes represented by these five keywords are explained in subsequent chapters. In each of these chapters, I have translated relevant extracts from Tilak's articles. I have intentionally used the word, Bharat. It is important to remember that Tilak uses the word Hindustan, but I have used the word Bharat in translation.

The last chapters create a framework that will facilitate reforms in our country. There is a very brief discussion of the decolonial and civilisational approaches.

This book is principally a research work that dovetails the self-reliance and Tilak school of thought. It is represented in a specific manner to attract the attention of the general reader and the scholar.

The constitution of this book has evolved from the discussions with my mother. I am unable to express my gratitude towards my *aai* and *baba* in words. Indeed, language is an extremely restricted medium to express your emotions towards your parents!

I am very fortunate to be in the company of eminent intellectuals like Pranav Athalye, Shubham Sarnaik, Chaitanya Kamat, Nikhil Joshi, Vinit Raje, Goutham R, Nikhil Dravid, and Onkar Tamhankar. I am grateful to these people for their help. I have learnt a lot from the discussions with these people. Special thanks to Pranav for resolving critical doubts. Special thanks to Shubham Sarnaik for providing a few essential references.

This book would not have been possible without the help of Unmesh Joshi. I owe a lot to him. He has guided me in a dense forest of Bharatiya philosophy! His discourses on *dharma*, philosophy and culture were instrumental in providing a creative impetus and intellectual basis for my book.

I want to thank Onkar Paldhe, Adwait Wakankar, Nihal Khambete and Cibi Raj Singarvelu for their support and help. Onkar is a witness to uncanny circumstances which lead to this book. Adwait is my dearest friend. Apart from the name, we have a lot of common interests! Our friendship has lasted for a decade. He is a witness to my intellectual evolution and the first appreciator of my writing style. I would be remiss if I did not acknowledge the contribution of professor Surendra Datar. He was my professor during my graduation. He has not played any active role in the formation of the book. But he acted as my mentor during my graduation years. I have learnt a lot from him.

I have written half of the book in *Tilak Ali* in Ratnagiri. I was living on rent in the flat owned by *Shri Vidyadhar Agashe*. It is a divine coincidence that during the period of writing the book, I was residing near the place where Tilak was born! The credit for this divine coincidence goes to professor V V Bhide and my dear friend Kapil Kelkar. I have written the remaining part of the book at my maternal grandfather's house. The loving memory of my maternal grandfather (*Dattatreya Datar*) and grandmother (*Vijaya Datar*) brings tears to my eyes!

Finally, I offer my profound reverence and veneration to the *gurutattva*. It is this divine principle that is guiding me on my journey. I hope this book will be a catalyst for change and play a significant role in the reawakening, rejuvenation and renascence of the great Bharatiya civilisation.

Alibag

मार्गशीर्ष कृष्ण द्वादशी शालिवाहन शके १९४४

December 20, 2022   **– Adwait Bhushan Athawale**

Chapter 1

Introduction

History and the present time are closely related. As time passes, memories fade away. Historical research is all about finding various threads of events that occurred in history, coordinating these events, determining the causality of events, and presenting them in pure and explicit form. Human behaviour is such that he reminisces past experiences before starting new endeavours. These experiences help persons and nations in times of crisis. A person receives inspiration and gains enthusiasm from examples in history. A nation needs to rewrite its history from time to time. History benefits nations if its presentation is changed vis-à-vis changing times and conditions.

There are two fundamental aspects of history one is research, and the other is the conclusion. In research, new historical sources are constantly searched and updated to present them in pure form. In the conclusion part, a principle is determined from these sources. The primary aim behind the study of history is to draw conclusions from the information contained in historical sources, present these conclusions in front of people, and make them conscious. Hence, it is the duty of intellectuals to rewrite and restructure history to give a new direction to the present socio-political discourse.[1]

In the past two years, much discussion has been taking place in the public discourse about the notion of self-reliance (*Aatmanirbharata*).

---

1   The views expressed in these paragraphs are based on an article written by the historian Govind S Sardesai. The article appeared in the magazine *Lokshikshan* in December 1932. The title is '*Rashtriya Itihas*' (राष्ट्रीय इतिहास) (National History). It represents the historical philosophy of G S Sardesai. It is reprinted in volume one of *Marathi Riyasat* (मराठी रियासत खंड १), published by '*Popular Prakashan*' in 1988.

Prima facie, it appears that self-reliance is a novel idea. But after a deep analysis of history, it becomes clear that it is an invariant principle which takes different names and forms vis-à-vis changes in space and time. Hence, it is important to trace the form of self-reliance in the history of Bharat. In the past 75 years, traditionally, there has been a focus on the history of the freedom movement to find references which would be relevant to present times and conditions. Respecting tradition, this book explores the form of self-reliance in the history of the freedom movement. But first, it is important to build theoretical foundations of self-reliance.

The most basic unit of society is the individual. This individual is an integral part of the family, the basic collective unit of society. An individual, family or society have necessities, desires, and interests. One of the necessities is security. To fulfil this necessity, a separate institution exists called a military. To maintain such an institution, money is needed, which is collected by levying taxes. The institution which levies and collects taxes is the government. Tax collection generates revenue that is expended on various organisations like the military. Another basic necessity of society is the administration of justice. For this, there exists a separate institution called a judiciary. It can make, interpret, or enforce the law. But in countries where the doctrine of separation of power is implemented, the role of the judiciary is limited to interpretation and, of course, adjudication. The making of the statutory law is the duty of the legislative body, and enforcement of the law is of the executive body. To manage different departments and implement the policy, an administration is needed. Also, there is a need for society to regulate relations with foreign elements. The regulations of relations with foreign elements are achieved by diplomacy. Thus, the government is a set of political, military, administrative, diplomatic, fiscal and judicial institutions. The government is an instrument through which society attempts to fulfil its necessities.

An individual has many desires. Similarly, family and society also have desires. To fulfil his desire, an individual must earn money. The abstract form of desire gains concrete and materialistic form in the form of goods. The desire to acquire goods translates into demand; to satisfy the demand, the production of goods begins. Often, demand is dispersed in a particular geographic region. Hence, there is a need for the distribution of goods. Hence, well-organised logistics and efficient supply chain management are needed to distribute goods properly. There is also a need for excellent transport infrastructure. With this, goods reach directly to the consumer or to the market where consumers can buy goods. To purchase goods, the consumer needs a medium of exchange, which is currency, often printed by the central bank. When the consumer pays money and buys goods from the trader, trade happens, and the transaction is generated. The production, distribution and consumption of goods (and services) constitute the economy. The economy governs the distribution of resources. Ultimately, it means it is the society which drives the market.

Now there are two agencies, one is the (concrete) government (or (abstract) state), and the other is the market. The natural question is about the jurisdiction of both. The first question is whether the government should interfere in the market (economy). As I have explained before, the government is necessary to fulfil the basic necessities of society, which are the maintenance of law and order, efficient delivery of justice, entering into diplomatic relations, security, etc. Now the question is whether the government is responsible for fulfilling individual desires and if the answer is yes, then to what extent.

Suppose that it is the responsibility of the government to fulfil individuals' desires. Then, the government enters into the economic domain. Slowly, it takes the place of the market. This omnipresence of the government gives draconian power in its hands. Also, it kills the entrepreneurship of the people. Slowly, the government starts controlling society and becomes dictatorial. Hence, the government should not play any active role in the economy. So, what should be the role of the government? The government should play a passive role in an economy. As explained previously, for efficient logistics and supply chain management, excellent transport infrastructure is needed in the form of roadways, waterways, and seaways. The government should set up this infrastructure on a massive scale. Even in this case, the government should accommodate the private sector. Also, the government should provide incentives to the private sector and give an impetus to entrepreneurship. Apart from such measures, the government should not have any role in the economy.

The second question is about the market. Society drives the market. But the other way is also possible, i.e., the market driving the society. The question is whether it is desirable. Those are individual desires which drive the market. The sole aim of the producer (manufacturer) is to maximise the profit. Hence, it is obvious that the market promotes radical individualism. Individual desires have constraints of family and society. For the grand interest of family (or society), an individual needs to surrender some of his desires. But radical individualism breaks all family bonds or societal bonds and removes all constraints on individual desires. Slowly, individuals get addicted to fulfilling their desires, and hence, the market gains draconian power to control their desires and, ultimately, society. This is not desirable. Hence, society should drive the market and not vice versa. We should avoid radical individualism and fanatic collectivisation!

Individuals express their thoughts, opinions, or ideas through language. A language is a medium through which thoughts, opinions, or ideas flow. It is a bridge which connects two individuals or individuals with society. It is a great unifying force. It governs all types of transactions in society. It preserves thoughts and ideas. It is a medium of instruction through which different sciences and arts are learned. The human mind expresses itself through language. This expression in the form of words is literature. The expressions of the human mind are spiritual, intellectual, artistic, and ethical.[2] These expressions, coupled with traditional beliefs and practices, constitute a culture. Culture is a

---

2   Aurobindo, S. (2016). *The renaissance in India.* Sri Aurobindo Ashram (1920). p.12.

definitive and distinctive characteristic of a society or nation. Culture is a substratum of identity. When this identity manifests into institutions created by society on a grand scale and reaches an epitome, it is called civilisation.

Each individual possesses knowledge and culture. He keeps on adding to it throughout his life. Society is enriched by multiple individuals' experiences, knowledge, beliefs, traditions, practices, and values. To preserve its identity, society needs to pass on knowledge, culture and values to successive generations, and the medium of transmission is the education system.

An individual has to discern between good and bad throughout his life. His choices reflect the nature of ethics that he and the society (of whom he is part) follow. Ethics provides a framework which declutters the situation and shows the path of the truth and duty. There should be a reflection of ethics and philosophy (as ethics is a branch of philosophy) in the institutions created by society.

After this rigorous analysis, it is possible to understand the notion of self-reliance. Self-reliance simply means dependence on our own abilities (rather than depending on the abilities of others). The word 'self' in self-reliance indicates a separate and distinctive identity.

Consider an individual who is a part of society. He performs certain actions in his life, taking specific decisions that impact his own life and society. This individual is said to be self-reliant when he performs actions and takes decisions on his own. This does not mean that he does not take help from other individuals. But it simply means that, in general, he relies on his own abilities and, if required, takes the appropriate help. But it is important to note that this 'help' taken by a self-reliant individual does not affect his course of action or decision. In other words, nobody can control or dictate the actions and decisions of the self-reliant individual. This does not mean that individual is isolated or remains aloof from society, but it simply means that instead of being a mere consumer, he becomes a contributor to society. Such individual lives with dignity and pride and receives respect from other members. Such individuals become an inspiration for others. A society consisting of such individuals is vibrant and strong.

The individual is also a part of the family. A family is a part of society. The principle of self-reliance also applies at the family level and subsequent levels up to a nation. The nation is a set of people with a common cultural ethos. A self-reliant nation depends on its own abilities. It does not mean that such a nation is autarkic. But instead of being a mere 'consumer', it becomes a contributor to the world. There are five pillars of self-reliance: government, economy, language, culture, and education. The base of self-reliance is self-belief. I have deliberately assumed that the word 'self-belief' is synonymous with the word 'self-pride', even though I know there is a subtle difference between the two words. S. Gurumurthy perfectly explains the difference between these two words in his essay in a book titled 'Aatmanirbhar Bharat A Vibrant and Strong India'. Self-belief is belief in own abilities.

A nation has its distinctive characteristics. These characteristics are reflected in its institutions. Its society and politics provide in their forms an outward frame in which the more external life works out what it can of its inspiring ideal and of its special character and nature under the difficulties of the environment.[3] I have already described the structure and function of the government and the economy. Territorial sovereignty is not enough for the nation to become self-reliant. The government should maintain law and order, create infrastructure, maintain national interest in the global arena, provide impetus to manufacturing and entrepreneurship, etc. This creates a stable and secure environment for people to optimise and maximise their creative abilities. Each individual possesses different abilities. Hence, optimisation and maximisation embrace all spheres of life, such as economy, culture, language, etc. This gives sovereignty in the field of ideas, culture, economy, language, education, etc. A nation

---

3   Aurobindo, S. (2016). *The renaissance in India*. Sri Aurobindo Ashram (1920). p.107.

with territorial, political, economic, linguistic, cultural, and educational sovereignty is a self-reliant and truly independent nation.

Now I shall explain the meaning of slavery and colonialism. Materialistic hunger is a peculiar phenomenon. A nation devoid of ethics and morality has no restraint on materialistic hunger. If the nation cannot feed this materialistic hunger of its people, then people belonging to that nation are compelled to search for (and dominate) new territories. Thus, people search for new territories, and most of the time, their primary reason is trade. In new territories, these people establish colonies, slowly expand their sphere of influence, and ultimately control institutions like the government and economy. This is colonialism. It is the material manifestation of abstract materialistic hunger. Again, as self-reliance has manifestations in five spheres, so has coloniality.

The basic heinous aim of the coloniser is to exploit resources and drain out the wealth of the colony to satisfy his materialistic hunger. To achieve this aim, the basic requirement is direct or indirect political domination. Once achieved, the next step is creating the mechanism through which resources can be uninterruptedly exploited, and wealth can be drained. The coloniser establishes the government to achieve its aim. With the help of the government machinery, the coloniser extracts wealth and exploits resources, and if native people resist his odious, iniquitous and despicable motives, he brutally crushes the resistance. This is the complete picture of political and economic subjugation.

But political and economic subjugation are the most tangible forms of colonialism. There are subtler variants, such as cultural, linguistic, and educational domination. A coloniser needs to administer the colonised nation. So, he needs people who possess administrative capability. If a vast country is colonised, it needs a native administrative class. The coloniser has two options. The first option is to pick such people from the administrative class of the regime which he has defeated. But normally, this option is avoided. So, the only remaining option is to create a new administrative class. To create a new administrative class, the coloniser starts the education system. This education system produces loyal servants who cannot think independently but can administer the country as per the directions of the coloniser. This colonised 'educated' class becomes the elite class in the native society. This colonised intelligentsia possesses a significant influence and power. Intelligentsia consists of bureaucrats, judges, lawyers, journalists, teachers, writers, etc. These people control and regulate different socio-political and cultural narratives. The colonial education system colonises this class.

As I have explained before, an education system is a medium of transmission of knowledge, culture, and values from one generation to the next. Hence, the introduction of foreign education system destroys the indigenous education system, resulting in the loss of the knowledge, culture, and values of colonised societies. Also, as the education being received is foreign in nature, foreign cultures and values intrude into the indigenous worldview of indigenous societies. Soon, it completely changes the indigenous worldview of the educated class. Slowly, the educated class ceases to feel the evil of colonialism. This is the beginning of slavery, and it deepens when evil is accepted as good.[4]

This educated class gets administrative positions in the government run by the coloniser. This class gets extra power in their hands. The rest of the uneducated people watch the concentration of the power in the hands of the educated class, although the real power is vested in the coloniser. The uneducated people 'realise' the importance of education. Slowly, the number of educated people increases and the degradation of indigenous knowledge systems, culture and values increases. One should not confuse this process with cultural assimilation. This is cultural subjection. Cultural subjection is where one's traditional cast of ideas and sentiments is superseded without comparison or competition by a new cast representing an alien culture which possesses one like a ghost.[5]

---

4   *Swaraj in Ideas* K C Bhattacharya.

5   Ibid.

Language is a medium through which culture transmits. It is easy for a coloniser to carry out an administration in his language. Hence, the coloniser's language becomes the official language. As the basic aim behind imparting education is to create an administrative class, naturally, the foreign language becomes the medium of instruction. This kills the indigenous languages as the educated class gets addicted to the foreign language. Also, as the educated class forms the elite core, foreign language gains prestige. This attracts the rest of the uneducated class, and they also start learning the coloniser's language. This also further strengthens the entrenchment of coloniality.

The base of self-reliance is self-belief. It is important for the coloniser to kill this self-belief of a colonised society to kill its fighting spirit and reduce it to a docile, pliant, and compliant state. Colonisers subtly achieve it through the education system. As colonised society has lost the battle with the coloniser, their morale is dropped. Coloniser subtly weaves an inferiority complex in the minds of colonised people by promoting self-hate through the education system. Colonisers set up the education system in such a way that students would not receive any inspiration from their history. Students moulded in such an education system obviously hates their history and culture and become obedient servants of the coloniser. This ultimately results in the surrender of an 'individuality' of culture, and the distinctive identity of the indigenous culture vanishes. This is the ultimate triumph of colonialism and the epitome of slavery.

Bharat experienced British colonialism in the nineteenth century. British conquered Bharat by defeating the Maratha empire. British started consolidating their rule in Bharat. They created the government machinery to extract wealth out of Bharat and exploit its natural resources. They also began imparting education to make loyal servants with English as a medium of instruction. Slavery deepened, and coloniality was entrenched! But the Bharatiya people offered multifaceted resistance to British domination in each dimension. This resistance is called the freedom movement.

The freedom movement was a multidimensional and collective effort. Many individuals contributed to it. As Bharat was reduced to a dependent nation, naturally, the notion of self-reliance formed the core of the freedom movement. Self-reliance has five pillars which stand on the base of self-belief. Lokmanya Tilak was one of the rare people in the freedom movement who fought against political, economic, linguistic, cultural, and educational slavery. His strategic response to omnipresent and draconian coloniality is encoded in his articles and speeches. A deep inquiry into Tilak's thoughts leads to the conclusion that Tilak's thoughts form the theoretical edifice of *Aatmanirbhara* Bharat.

In this book, I have critically analysed Tilak's thoughts on each sphere of self-reliance. Self-reliance is an invariant principle. But its manifestation into the names and forms is variant vis-à-vis time and conditions. I have given a specific name to each pillar of self-reliance. These names are taken from Tilak's articles. For the analysis, I have relied on three primary sources. The first source is articles written by Tilak and speeches given by him. As articles written by Tilak are in Marathi, I have translated relevant portions of these articles. The second source is Tilak's authoritative biography written by N C Kelkar. As Kelkar was Tilak's contemporary and trusted deputy, the biography is an extremely valuable resource for analysing Tilak's thoughts. The third resource is 'Reminiscences and anecdotes of Lokmanya Tilak' by S V Bapat. These are works collected and edited by S V Bapat, a contemporary of Tilak.

From Tilak's thoughts, I have constructed the grand edifice of *Aatmanirbhara Bharat*. I hope readers will draw inspiration from Tilak's vision of *Aatmanirbhara Bharat*.

Chapter 2

Tilak and His Times

Part One

The political leader gets influenced by the situation prevailing at his time. His thoughts have a definite reference to time. The leader has to accept or fight against the socioeconomic conditions of his time. He cannot ignore them. The leader's ideology gets affected by his personality, ethos, philosophy, and life values.[6]

Tilak was a nationalist and philosophical leader. His time was the time of British domination of Bharat. The time of Tilak witnessed an unprecedented transformation. It was a time of great interchange. Coloniality was entrenched in all spheres of life through institutions set up by the British. Tilak's life was all about the fierce struggle against this omnipresent coloniality. Thus, it is critical to understand Tilak and his times.

Tilak was born on the 23rd of July in 1856 at Ratnagiri. His public life began in January 1880 with the inauguration of the New English School. But to understand the life and philosophy of Tilak, one needs to understand the pre-Tilak history of Maharashtra.

British became masters of Bharat after the end of the Maratha empire and started consolidating power. They needed an administrative class to govern the huge country. Hence, they introduced the education system. Education institutions were set up, and the systematic destruction of Bharatiya institutions, culture, and traditions started.

---

6   टिळक विचार ५-६. This book was written by B K Kelkar. The citation is taken from the E-book version of the book published by the *Shri Charitable Trust*.

Slowly English language took the place of Sanskrit and Marathi. In 1858, Edwin Arnold wrote that most of the advanced students were better scholars in English than in Marathi.[7] In 1856, the Bombay University Act was passed. When Tilak passed LLB, there were about 5000 schools and nearly 300000 students in the Bombay Presidency. The educational institutions comprised eight colleges, 48 high schools, 177 middle schools, one art school, 284 girl schools and the rest of primary schools.[8] In Tilak's biography, his biographer N C Kelkar has cited one letter confirming that people were slowly becoming acquainted with the evils of that system.[9]

The knowledge of the sins of that system does not seem to have become deep enough to produce a reaction against the very spread of education. The development of literature was also not remarkable. Printing presses were few. Newspapers were few. Important newspapers were *Dnyanpraksh, Subodh Patrika, Dnyanodaya, Induprakash, Vartamandipika, Prabhakar, Darpan, Purnachandrodaya,* etc. Kelkar has cited one letter that appeared in *Dnyanpraksh,* which shed some light on the condition and style of newspapers in Maharashtra.[10]

The spread of education was gradually affecting men and manners in Maharashtra. A change was visible in the dress and daily behaviour of people.[11]

Tilak had commented on the socio-political situation. On 18th March 1901, he delivered a lecture in memory of *Vishnushastri Chiplunkar's* death anniversary. It is given below: "Education alone

---

7   Kelkar. (1928). *Life and Times of Lokmanya Tilak.* pp.64.

8   Ibid, pp.64-65.

9   केळकरकृत लो. टिळक यांचे चरित्र, खंड क्र. १,पृ.क्र.६६.

10   केळकरकृत लो. टिळक यांचे चरित्र, खंड क्र. १,पृ.क्र.७४-७५. To get a clear idea about the overall account of literature prevalent in Pre-Tilak Maharashtra, refer to the same chapter from the same reference. Interested readers should also read *Chiplunkar's Nibandhmala.*

11   केळकरकृत लो. टिळक यांचे चरित्र, खंड क्र. १,पृ.क्र.७५. Here, Kelkar cites one article in *Dnyaprakash* dated 18th of September 1871 in which a realistic account of changing manners, dress and customs is given.

does not necessarily grant societal leadership. After the end of *Peshwai*, the respect gained by old historic princely families was lost. The government used newly educated people to build government machinery. But these freshly educated people received an education that lacked the education of *dharma* and *niti*. Thus, the minds of these people were in a hopeless condition. Their old ties had been cut off. They had received an education that was meagre and faulty. These people with half-baked intellect took jobs in governments. Their power was increased, and they started ridiculing and condemning society. In between 1837 and 1874, two generations of educated people passed. First-generation could be *Gopal Hari Deshmukh's* generation, whose condition is expressed above. The social constraints loosened as the second generation of educated people like M G Ranade and *Kunte* came into public life. English education carried out the divorce of morality, *dharma*, education, scholarship, personal behaviour, family status and public life. So, these educated people started picking holes in the prevalent social conditions. Foreign teachers and missionaries helped in this destructive work. It was not realised that building new systems like *Brahmo Samaj* or *Prarthana Samaj* was not the proper way to protect society against such attacks. The people noticed the bizarre manners and grotesque ideas of the crusading reformers. So, people turned against them. Soon, the second generation of educated people assumed leadership. This generation realised that nation could not be advanced only by religious and social reforms. It was also recognised that government service is not the only channel to serve society. The qualities of mature judgement, profound study, irreproachable conduct, moral courage, and sacrifice aroused significantly in this generation."[12,13,14]

The most important political leader before Tilak was Mahadev Govind Ranade. Ranade founded many public institutions in

---

12   Kelkar. (1928). *Life and Times of Lokmanya Tilak*. pp.73-75.

13   केळकरकृत लो. टिळक यांचे चरित्र, खंड क्र. १,पृ.क्र. ८०-८१.

14   Similar descriptions can be found in his early *Kesari* editorials.

Maharashtra. There was almost no public movement in Pune with which he was not associated. He was also associated with many founders of the Indian National Congress. Although Tilak and Ranade were opponents, Tilak respected Ranade and felt gratitude and reverence for him. It was reflected in the obituary article written by Tilak in *Kesari*.[15]

Politics was beginning to shape itself under the omnipresent influence of Ranade. The organised political and social agitation through institutions was started in Pune with the beginning of *Sarvjanik Sabha*. Further, a network of such institutions was built up in Maharashtra.

This was the situation in Maharashtra when Tilak began his public life. Foundation was done. With his eagle eye Tilak surveyed the whole situation, created his plan of action, and started the construction. As the work proceeded, assistants and co-workers flew around him.[16]

In the next part, I will try to sketch the life of Tilak. However, the main idea is not to write the biography of Tilak but to obtain fundamental elements in the Tilak school of thought.

---

15   *Kesari*, 22nd January 1901.
16   Kelkar. (1928). *Life and Times of Lokmanya Tilak*. pp.80-81.

Part Two

Tilak was born into a *dharmic* family. His father, Gangadhar Ramachandra Tilak, was a Sanskrit scholar. He was first the headmaster of primary school and then became assistant deputy educational inspector. He was known for his learning. *Gangadharpant* and R G Bhandarkar were friends. Bhandarkar had given a speech in which he illustrated the qualities of Tilak's father.[17] Tilak's mother, *Parvatibai*, was a devoutly religious woman. Tilak was originally named Keshav. But her mother used to call him *Bal*. To perpetuate the memory of his mother, Tilak continued this name.[18]

In 1866, *Gangadharpant* was transferred to Pune. Tilak's mother died the same year, and he lost his father in 1872. His uncle raised him. Tilak was born a scholar and was well-trained in Sanskrit, mathematics, and Marathi by his father. In 1871, his marriage took place. He took admission to Deccan college in 1873. He had an independent way of thinking. He used to give short but definite time to his study; the rest was spent reading and discussing with his friends. He spent the first year building his body. He attended lectures only if he thought them worthy of attending. He passed the B.A. examination in first class in 1876.

In 1877, Tilak appeared for the M.A. exam but failed. Then, he pursued L.L.B. and passed the L.L.B. examination in 1879. While studying for L.L.B., he paid particular attention to Hindu law (*Hindu Dharmashastra*). It appears that during that period, Tilak came in contact with Agarkar and became close friends.

If one glances through Tilak's opinions at his young age, it can be seen that he had an inner urge to serve society. To serve society, there were two ways open to him. The first was to advise the old generation, and the second was to educate the new generation. The first way

---

17 केळकरकृत लो. टिळक यांचे चरित्र, खंड क्र. १,पृ.क्र. १६.

18 बापटकृत लोकमान्य टिळक यांच्या आठवणी व आख्यायिका, खंड क्र. १ पृ. क्र. २६९.
   The citation is from the special edition published by *Param Mitra* publications.

was difficult, often impossible. It is always better to guide the young generation. Their minds can be trained and moulded to take a suitable shape. Tilak might have decided to begin his public life by launching a school for these reasons.[19]

There is no evidence to recollect Tilak's opinions about the profession of teaching and contemporary teachers. Tilak got his inspiration for starting the school from *Vishnushastri Chiplumkar*. The views of *Chiplunkar* are well-documented. They are scattered in his famous *Nibandhmala*. But the integrated version of his ideas can be obtained in the magazine *Shalapatrak* dated January 1872.[20] He wrote an article about the duties of teachers. It is given below:

It appears today that the learning and love of knowledge have spread much. But it is an illusion. People learn for the love of government service. They do not even have a common liking for it. Along with university gowns, they doff all sense of patriotism, love of learning and hatred of vices. What to expect from others if the teacher thinks at such a low level? The teaching profession is to be followed only when no other option is available. This is the current mindset of pupils and teachers. One dark chain of selfishness binds both the teachers and the taught together. The curriculum is also hedged around. Even the breath of *dharma* is not allowed to enter and 'contaminate' the school atmosphere. But if teachers instil a passion and respect for learning into students and inspire them to acquire the teaching, then students will turn out to be sterling and indomitable patriots.[21]

Tilak's ideas ran parallelly with those of *Chiplunkar* though there were some minor differences in some cases. Both shared the same vision of national education. *Chiplunkar* became famous, especially among young people, because of his *Nibandhmala*. As he had resigned from the government service, he was thinking of starting a private

---

19   Kelkar. (1928). *Life and Times of Lokmanya Tilak.* pp.82-85.
20   केळकरकृत लो. टिळक यांचे चरित्र, खंड क्र. १,पृ.क्र. ९८ - ९९.
21   Kelkar. (1928). *Life and Times of Lokmanya Tilak.* pp.85-86.

school. There were two options in front of *Chiplunkar*. One was to take an old school in his hand, and the second was to assemble a new team of teachers and co-workers. He examined two senior schools. His mind was oscillating between those two schools.

At the same time, Tilak, Agarkar, and others in Deccan College deliberated their future work. *Nibandhmala,* which began in 1874, had already revolutionised and shocked the thought process in Maharashtra. The government was sceptical of *Nibandhmala,* and already it was seen as a seditious magazine.

It can be safely assumed that Tilak did not receive the inspiration of patriotism from *Chiplunkar.* The patriotic flames of *Chiplunkar* and Tilak were lightened up independently, and destiny brought them together. Some enthusiastic followers of Agarkar often claim that Tilak received the inspiration of patriotism from Agarkar. But this is a useless and hopeless argument.[22,23]

When Tilak and Agarkar heard about *Chiplunkar's* desire to start a new school, they met him in September 1879. They agreed that it was more appropriate to establish a new school rather than undertaking an old school. The whole incident is described in *Chiplunkar's* letter dated 13th September 1879.[24]

The school opened on 2nd January 1880. *Bhagwat* and *Karandikar,* initially included in the prospective, had withdrawn from the scheme. Agarkar failed in his M.A. The critics viewed this school as a romantic, childish, and foolish act. The ambition of *Chiplunkar* was to close down Poona High School. It remained unachieved in his lifetime, but the government closed that high school in March 1922.

Along with Tilak and *Chiplunkar,* people like *Madharao Namjoshi, Vasudev Shastri Khare, Nandgirkar Shastri, Hari Krishna Damle* and *Krishnarao Mande* joined the New English School. The idea of national

---

22   केळकरकृत लो. टिळक यांचे चरित्र, खंड क्र. १,पृ.क्र. १००-१०१.

23   Kelkar. (1928). *Life and Times of Lokmanya Tilak.* pp.88-89.

24   केळकरकृत लो. टिळक यांचे चरित्र, खंड क्र. १,पृ.क्र. १०१-१०२.

education was inherent. *Chiplunkar's* address to students before the school closed on May vacation proves it.[25]

New English School developed rapidly. In the first five years, the *Jagannath Shankarsheth* Scholarship was the monopoly of the New English School. The sole credit of that monopoly went to the *Vaman Shivram Apte*, who was then superintendent. Many positive reviews were received from the government and Anglo-Indian newspapers.[26]

The most natural development of the New English School should have been College. But it was not easy. The other development was the printing press and newspapers. *Chiplunkar* was an established, popular and critically acclaimed writer. *Namjoshi* was the editor. Agarkar had an excellent command of the language. *Apte* was also a writer. The idea of the press and newspaper originated in the minds of *Chiplunkar* and *Namjoshi*.

A press was established and named *Arya Bhushan Press*. The first work of the press was to print the 66th edition of *Nibandhmala*. After that, it was decided to launch two papers, *Mahratta* in English and *Kesari* in Marathi. *Chiplunkar*, Tilak, Agarkar, Apte, Namjoshi, and Garde signed the first announcement of *Kesari*. Tilak became in charge of *Mahratta* and Agarkar of *Kesari*. The first issue of *Kesari* appeared on the 4th of January, 1881. *Mahratta* was two days older than *Kesari*.

In the early years, *Chiplunkar* used to write articles on literary subjects. Agarkar wrote articles on historical, economic and social fields. Tilak wrote articles on law and *dharmashastra*. There was no official declaration of authorship in newspapers in the early years. Still, it is possible to trace the authorship by discerning the style.[27,28]

Now I will briefly explain an incident that gave immense popularity to Tilak. The incident is known as the Kolhapur case. A defamation suit

---

25   उपरोक्त पृ.क्र. १०४-१०६.
26   उपरोक्त पृ. क्र. १०९-११०.
27   केळकरकृत लो. टिळक यांचे चरित्र, खंड क्र. १,पृ.क्र. ११३-१२५.
28   Kelkar. (1928). *Life and Times of Lokmanya Tilak*, pp.103-115.

was filed against Tilak and Agarkar, and both were imprisoned. The story is intricate and exciting.

As expected, *Kesari* and Mahratta started writing on political affairs after the inauguration. The articles in *Kesari* were not only limited to the British government but there were articles discussing the political affairs of native states. *Kesari* was strongly opposing the unnecessary interference of the British government in the affairs of native or princely states.

Articles in *Kesari* criticised the native minister in *Baroda* state and his leaning toward the British and conspiracy against young Maharaja *Sayajirao*. The criticism was bitter, but those articles were ignored and did not bring any legal or political action.

The Kolhapur princely state was another matter. The king of that state was suspected to be a lunatic. There was widespread anger against the British and minister *Barve* in Kolhapur state. Coincidentally Barve was the same person under whom *Gangardharpant*, the father of Tilak, worked. *Gangadharpant* and *Barve* were against each other. Public opinion was with *Gangadharpant* and not with *Barve*. It was purely an accident that this hostility between *Barve* and Tilak survived long.

In the *Baroda* state affair, *Kesari* took the side of the king of Baroda. So, people who favoured the king of Kolhapur started sending letters to *Kesari* about the Kolhapur case and the ill-doings of Barve. There was widespread anger against Barve. Hence, the office of *Kesari* was flooded with letters against him. We have no authentic record to prove whether the criticism was justified or not.[29]

In Pune, speeches were arranged to inform the people about the condition of the king and *Barve* and harsh language were used. *Kesari* reported one speech and started attacking the Kolhapur administration.[30] Some private letters (which afterwards were proved

---

29   Ibid, pp.121-122.
30   केळकरकृत लो. टिळक यांचे चरित्र, खंड क्र. १,पृ.क्र. 131-132.

fictitious) were shown to the editors of *Kesari* and *Mahratta.* With reference to those letters, *Kesari* launched an attack on *Barve*.[31] Anglo-Indian newspapers took the side of *Barve* and painted him as a selfless and innocent minister.[32] The actual letters were not reprinted in *Kesari*. The letters were published in *Dnyanprakash. Barve* filed a defamation suit against the editors of *Kesari* and *Mahratta.* Legally Tilak was responsible for *Mahratta* and Agarkar for *Kesari.* But the articles which were responsible for defamation were penned by *Apte!*[33]

The public opinion was with Tilak. But the principal question was not how *Barve* handled the administration of state or how he behaved with the king but how Tilak and Agarkar put faith in fictitious letters and wrote strong articles against *Barve*.[34]

A brief sketch of events can be constructed from the account given by various witnesses in the case. The letters fell into the hands of V G Ranade (editor of *Dnyanprakash*) through a confident man who had gone to the house of *Ainapurkar* at Kolhapur, who had letters addressed by *Barve.* V G Ranade handed those letters to Nana Bhide. Bhide showed those letters to his friends in Pune. M G Ranade also saw them. The letters were kept in the custody of M G Ranade. Bhide confessed in court that M G Ranade was perfectly convinced of the truthfulness of those letters. But M G Ranade refused to give his opinion on those letters in court. It was reported that he threatened to wash his hands if questioned in court.[35,36,37]

As letters were fictitious, Tilak and Agarkar submitted an apology to *Barve.* But Tilak and Agarkar were sentenced to four months of

31   उपरोक्त पृ. क्र. 132.

32   Kelkar. (1928). *Life and Times of Lokmanya Tilak.* pp.123-124.

33   Ibid, p.125.

34   Ibid, pp.127-128.

35   Ibid, pp.128-130.

36   For more details, please refer: केळकरकृत लो. टिळक यांचे चरित्र, खंड क्र. १,पृ.क्र.136-140.

37   In his book written in jail, Agarkar has bitterly criticised Ranade for his behaviour. See: केळकरकृत लो. टिळक यांचे चरित्र, खंड क्र. १,पृ.क्र.139-140.

simple imprisonment on the 15th of July 1882. They were sent to *Dongri* Jail.[38][39] The judgement did not affect public opinion. It enhanced the popularity and prestige of Tilak. Kolhapur king died in a suspicious state in Ahmednagar fort on 25th December 1883, and the matter was closed.[40]

Tilak and Agarkar were released from jail on the 26th of October, 1882. They were treated as heroes by people. A grand welcome ceremony was arranged. Tilak earned a place in the people's hearts, and it lasted throughout his life and even after his death.

On 17th March 1882, *Chiplunkar* passed away suddenly. His death was a shock to Tilak and his co-workers. It was a significant loss to Maharashtra's public and intellectual life and the *Marathi* language. The associates of *Chiplunkar* carried his work. Tilak, Agarkar, *Apte*, and *Namjoshi* contributed in different fields and served the nation and society. The seed sown by Chiplunkar soon evolved into a large tree.

The most natural evolution of the New English School should have been into the college. In 1882, an education commission was appointed. *Apte* appeared in front of that commission on behalf of the New English School and expressed his views in front of the commission. The views represented explicitly highlight the colossal and throughout understanding of education.

Missionaries in India and England had started an agitation against the educational administration of India. The reason behind the agitation was that the government schools were competing with missionary schools to such an extent that the latter was threatened with extinction and the secular educational institutions were Godless

---

38   Kelkar. (1928). *Life and Times of Lokmanya Tilak.* pp.131-132.

39   Agarkar has written a book on their stay in Dongri jail. In that book, one finds a detailed description of jail life.

40   For more details, see: केळकरकृत लो. टिळक यांचे चरित्र, खंड क्र. १,पृ.क्र.146-149.

and irreligious.[41,42,43] This evangelical agenda of missionaries was not a new thing. It is captured in the petition to the British Parliament by William Wilberforce.[44]

The agitation led to the appointment of the Hunter Commission. The critical problems which were to be examined by the commission were:

1. the role of government institutions in the educational commission of India

2. the relationship of government to private enterprises

3. the place of missionary effort in Indian education.[45]

In his appearance before the commission, Apte stressed the following: 1. To increase the number of schools and colleges 2. To make education affordable, 3. To reform the education given in government schools 4. To provide freedom to private schools 5. To grant autonomy to aided schools 6. To make the mother tongue a medium of instruction rather than the English language 7. Not to import education policies from England and apply policies framed in Bharat 8. To generate textbooks in Bharat and to encourage their use 9. Higher education should remain in the hands of the Bharatiya people. *Apte* called it national education. National education aims to create patriotic and dutiful individuals and not to create 'graduates' in western civilisation. *Apte* thought that individuals with national

---

41   Syed, N., & Naik, J. P. (1943). History of education in India-During British Period; McMillian &Co. *Ltd, Bombay*.p.193.

42   Here, the word irreligious is used to complain that the government was not spreading the Christian religion through education.

43   To understand the background, see;
       Syed, N., & Naik, J. P. (1943). History of education in India-During British Period; McMillian &Co. *Ltd, Bombay*. pp187-192.

44   House of Commons (19 February 1813), 'Petition Respecting the East India Company, from the Society in Scotland for Propagating Christian Knowledge', H.C. Deb, vol. 24, cc 654–655.

45   Syed, N., & Naik, J. P. (1943). History of education in India-During British Period; McMillian &Co. *Ltd, Bombay*.p.193.

education would increase the nation's socio-political status, leading to a slow and peaceful revolution. [46,47]

In the school report of 1883, the direction towards college is evident. It is given below:

We have undertaken this work with the firmest conviction and belief that of all agents of human civilisation, education is the only one that brings about the material, moral and religious regeneration of fallen countries and raises them to the level of most advanced nations by slow and peaceful revolutions.[48]

Deccan Education Society was formally constituted on the 24th of October 1884 in a public meeting under the presidentship of Sir William Wedderburn. The board members were *Mandlik*, Wedderburn, Wordsworth, *Telang* and others. Bhandarkar praised all the seven individuals associated with New English School. Those seven individuals were: Tilak, *Apte*, Agarkar, *Namjoshi*, *Gole*, *Dharap* and Kelkar. He made particular mention of Tilak.[49]

Fergusson College opened on 2nd January 1885. It grew rapidly. Kelkar gives an account of Fergusson college's growth in Tilak's biography.[50] Tilak taught Sanskrit and mathematics at Fergusson College.

Tilak and Agarkar differed in the textures of temperaments and posturing of minds.[51] In the early years, the difficulties of differing points of view were avoided skillfully. But as years passed, this harmony waned away.

Tilak and Agarkar held completely divergent views concerning social reform. Agarkar was aggressive, extremely outspoken, and

---

46 केळकरकृत लो. टिळक यांचे चरित्र, खंड क्र. १,पृ.क्र. 165-166.

47 Apte's arguments and defence were so convincing that Hunter praised New English School. See: केळकरकृत लो. टिळक यांचे चरित्र, खंड क्र. १,पृ.क्र.110.

48 Kelkar. (1928). *Life and Times of Lokmanya Tilak*. p.144.

49 Ibid, p.145.

50 केळकरकृत लो. टिळक यांचे चरित्र, खंड क्र. १,पृ.क्र.164-173.

51 Kelkar. (1928). *Life and Times of Lokmanya Tilak*. p.152.

over-zealous. He wanted a complete revolution in Hindu *dharma*. He also wanted to reconstruct the social order. He was in favour of support from the state to reform Hindu *dharma*. Tilak vehemently opposed the views expounded by Agarkar. Tilak was not against social reform but thought it should evolve organically from within. He was strictly against the social reform induced by the state, which in turn was controlled by a foreign power like the British using law. This was the central point in the social controversy. The other issue was the priority of political reform. On the same topic, justice *Telang* gave one speech in public in which he supported the political reforms in favour of social reforms. The speech of Telang was reported in one article in *Kesari*, and the ideological position of Telang was carried forward by Tilak in his usual rationalist approach.[52] The majority of the Deccan Education Society was with Tilak.

Soon, various social issues surfaced. Between 1884 to 1887, a fierce battle of opinions was fought between reformist Agarkar and nationalist Tilak. When M G Ranade, Bhandarkar, favoured state-sponsored reform, Tilak launched a splendid attack through *Kesari*.[53] Finally, Agarkar resigned from *Kesari*. He founded another newspaper *Sudharak* to run his extremist propaganda. He took the help of Gopal Krushna Gokhale. Ironically, Gokhale used to tell his friends that he joined the Deccan Education Society in 1885, and Tilak was his inspiration![54] Later, Gokhale was groomed by M G Ranade. Gokhale was Ranade's political successor.

On 25th October 1886, Tilak became the editor of *Kesari*. He continued his rivalry with Agarkar. Agarkar died on 17th June 1895. Tilak wrote an extremely emotional obituary article.[55] He had become highly emotional when he wrote that article. He also delivered another

---

52   आधी कोण? राजकीय की सामाजिक?

53   केळकरकृत लो. टिळक यांचे चरित्र, खंड क्र. १,पृ.क्र.174-202.

54   उपरोक्त पृ. क्र.199.

55   *Kesari*, 18th June 1895.

article in remembrance of Agarakar on his first death anniversary.[56] Both articles are fine examples of Tilak's sportsmanship and chivalrous tribute to a dead hero. In both articles, Tilak highlighted the excellent qualities of Agarkar.

Most people in the Deccan Education Society were on Tilak's side when the controversy over social reform broke out. But on the question of the internal affairs of the institution, the majority was against the Tilak. Finally, Tilak resigned from the Deccan Education Society on 15th December 1890 with a detailed and lengthy document in which he expounded the reasons behind his resignation. It is reprinted in his biography.[57]

Tilak had firmly established himself as the public leader after M G Ranade. In 1885, Indian National Congress was established. Slowly Tilak and Gokhale were establishing themselves as national leaders through the congress platform. Crawford case is another incident that stamped the authority of Tilak in the public domain.

Crawford was the revenue commissioner, and his conduct was corrupt. (Coincidentally, Tilak's father had lost one thousand rupees in a sawmill, which Crawford did not repay.[58] But it cannot be said that Tilak took personal vengeance on Crawford.) Crawford was charged with corruption. He took bribes from *mamlatdars*. A commission was appointed, and several *mamlatdars* confessed that they had given bribes to Crawford. Crawford was acquitted of the corruption charge but declared guilty of accepting loans and was suspended. *Mamlatdars* who confessed their crime of giving bribes were declared guilty. This is how the British justice system used to work.

Tilak took a stand and stood firmly with *mamlatdars*. He organised a public meeting on 1st September 1889. At this meeting, Tilak made his maiden public speech.[59] He continued his efforts for *mamlatdars*. He

---

56   *Kesari*, 4th July 1896.
57   Kelkar. (1928). *Life and Times of Lokmanya Tilak*. pp.528-560.
58   केळकरकृत लो. टिळक यांचे चरित्र, खंड क्र. १,पृ.क्र. 13-19.
59   उपरोक्त, पृ.क्र.227-229.

made petitions to the parliament. Although the actions were fruitless, his honest efforts brought some relief to *mamlatdars*.[60]

Tilak became the owner of *Kesari* in full title in 1891. The details of that event are not explained here. Interested readers should read cited sources.[61,62] Between 1890 and 1897, Tilak was involved in various controversies. He again clashed with moderate stalwarts like *Telang*, Bhandarkar and Ranade. His intellectual calibre and deep knowledge of *dharmashastra* became evident when he single-handedly defeated Bhandarkar, a great Sanskrit scholar, in an intellectual debate through editorials in *Kesari* in the age of consent bill controversy.[63,64]

I will briefly explain the controversy of *Sharda Sadan*, established by *Pandita Ramabai*. *Ramabai* was a strange woman. Her biography is peculiar and interesting.[65] She was a Sanskrit scholar. She first visited Pune in 1882. Due to her scholarship, people like Ranade and Bhandarkar got impressed. In 1882, she established *Aryamahila Samaj*, whose main aim was to bring the overall development of women. People like Ranade and Bhandarkar supported that institution.[66] She came back to Pune and came in contact with Christian missionaries. With their support, she travelled abroad and became a Christian. She travelled to the USA. After that, she returned to Bharat and established *Sharda Sadan* on 11th March 1889. American Missionary Organisation funded her institution.[67]

---

60   For more details about Tilak's action to resolve this issue, see:
      केळकरकृत लो. टिळक यांचे चरित्र, खंड क्र. १,पृ.क्र.227-234.
61   केळकरकृत लो. टिळक यांचे चरित्र, खंड क्र. १,पृ.क्र.236-248.
62   Kelkar. (1928). *Life and Times of Lokmanya Tilak.* pp.182-187.
63   केळकरकृत लो. टिळक यांचे चरित्र, खंड क्र. १,पृ.क्र.259-262.
64   One should not doubt the scholarship of Bhandarkar. Tilak had huge respect for Bhandarkar. Please see:
      बापटकृत लोकमान्य टिळक यांच्या आठवणी व आख्यायिका खंड 1 पृ. क्र. 156.
65   To read her brief biography see: केळकरकृत लो. टिळक यांचे चरित्र, खंड क्र. १,पृ.क्र.313-316.
66   केळकरकृत लो. टिळक यांचे चरित्र, खंड क्र. १,पृ.क्र.316.
67   Kelkar. (1928). *Life and Times of Lokmanya Tilak.* pp.217-218.

Ramabai said that the primary goal of *Sharda Sadan* was to support and educate widows. She also said that the institution would not force Christianity on its members. Again, pro-reform moderates like *Telang*, Bhandarkar, and Ranade supported that institution. They became advisors to *Sharda Sadan*.[68]

Kesari published one letter in Christian Weekly from New York dated 21st December 1889. In that letter, it was said that two out of seven child widows in *Sharada Sadan* had expressed their inclination towards Christianity. Further, it was declared that the *Sharda Sadan* might be regarded as a Christian institution.[69] Controversy broke out. People were angry. Tilak attacked Ranade and other advisors to *Sharda Sadan*, who were indirectly helping the conversion agenda of *Ramabai*. Ranade wrote one article in *Dnyaprakash* and said that he and Bhandarkar had verified all the objections and supported *Ramabai*.[70] Immediately, Tilak attacked Ranade in *Kesari* and accused him again of deceiving the public and supporting proselytising agenda of *Ramabai*.[71] Tilak published various pieces of evidence that further confirmed the real face of the mission.[72] Finally, on 13th August 1893, Ranade, Bhandarkar and others cut off all connections with *Sharda Sadan*. The resignation letter is proof of the short-sightedness of moderates like Ranade, Bhandarkar and *Telang*.[73]

Tilak emerged victorious again. This time Ranade and Bhandarkar was crushed, and their short-sightedness and weak leadership qualities were exposed in front of the public. After a few years, Sharda Sadan openly became Christian, and their centre was shifted to Pune, and the institution was renamed Mukti Sadan.

Some incidents are ignored in Tilak's life. Bapat Commission is one of them. This incident captures the inherent qualities in Tilak, such as

---

68   Ibid, p.218.

69   Kelkar. (1928). *Life and Times of Lokmanya Tilak*. p.218.

70   केळकरकृत लो. टिळक यांचे चरित्र, खंड क्र. १,पृ.क्र. 325.

71   उपरोक्त, पृ.क्र. 325-326.

72   उपरोक्त, पृ.क्र.325-327.

73   Kelkar. (1928). *Life and Times of Lokmanya Tilak*. p.221.

self-sacrifice and legal acumen. I will not explore this topic. Interested readers should read cited references.[74,75]

Tilak was the originator of the concept of national festivals. National consciousness manifests itself in different forms. It may take the form of developing and strengthening the mother tongue, the revival of culture, historical research, hero-worship of historical personages, patriotic songs, etc.[76] To regenerate national consciousness, Tilak started national festivals. First was the Ganpati festival. It was being celebrated at the family level. Tilak expanded the individual celebration to embrace a more significant number of people.[77] The second festival was *Shivjayanti*. *Shivjayanti* means the birth anniversary of the great king *Chhatrapati Shivaji Maharaj*.

Maharashtra has a glorious history, and *Chhatrapati Shivaji Maharaj* and his *Swarajya* is a glorious epoch not only in the history of Maharashtra but in the history of *Bharatvarsha*. He lifted the country from slavery by founding his kingdom, i.e., *Swarajya*. His inspiration was such that after the death of Aurangzeb, Marathas dominated the whole of Bharat. The British succeeded the Marathas as the ultimate power in Bharat.

The word *Swarajya* used by *Shivaji Maharaj,* has the most profound significance. The term was central to the freedom movement and Tilak's life. *Swarajya* is translated as self-rule. *Shivaji Maharaj* realised that dream, and for almost one hundred and seventy-two years, Marathas lived that dream and ended the domination of the Mughals. Freedom had to be political first, but it had to be cultural. *Shivaji Maharaj* brought political freedom by re-establishing the indigenous empire after the fall of *Vijayanagar.* He also sought cultural freedom. He began dropping out Persian and Arabic words from Marathi. This was the first time the *Swarajya* word was used in the known political history of Bharat, and

---

74   Ibid, p.244-254.

75   केळकरकृत लो. टिळक यांचे चरित्र, खंड क्र. १,पृ.क्र.369-383.

76   Kelkar. (1928). *Life and Times of Lokmanya Tilak.* p.279.

77   Ibid, p.282.

the second was when Tilak fought against the British! *Shivjayanti* was, in a way, a tribute offered to *Shivaji Maharaj* by Lokmanya Tilak.[78] The festival was a huge success. It made its way to the corner of Maharashtra, and even today, it is celebrated on a large scale in Maharashtra. One should offer such tribute to their inspiration the way Tilak offered to *Shivaji Maharaj*, who is undoubtedly the '*Rashtrapurush*' (the man who defines the nation and its nationality) of *Bharatvarsha*.

Between 1890 and 1895, Tilak was involved in congressional activities.[79] In 1895, he got elected to the Pune municipality. In the same year, he became a councillor in the Bombay council. He was re-elected in 1897. His work in committee is discussed in his biography.[80]

The tenth Congress session was held in Madras under the presidentship of Alfred Webb, and Hume was secretary. It was decided that the next session would be held in Pune in 1895. Pune had gained prominence in national politics. But Congressmen were suspicious about how the session would be passed away without any horrible incident. Tilak had expressed his objections to Bombay people in a humorous style in *Kesari*.[81]

The Influence of the nationalist party of Tilak was increasing day by day. Tilak's prestige was also growing. He had emerged as a mass leader. Moderates were envying Tilak. Tilak had defeated them in every controversy. Tilak also had entered the Legislative council. Two factions were evident in politics. Ranade, Gokhale and others led the moderate faction. The nationalist faction was under the dynamic leadership of Tilak. Pune was the centre of political polarisation and soon became the centre of a clash between two political sections.

The issue was of national conference and social conference. The nationalist party was against holding a national and social conference

---

78   For a detailed description of the history of *Shivjayanti*, see:
केळकरकृत लो. टिळक यांचे चरित्र, खंड क्र. १,पृ.क्र.425-439.

79   Kelkar. (1928). *Life and Times of Lokmanya Tilak*. pp.255-266

80   Ibid, pp.267-278.

81   केळकरकृत लो. टिळक यांचे चरित्र, खंड क्र. १,पृ.क्र.440-441.

under the same pandal. Moderates were in favour of it. Tilak was working as the secretary of the working committee of Congress. Tilak valued the successful holding of Congress much higher than the dispute of pandal.[82] He knew that if controversy broke out in the Congress session, then it would hurt the reputation of Pune. He was trying hard to coordinate two factions.[83] But the moderate faction demanded his resignation from the post of secretary. There was an attempt to kidnap his 'secretary office' from his house when he was in Bombay![84]

In Bombay, the moderate party was dominant. Members of Congress like Pherozeshah Mehta in Bombay got anxious about controversies in Pune. They decided to form a board of seven secretaries, two from Tilak's party, two from the moderate party and three from Bombay. Three secretaries from Bombay were moderates. This arrangement was made to keep Tilak in the minority.[85]

Tilak favoured securing support for Congress from all sections of society. He pitched his position further in the committee. But he was in the minority. There were other issues also. Finally, Tilak resigned from the post of secretary with a noble motive that a Congress session should be held at Pune at any cost. After Tilak's resignation, there was no one on the committee to oppose the moderate's agenda. Moderates were enjoying the absolute majority. They started pushing their agenda further. But they lacked the support of the public. The people of Pune were against holding a social conference in the pandal of Congress. People started raising their voices against the autocratic rule of moderates.[86,87] Soon, moderates received empirical evidence of public anger.

---

82   Kelkar. (1928). *Life and Times of Lokmanya Tilak.* p.299.

83   केळकरकृत लो. टिळक यांचे चरित्र, खंड क्र. १,पृ.क्र.443-444.

84   उपरोक्त, पृ.क्र.450.

85   Kelkar. (1928). *Life and Times of Lokmanya Tilak.* p.301.

86   Kelkar. (1928). *Life and Times of Lokmanya Tilak.* p.302-303.

87   केळकरकृत लो. टिळक यांचे चरित्र, खंड क्र. १,पृ.क्र.451-452.

S V Date was a recognised personality in Pune. He agreed with the nationalist party that social conferences should not be held in the pandal of Congress. His association with Tilak disturbed moderates. Associates of Ranade gave promise to Date of not holding a social conference in the pandal of Congress.[88] But later, moderates forswore their commitment.

Date got angry. He called the public meeting. A vast mob was present. It is said that about ten thousand people attended the meeting. Date gave a long speech. He severely criticised Ranade and other moderates. His arguments were straightforward and valid. He was not against holding Congress in Pune but against the idea of holding a social conference in the pandal of Congress. He said that moderates were abusing public opinion. He further said that the Congress session would be a bear garden if moderates continued abusing public opinion; the fire would be set up to Congress pandal.[89]

Moderates were terrified after his thundering speech. They never expected such an aggressive response from the public. They were behaving like an autocrat due to secretaries from Bombay. They imagined fire set up to pandal that was yet to set up! Date kept visiting the site where the pandal was being set up and kept passing comments of setting fire to the pandal! Fire extinguishing apparatus was set up near the pandal!

Ranade received numerous letters. Newspapers like London Times, *Amrutbazar Patrika*, The Hindu, Patriot, and National Guardian expressed their anger towards the obdurate behaviour of Ranade. As days passed, public opinion got inflamed against the social conference. Finally, Ranade declared on 28th November that the social conference would not be held in the pandal of Congress.[90]

---

88   उपरोक्त पृ.क्र. 458-459.
89   उपरोक्त पृ.क्र.459-461.
     Kelkar. (1928). *Life and Times of Lokmanya Tilak*. pp.304-305.
90   केळकरकृत लो. टिळक यांचे चरित्र, खंड क्र. १,पृ.क्र.461-462.
     Kelkar. (1928). *Life and Times of Lokmanya Tilak*. pp.305-306.

Again, Tilak had achieved a massive win against Ranade, Gokhale and other moderates. The aristocratic and elitist attitude of moderates was exposed to people. After this controversy, the Congress session was held in Pune with remarkable success. Here also, Tilak defeated moderates through his skilful and dexterous diplomacy. The president of Congress was Surendranath Banerji. He was coming to Pune. He reached *Dhond* and Gokhale reached the station to welcome and receive the president. A grand welcome ceremony was arranged at Pune Railway Station. Banerji was sleeping in his carriage. So, Gokhale waited. Tilak had given his welcome letter to his nephew *Dhondopant Vidwans*, his trusted deputy. *Vidwans* waited as soon as Banerji opened the Railway door and gave him Tilak's letter. Gokhale arrived there and was shocked when he saw Tilak's letter in the hand of the president. On the following day of the Congress session, Tilak organised a grand meeting for the memorial movement. He invited Banerji and Pandit Madan Mohan Malviya. They came and addressed the vast mob. Thus, with dextrous diplomacy, Tilak outsmarted Gokhale, Ranade and other moderates dominating Congress.[91] There were two noted incidents. As people were on Tilak's side, Gokhale used the word 'brute force' to describe public opinion. Tilak used this opportunity and attacked Gokhale in his articles. Another intellectual skirmish took place between Gokhale and Tilak. Gokhale's attempt to insult the public was exposed.[92] After this, some members from Gokhale's party sent a news item to The Hindu of Madras that Tilak took the aid of students to launch a dispute at Pune. Tilak filed a defamation suit against the editor of Hindu. His motive was just to expose disgraceful tactics used by Gokhale's party, and thus the case was not launched.[93]

---

91   केळकरकृत लो. टिळक यांचे चरित्र, खंड क्र. १,पृ.क्र.463-465.
     Kelkar. (1928). *Life and Times of Lokmanya Tilak.* pp.307-309.

92   केळकरकृत लो. टिळक यांचे चरित्र, खंड क्र. १,पृ.क्र.465-468.
     Kelkar. (1928). *Life and Times of Lokmanya Tilak.* pp.309-311.

93   केळकरकृत लो. टिळक यांचे चरित्र, खंड क्र. १,पृ.क्र.468-470.
     Kelkar. (1928). *Life and Times of Lokmanya Tilak.* pp.311-312.

Between 1890 and 1897, Tilak was involved in direct conflict with Ranade, Gokhale and others. He gave a tough fight in every controversy. Ranade was ultimately defeated when Tilak captured *Sarvajanik Sabha*. *Sarvajanik Sabha* was established on 21st April 1870, to mediate between people and government. Ganesh Vasudev Joshi was a principal member of *Sarvajanik Sabha*. For many years, *Sarvajanik Sabha* was controlled by Ranade. It had its quarterly journal and was managed by a president, two secretaries and a large executive committee.[94]

Ranade was the patron of *Sabha*. Ironically, his name was not mentioned in the membership list.[95] Slowly, *Sabha* established itself at par with the Bombay Association and British Indian Association. Meanwhile, *Sitarampant Chiplunkar* (uncle of *Vishnushastri Chiplunkar*) became the leader of *Sabha*. Gokhale succeeded *Chiplunkar* as secretary. In the annual general meeting of the *Sabha* on 14th July 1895, Tilak was in the majority. From Ranade's party, only Gokhale was retained in the executive committee. But Gokhale was weak as he lacked the majority to implement moderate policy.

Malicious propaganda was inflicted on Tilak. He defended vigorously. He continued his argument and said that the interplay between the majority and minority is not new. He also pointed out that in Bombay, institutions split when the issue of difference of opinion arose. In this case, however, he captured the existing institution instead of establishing a new one.[96]

Moderate newspapers and moderate henchmen started running malicious propaganda against Tilak. He was described as an egoist, a megalomaniacal demon, the destructor of institutions, incapable of doing nothing. Solid prophecies were uttered about the future of *Sarvajanik Sabha*.[97] Tilak proved with facts and figures the mishandling

---

94   Kelkar. (1928). *Life and Times of Lokmanya Tilak*. p.314.
95   केळकरकृत लो. टिळक यांचे चरित्र, खंड क्र. १,पृ.क्र.473.
96   Kelkar. (1928). *Life and Times of Lokmanya Tilak*. pp.315-316.
97   Kelkar. (1928). *Life and Times of Lokmanya Tilak*. pp.317-318.

of the journal by Gokhale when he was the secretary and editor.[98] Gokhale retired in August 1896. Tilak appointed persons of appropriate calibre, and the work of *Sabha* was continued. He continued writing in the journal published by *Sabha*. He wrote a brilliant article on the topic 'Decentralisation of Finance'. This article is an explicit example of the profound intellect of Tilak. It proves that Tilak could write adroitly on any matter topic. Doubts were being raised by Tilak's opponents about his ability to understand the minute details of financial administration. He was compared with Ranade, an economist and dextrous commentator on financial administration and its statistical interpretations. That article of Tilak erased all the doubts about his ability and proved that he could even match, if not surpass, Ranade on his turf of financial administration.[99]

The capture of *Sabha* was a jolt to Ranade. For twenty years, he was the sole authority in *Sabha*. He had found his ideological and political disciple in the form of Gokhale, who was forwarding his line of politics. But between 1890 to 1897, Tilak inflicted an embarrassing defeat on Ranade and his socio-political positions. A new sun had risen, and its blazing flames were burning the prospectus of policies advocated by Ranade, Gokhale and other leaders. Anxious Ranade arranged meetings with his supporters. After deep deliberations and discussions, all agreed to set up a new institution to rival *Sarvajanik Sabha* and counter Tilak. Ranade and his supporters declared the establishment of the *Deccan Sabha* on 31st October 1896. The promoters of *Deccan Sabha* used two words that would play an essential part in the socio-political and intellectual life of the nation. Those two words were: moderates and liberals.[100] Ranade and his followers used those two words to distinguish themselves from Tilak.

---

98   केळकरकृत लो. टिळक यांचे चरित्र, खंड क्र. १, पृ.क्र.481-482.

99   उपरोक्त पृ.क्र.482-483.

100   The entire declaration is reprinted in the following: Bhagwat and Pradhan. (2008). *Lokmanya Tilak A Biography*. Jaico Publishing House. pp.156-157.

Liberalism was used to connote the reformist aspect, and moderation to connote the political element.[101]

The capture of *Sarvajanik Sabha* marked the end of Ranade's era. Tilak also captured his last fort. Tilak established himself as the true leader of the people. He increased his mass base. He also stamped his presence in national politics. After defeating moderates and liberals in Pune, he was set to fight against the British. The British government was sceptical about Tilak. Their suspicion increased when Tilak started the *Shivjayanti* festival because they had to fight with Marathas in three wars, and *Chhatrapati Shivaji Maharaj* was the founder of the Maratha empire. Therefore, an attempt to celebrate his birthday was naturally seen as rebellious.

A famine struck in Maharashtra in 1896. Tilak was in council and also had captured *Sabha*. The scope of work in the council was limited. In those days, there were many constraints on the authority of councillors. The first mention of famine was on 29th September of *Kesari*.[102] Famine gradually increased. But the government did not recognise famine. From 20th October, Tilak increased the intensity of criticism. He told people to be conscious of their rights to implement the famine code. There was a famine in 1876-1877 in Maharashtra. Ranade had sent journalists through *Sabha* throughout Maharashtra and published famine narratives in those times. Tilak replicated Ranade's strategy. After that, *Sabha* sent a report to the government. Tilak wrote a few articles that criticised the famine code and showed loopholes.

Another constructive activity of Tilak in famine was his fight for weavers. He fought for weavers in the Solapur district. He pointed out a few provisions in the famine code. But as usual, the great British government ignored his suggestions. With the help of wealthy merchants in Solapur, Tilak proposed establishing Weaver's guild. This

---

101 केळकरकृत लो. टिळक यांचे चरित्र, खंड क्र. १,पृ.क्र.486-487.
   Kelkar. (1928). *Life and Times of Lokmanya Tilak.* p.324.
102 केळकरकृत लो. टिळक यांचे चरित्र, खंड क्र. १,पृ.क्र.501.

improved the condition of weavers and their guilds. This enhanced the condition of weavers and their families. Weavers carried out activities on the plan sketched by Tilak. They came out of poverty and became prosperous.[103] Tilak continued his service to society, translated the famine code from English to Marathi, and distributed it to people. Tilak criticised bureaucrats and started agitation against famine.

Unfortunately, 1896 was the year of disasters. The plague followed famine. The epidemic made its first appearance in Mumbai in October 1856. Slowly, it spread in Maharashtra. It reached Pune. The government started implementing stringent measures. Tilak heavily criticised the government and advised decentralisation of power and empowerment of local bodies.[104] On the 4th of February, district magistrates were given military powers. They became the ultimate authority in their district. Special plague officials were appointed. There were two options first, quarantine and second, hospitalisation. These measures turned out to be instruments of ultimate torture. Rand was appointed as a plague officer in Pune on 17th February. Tilak advocated a mild segregation policy and separate private hospitals.[105] Tilak criticised the government and people for neglecting to adopt necessary preventative measures. Rand started implementing his horrible and draconian plague policy. He appointed European soldiers to inspect houses.[106] These soldiers began their inspection with arrogance.

Rand and his soldier gang started an era of horrible oppression. Anger was rising in public. Tilak attacked the government through *Kesari* and compared the Curzon regime with the Mughal rule.[107] The comparison was perfect because the Mughal reign was the epitome of intolerance, injustice, repression and suppression. But Tilak was not merely a crying critic but a *'karmayogi'*. He was instrumental in

---

103 बापटकृत लोकमान्य टिळक यांच्या आठवणी व आख्यायिका. खंड 2 पृ. क्र. 371.
104 Kelkar. (1928). *Life and Times of Lokmanya Tilak*. p.354.
105 केळकरकृत लो. टिळक यांचे चरित्र, खंड क्र. १, पृ.क्र.523.
106 उपरोक्त पृ.क्र.525.
107 Kelkar. (1928). *Life and Times of Lokmanya Tilak*. p.358.

the construction of a private hospital in Pune.[108] He outshined all do-nothing politicians and armchair critics. It was established that Tilak was not merely a constructive critic but a constructive leader. He raised his concern about the behaviour of so-called educated people. He was obliged to question since those so-called educated people had flown away from Pune when a plague hit it. People from both ideologies fled. But there was a severe leadership crisis in the moderate and liberal parties. The leadership qualities of Tilak came in front of people. He did constructive work and gave appropriate channels to the working abilities of people. Still, some mischievous moderates questioned Tilak about his work in the plague.[109] Soon, the plague epidemic slowed down and finally ended. People returned to Pune. Life was coming back to normal. But Pune was heading towards the storm.

Tilak wrote a beautiful article explaining the importance of hero-worshipping and the work of *Chhatrapati Shivaji Maharaj*. After the plague epidemic, *Shivjayanti* was celebrated on a grand scale. Lectures on Mahabharata and *Shivaji Maharaj* were arranged. *Chhatrapati Shivaji Maharaj's* firm faith in *Swadesh* and *Swadharma* was highlighted in those lectures. Professor Bhanu defended *Shivaji Maharaj* on the assassination of Afzal Khan. A detailed report was published in *Kesari*. In the issue of 15th June, one poem with reference to the *Bhawani Talwar* was published. Tilak's opponents were waiting for this opportunity. With the pen name of 'justice', one person wrote a letter to the Bombay Times and said that Tilak was attempting sedition.[110]

On the 22nd of June, Rand returned home from dinner for the jubilee function. He was shot down, and news of Rand's murder spread like flames. The government was terrified. Anglo-Indian newspapers started barking as they were loyal subjects of the government.[111]

---

108 Ibid, pp.358-359.

109 केळकरकृत लो. टिळक यांचे चरित्र, खंड क्र. १,पृ.क्र.531-535.

110 उपरोक्त पृ.क्र.541-542.

111 Kelkar. (1928). *Life and Times of Lokmanya Tilak.* p.370.

Lamb, then collector of Pune, addressed one gathering in Pune and indirectly accused Tilak of sedition. Tilak was well aware of the future. But it never affected the tone of his writing. It was straightforward and pinpointed, as usual. One cannot find even an inch of fearful and trembling expressions in *Kesari*. He continued his policy of criticising the government. On the 6th of July, he thundered an article titled 'Is government's head on their shoulders?' He severely criticised the government and also taunted Anglo-Indian newspapers.[112] His blazing writings infuriated the government.

Tilak came to Bombay to gather more information about the government's motives. At those times, Gokhale was in London. The news of Rand's murder was being discussed in London. A representative of Manchester Guardian questioned Gokhale. Gokhale bluntly said that the murder resulted from extreme repression to which Pune people were subjected. He further said that the conduct of British soldiers and officers was misogynist. They harassed and harmed the modesty of women. Gokhale continued further and said that one woman even attempted suicide.[113]

These 'extreme' views by 'moderate' Gokhale created a storm in London. The Secretary of state declared that Gokhale's remarks were wrong. There was indeed a slight exaggeration in the views expressed by Gokhale. He relied on information supplied by his friends and followers. He met the same fate as Tilak and Agarkar in the Kolhapur case. The shameless British government declared that the British government in India never oppressed people in a plague epidemic. Gokhale returned to Bharat and apologised to the government. On the 27th of July, a suit was filed under section 124A of the Indian Penal Code against Tilak before a magistrate. Arrest and search warrants were issued in the name of Tilak. Tilak was staying at his friend's house in Mumbai. At night, officers came and showed him the warrant. The

---

112 केळकरकृत लो. टिळक यांचे चरित्र, खंड क्र. १,पृ.क्र.545-546.
113 केळकरकृत लो. टिळक यांचे चरित्र, खंड क्र. १,पृ.क्र.546.

stability of his mind was not disturbed, and, with usual coolness and calmness, he surrendered.[114]

Tilak applied for bail, but Justice Parsons and Ranade rejected his bail application. Finally, he was released on bail by Justice Badruddin Tyabji. When his bail was announced, there was applause in the overflowing courtroom. People like *Dwarkadas Dharamsi* came forward to provide financial securities. There were discussions in public about the conduct of Ranade as a judge.[115] The financial position Tilak was not good. He could not finance his defence. His friends published a defence fund advertisement before he was released from bail. It was not a case against Tilak as an individual, but it was seen against the Bharatiya public. The idea of a defence fund reached Bengal. Shishir Kumar Gosh, Surendra Kumar Ghosh and Surendranath Banerji worked hard to raise funds.[116] They also send barristers Pu and Gerth for Tilak's case. Tilak arranged papers and prepared briefs for his defence.

The case was opened on 8th March. Justice was Strachey. Nine juries were chosen. There were five Europeans on the jury. Hearing commenced. The main question to be examined was whether or not the nature articles written by nature had a seditious spirit. For that, a rigorous analysis of those articles was necessary. Those articles were written in the Marathi language, and the judge and majority of juries were British! They did not understand even a single word of Marathi, and they were expected to judge such an issue, which was incomprehensible to their intellect. This was a classic example of a great British justice system working at its best!

As the hearing proceeded, it became a lecture on grammar, semantics and linguistics. Different shades of meanings of Marathi words were discussed at great length. The court asked Tilak to explain the implications of various words and why and how he used those

---

114 Kelkar. (1928). *Life and Times of Lokmanya Tilak*. pp.376-377.

115 केळकरकृत लो. टिळक यांचे चरित्र, खंड क्र. १,पृ.क्र.551-553.

116 उपरोक्त पृ.क्र.556-558.

words. There was a rumour that the government had decided to call Dr. Bhandarkar to elucidate certain words and translations. But he was not called. If he had been, it would have been a great dual between two intellectual giants, one with profound education and the second with gifted but infallible intellect.[117]

Finally, Tilak was declared guilty on 14th September by juries, the majority of six. The judge accepted the majority verdict. Tilak was sentenced to eighteen months of rigorous imprisonment. An appeal against the judgment was submitted. It was heard by the bench of three justices, Farren, Candy and Strachey. Strachey was sitting on the bench when the appeal was against the judgement![118] It was carried to the privy council for special appeal.

As Tilak was imprisoned, N C Kelkar carried out the declaration of both papers. Along with *Krushnajipant Khadilkar*, Kelkar successfully continued the running of both newspapers. Bharatiya newspapers heavily criticised the government, while Anglo-Indian newspapers expressed their joy. The difference between Bharatiya and anti-Bharatiya got highlighted in that case. Protests erupted in Maharashtra. Mill workers went on strike; students bunked lectures. Pro-government agencies tempted Tilak to submit an apology to be released from imprisonment. But Tilak indignantly declined to tender an apology. His decline of apology was in stark contrast with the mealy-mouthed behaviour of Gokhale. There were rumours that moderate party people helped the government against Tilak.[119]

Chaphekar brothers, who had assassinated Rand, were caught, sentenced to death, and became martyrs. Tilak's appeal in front of the privy council was also rejected. Tilak was jailed in the year 1897. If one compares jails after 1920 and jails in 1897, one will notice stark differences. Hardships were more in 1897.[120] Kelkar sketches the jail

---

117   Kelkar. (1928). *Life and Times of Lokmanya Tilak*. pp.393-394.
118   Kelkar. (1928). *Life and Times of Lokmanya Tilak*. p.400.
119   Ibid, pp.404-405.
120   Ibid,411.

life of Tilak.[121] He was released from prison on 6th September 1898. The news spread to the whole of Bharat. One English newspaper computed that at least ten thousand people visited his house.[122]

Tilak took a long break as his health deteriorated greatly due to the hardships he faced in prison. He was invited to the Madras session of Congress in 1898. He attended it and did not give a speech. His opponents criticised him and accused him of promising the government that he would not speak against the government. After the Madras session, Tilak travelled to *Rameswaram* via Madras. In between travel, one of the correspondents of the South Indian Post questioned him about his silence. Tilak answered that he did not speak because his health was not well, and once he said invitations would fly towards him, he would not be able to conduct requested lectures. From *Rameswaram*, he went to *Srilanka*. Similarly, after attending the Lucknow Congress session in 1899, he went to Myanmar. He gave one long speech in Pune in 1900 on his travel experiences. The lecture is proof of the ability of Tilak to notice minute details in society, customs and traditions.[123]

The enormous grand temples in Madras profoundly affected Tilak's mind. He said that the colossal nature, grandeur and splendour of *Hindu Dharma* could be realised after visiting such temples. He further commented that those institutions were instrumental in keeping unity among Hindus and that unity is natural and inherent.[124] After Madras, he visited *Thanjavur*, which was in Madras province. *Vyankoji*, a brother of *Chhatrapati Shivaji Maharaj*, once governed *Thanjavur* Maratha rulers governed it until 1855 when taken over by the British. It was a cultural centre. Tilak visited the Marathi people in *Thanjavur*. He was delighted when he witnessed the retention of the pride and love for the Marathi language of those people. He whole

---

121 Ibid,411-135.

122 Ibid,434.

123 केळकरकृत लो. टिळक यांचे चरित्र, खंड क्र. १,पृ.क्र.650.

124 उपरोक्त पृ.क्र.651.

heartedly praised them. The English language spread in Madras, but people from that province were still deeply rooted in their culture, tradition and *dharma*. Observing this, Tilak felt great satisfaction. He visited Pondicherry. He observed that the English language was not much used at Pondicherry. He inferred that there was little connection between the English language and governance.[125]

Finally, Tilak assumed the editorship of *Kesari* on the 4th of July, 1889. The title of the editorial was striking. He thanked all the people for whom him using money and other ways. The grand battle of Tilak with the British had just begun. When Tilak assumed the editorship of *Kesari,* Lord Curzon was appointed as the viceroy of India. The time was critical. British-Afghan war was going on. The famine effect was evident, and there seemed to be no end to people's suffering. Discontent was fermenting in the minds of the Bharatiya people. When Curzon assumed tenure, people hoped for good administration and a promising future. His popularity increased in the first two years. Tilak commented on Curzon in 1901 when Curzon gave his budget speech. He said that Curzon was hopeless. Sadly, his words came true.[126]

Tilak attended Lucknow Congress on 27th December 1899. Tilak was welcomed and adored. His popularity was increasing day by day. Between 1900 and 1905, Tilak wrote on many issues. In those articles, he had to pen obituary articles which became classics. The two are of significant mention. Ranade died on 16th January 1901. In the obituary article, Tilak paid tribute to Ranade. He was in constant battle with Ranade. But he always knew the ability of Ranade and the importance of work done by him. He summed up the work of Ranade, highlighted his virtues and paid tributes.[127] The other important article is an obituary article on Swami Vivekanand. He mentioned the importance of the work of Vivekananda concerning nation and *dharma*. He briefly reviewed his life. He further made it explicitly clear that the only

---

125 केळकरकृत लो. टिळक यांचे चरित्र, खंड क्र. १,पृ.क्र.651.
126 केळकरकृत लो. टिळक यांचे चरित्र, खंड क्र. २, भाग १, पृ.क्र.3.
127 *Kesari,* 22nd January 1901.

precious thing left to Hindus is their dharma, and if Hindus ignore their dharma, they will be subjected to mockery and condemnation. He further reminded people about Vivekanand's message to understand the *dharma* and get back to core *dharmic* principles. He compared his work with that of *Adi Shankaracharya*.[128] Tilak continued his editorial juggernaut and enriched the Marathi language. Significant mention should be of articles about the philosophy of Herbert Spencer and its connection with Vedanta.[129]

In 1903, *Shivjayanti* was celebrated in Bengal on a colossal scale. Almost eight thousand people were reported. Two thousand people were standing on roads due to a lack of seats. The life and work of *Chhatrapati Shivaji Maharaj* were explained. As usual, some newspapers criticised the celebration. Bengali people ignored British tactics.

Between 1901 and 1903, Tilak participated in Congress sessions and provincial conferences. In 1901, the 17th Congress session was held in Kolkata. Dinshaw Wacha was the president. *Pandit Madan Mohan Malviya* introduced a resolution on the education commission, which was supported by Tilak.[130] He gave lectures on *Gita* at Nagpur. The next session of Congress was held in Ahmedabad. Tilak could not attend it because of illness. In that session, one person expressed his discontent about the inefficient working of Congress.[131] Tilak skipped the Madras Congress session in 1903 due to a court matter. He wrote an article in *Kesari* exposing the inefficiency of Congress. He directly questioned Congress about the usefulness of the method of constitutional agitation adopted by Congress. He also demanded an account of the success and work done by Congress in eighteen years. He further raised the critical question: if constitutional agitation is the only way to increase the nation's condition, why is

---

128 *Kesari* 8th July 1902.

129 *Kesari* 11th August 1896. *Kesari* 7th May 1901. *Kesari* 14th May 1901. *Kesari* 15th December 1903.

130 केळकरकृत लो. टिळक यांचे चरित्र, खंड क्र. २, भाग २, पृ.क्र.32.

131 उपरोक्त पृ.क्र.33.

it not benefiting us? He further said that if constitutional agitation is ineffective, we should drop it and try a new method. He favoured spreading the movement of Congress to the general public. He was not in favour of limiting Congress to one annual session.[132] Moderates were not in favour of the views propagated by Tilak. Battle lines were becoming apparent. Meanwhile, Tilak faced a lawsuit famously called the 'Tai Maharaj case'. For details of the case, please refer to the cited material.[133]

In 1904, a conference of socialists was arranged in Amsterdam. Dadabhai Naoroji attended the conference. He heavily criticised the British government. Moderate leaders in Bombay did not appreciate his views.[134][135] The twentieth annual Congress session was held in Bombay. Sir Henry Cotton was the president. Sparks flew between Phirozshah Mehta and Lala Lajpatrai. The differences between moderates and new leaders like Tilak and Lajpatrai were becoming acute. One important resolution passed by Congress in the 1904 session was establishing the diplomatic mission in London. Tilak recommended the name of Gokhale. Even though Gokhale was his ideological opponent, he knew Gokhale's diplomatic abilities and statesmanship. Gokhale did a remarkable job in London. He received a grand welcome when he returned and was honoured in a public meeting. Tilak made a speech and wholeheartedly praised Gokhale.[136] In Amravati, Tilak gave a speech about ancient Bharatiya polity and asked people to agitate for *Swarajya*.[137] The *Shivjayanti* was spreading in Bharat. In 1906, he visited Kolkata, where *Shivjayanti* celebrated with great enthusiasm. During that festival, *Swadeshi* was promoted.[138]

---

132 उपरोक्त पृ.क्र.36.

133 केळकरकृत लो. टिळक यांचे चरित्र, खंड क्र. २, भाग 3, पृ.क्र. 1-72.

134 केळकरकृत लो. टिळक यांचे चरित्र, खंड क्र. २, भाग 4, पृ.क्र.2.

135 उपरोक्त पृ.क्र.3-4.

136 उपरोक्त पृ.क्र.31-33.

137 उपरोक्त पृ.क्र.22.

138 उपरोक्त पृ.क्र.28-29.

Lord Curzon's rule was highly unpopular. Discontent was silently spreading in Bharatiya minds. The outburst of unrest took place when he attempted the partition of Bengal. Partition of the province was not a new thing. There was more than one province in Maharashtra, as in the Hindi heartland. In 1874, Assam was separated from Bengal. Even after that, the civil service was unhappy. They demanded the separation of Chittagong, Noakhali and Tipra from the Bengal province for administrative convenience and efficiency. The plan created controversy. Councillors also expressed their opposition.[139] The government put the proposal on hold.

When Curzon became viceroy, he reformed the proposal. The amendment was done to include *Dhaka* and *Mymensingh* districts. This amendment was carried out deliberately to ensure that Bengal province should shrink to an admissible extent. It was a straight division of Bengali-speaking people. There aroused a huge uproar. But Curzon continued his arrogant behaviour and did not put the partition plan on hold. Initially, officers like Andrew Freezer met Bengali landlords and eminent Bengali leaders. Lord Curzon himself went to East Bengal and tried to convince people. He tried to create a religious divide. He expected his mischievous tactics and magnificent personal charm to calm the rising Bengali discontent. But he was soon disappointed. Maharaja of *Mymensingh* expressed his anger to Curzon in their meeting. Still, Curzon was in no mood to step back. He further amended the plan to include *Faridpur* from west Bengal and *Barisal* from East Bengal. Ignoring rising public anger, Curzon demanded permission to partition Bengal province from Lord Morley, then secretary of state of India. Morley did not inquire about public opinion and granted consent. The partition of Bengal into two provinces was declared on 20th July 1905. The news struck like a bomb. Bengal remained awestruck for a moment and soon rose as one unit to resist the autocratic behaviour of the British. They viewed partition

---

139 केळकरकृत लो. टिळक यांचे चरित्र, खंड क्र. २, भाग 4, पृ.क्र 46-47.

as a sinister tool to divide Bengal and suppress the rising nationalistic sentiments in Bengal.[140]

The first meeting took place at the house of *Maharaja Jatindramohan Tagore*. The telegram of protest was sent to the British government. In that telegram, the logical and straightforward alternative was presented. Bengali leaders admitted that it was hard to administer a vast province like Bengal but suggested other ways to divide it. The partition could have been done so that Bengali-speaking people would not get divided. The government ignored the proposal. A large meeting was arranged in the town hall at Kolkata on 7th August. The protest was proclaimed, and soon it manifested itself in various forms. Newspapers like *Amrita Bazar Patrika* said that the partition was the murder of Bengali *Advait*. Curzon attempted the division of Bengal, but the whole nation united against the British government.[141] The movement against the partition of Bengal began. It was the first mass revolt against the British after the mutiny of 1857. The agitation started on 7th August. Kolkata was flooded with people. People from all classes gathered on the street. A boycott of British goods was declared, and a massive committee of around two hundred was formed to steer further movement.

The prediction of Tilak about Curzon had come true. He got delighted when he watched the ferocious response of the Bengali people. He was hopeless about the effectiveness of the method of constitutional agitation. He was keen on finding new ways of agitation. It does not mean that Tilak was against the constitutional agitation, but he knew its limitations. He favoured the simultaneous operation of constitutional and unconstitutional methods of agitation. He preferred reaching out to the common people instead of giving long but useless speeches in the Congress session. Moderates forced constitutional agitation as the only way to fight the imperialist British. They were not ready to change. Coincidently, when Tilak was searching for new

---

140 उपरोक्त पृ.क्र.48.
141 उपरोक्त पृ.क्र.49.

agitation methods, a tsunami of nationalism erupted in Bengal. He wrote an editorial titled 'Time of Emergency' and showed his strong support for the Bengal movement against the partition.[142]

Two methods of agitation surfaced in the Bengal movement. One was a boycott, and the other was *Swadeshi,* i.e., the use of goods manufactured in Bharat. Boycott, when combined with *Swadeshi,* becomes a lethal economic weapon. Tilak knew this fact. He also knew that common people could contribute to such movements. No records can trace the person who invented the boycott movement. The idea was realised on a mass level. Surendranath Banerji had ascribed the origin of the boycott movement to one meeting in the *Pavna* district.[143] *Swadeshi* was not a new thing. G V Joshi from Pune, one of the founders of *Sarvajanik Sabha,* attempted *Swadeshi* for a lifetime.[144] Newspapers were instrumental in the spread and perpetuation of the movement. The agitation gained momentum. Words like constitutional or legal were left behind. Nobody cared whether their protest was constitutional or not.[145]

The government tried to suppress the movement. But many government servants helped the movement. Universities issued circulars to students and asked them not to join the movement. Those circulars were thrown in the dustbin. The poem *Vande Mataram* written by poet Bankim Chandra Chatterjee became famous. The government banned singing *Vande Mataram.* But the ban became a joke as people were anxious to sing and go to jail. Officers used to get mad when they used to hear *Vande Mataram.* The song became a national song. The Bengal partition was scheduled to be executed on 16th October 1905. Bengali people decided to exhibit their protest in an intense and colossal manner. All agreed to build one big building to signify the unity of Bengal. It was named 'Federation Hall'. The Foundation stone was

---

142 केळकरकृत लो. टिळक यांचे चरित्र, खंड क्र. २, भाग 4, पृ.क्र 50-51.

143 केळकरकृत लो. टिळक यांचे चरित्र, खंड क्र. २, भाग 4, पृ.क्र.52.

144 केळकरकृत लो. टिळक यांचे चरित्र, खंड क्र. 1, पृ.क्र. 95.

145 केळकरकृत लो. टिळक यांचे चरित्र, खंड क्र. २, भाग 4, पृ.क्र.53.

laid by Anand Mohan Bose. At the same time, Curzon was compelled to resign. It was not due to Bengal partition agitation but internal bureaucratic politics. But it increased the enthusiasm of protesters.[146]

As agitation in Bengal started, Tilak also began writing blazing editorials in August 1905. As the boycott movement started, Bengali people shifted to Bharatiya attire and adopted a simple lifestyle. In 1906, the *Swadeshi* conference and exhibition were arranged at *Pandharpur*. There were differences between moderates about boycott and *Swadeshi*. In principle, moderates were not opposing *Swadeshi*. But they had considerable opposition to the nature and execution of the boycott movement. Even in the case of the *Swadeshi* movement, moderates showed pathetic interest. In Maharashtra, Tilak was successful in generating a tremendous response from people. On 20th August 1906, in *Sarvajanik Sabha*, the gathering of students was arranged. Tilak was the president. In that gathering, foreign clothes were burnt. One of the students was V D Savarkar, who also gave a fiery speech.[147] As usual, Tilak gave a philosophical touch to the boycott movement and called it *Bahishkaryoga*. Moderates raised concerns and tried hard to discourage people. They raised some stupid questions, which Tilak answered through his articles in *Kesari*.[148]

1905 Congress session was held at Banaras, and G K Gokhale was the president. Gokhale gave an aggressive speech. The aggressiveness in his speech surprised many people! Times even expressed the regret that Gokhale had made a huge mistake by leaving the moderate camp! Lala Lajpatrai also gave an aggressive speech. Curzon was compared with the Mughal despot *Aurangzeb*. *Swadeshi* and the boycott movement were appreciated. Moderates didn't support the boycott but at least didn't oppose it. The other influential agenda in front of 1905 was national education. The plan for national education and the work of Banaras Hindu University (BHU) received the forward push. On 31st October

---

146 उपरोक्त पृ.क्र.55-57.
147 उपरोक्त पृ.क्र.62-65.
148 *Kesari, 22nd August 1905, 5th September 1905, 12th December 1905.*

1905, in Banaras Town Hall, *Pandit Madan Mohan Malviya* represented the concept of a Hindu University. Surendranath Banerji approved it. Tilak also enthusiastically supported the idea.[149]

The 1906 Congress session was arranged in Kolkata. Bipin Chandra Pal recommended the name of Tilak for presidentship. *Dadasaheb Khaparde* suggested the name of Lala Lajpatrai. Moderates were terrified. Finally, the name of Dadabhai Naoroji became final. Tilak anticipated the bold and fiery speech from Dadabhai. He even predicted it in *Kesari* before the Congress session. His predictions came true. Dadabhai gave an extremely aggressive speech.

Phirozshah Mehta opposed the resolution of *Swadeshi*. But it was passed. Gokhale and other moderates opposed the resolution of the boycott. They were not in favour of using the platform of Congress for the boycott movement. Bipin Chandra Pal further contemplated the meaning of the boycott and exemplified its structure. After the Kolkata Congress session, Tilak gave a lecture at Kolkata square college on the presidentship of Bipin Chandra Pal. The topic was: 'New party and its directions.' In his speech, Tilak said: "Two new words had made their space in public discourse. But they have relative meanings. This is because the moderates might become extremists tomorrow, and extremists might become moderates tomorrow. We use those words specifically to show division within us. The path of petitions and requests is useless and hopeless. We should continue our protest till we gain our final goal of *Swarajya*."[150] The 1906 Congress session was remarkable in the history of the freedom struggle. The nationalist sentiment took over the Congress session. Tilak expressed his win with a roar in *Kesari* on 1st January 1907. He said that the ideology of the nationalist camp had influenced congress. This fact was also admitted by the Englishman, who said that Congress had gone into the hands of extremists.[151]

---

149 केळकरकृत लो. टिळक यांचे चरित्र, खंड क्र. २, भाग 4,पृ.क्र.42-44.

150 उपरोक्त पृ.क्र.79-81.

151 उपरोक्त पृ.क्र.74-75.

National education received a boost due to the Bengal partition movement. On 15th August 1906, National College and school were inaugurated in Kolkata. The aim was to embed qualities of character and national sentiment. In the same month, in Pune, *Maharashtra, Vudyaprasarak Mandali* was established. Deshmukh, *Khare,* and *Vijapurkar* founded *Samartha Vidyalaya.* Tilak was popular with students. Tilak began his public life in the field of education. He was among the founders of national education. According to Tilak, national education is one that creates a nationalist attitude.[152] He worked hard to spread national education. He started giving speeches to spread national education. On 14th September 1907, he gave a speech in Pune in which he said that government education was corrupting students' minds and that national sentiment must be awakened.[153] On 27th February 1908, Tilak gave another speech at Solapur in which he said the following:

"National education helps the student recognise the nationhood of nation. English is not our language. We are learning it because it is the language of our rulers. If it had been possible in my childhood to obtain education in my mother tongue, then I would have gained all the knowledge I had gained up to this age (When Tilak gave that particular speech, his age was approximately fifty-two.) at the age of twenty-five or thirty."[154] National education spread throughout Maharashtra due to the vigorous efforts taken by Tilak.

The provincial conference of Bombay province was arranged at Surat. Moderates dominated it. *Bhalchandra Bhatavadekar* was the president. In the presidential address, he criticised the nationalist party. He tried to push forward the moderate's agenda of petitions and requests. He also gave a certificate of liberalism to the government. Mehta opposed the resolution of national education brought by Kelkar. When voting took place, Kelkar gained the majority. But the president issued a veto. Tilak heavily criticised the provincial conference and also

---

152 केळकरकृत लो. टिळक यांचे चरित्र, खंड क्र. २, भाग 5,पृ.क्र.9.
153 उपरोक्त पृ.क्र.17.
154 उपरोक्त पृ.क्र.18-19.

Bhatavadekar's presidential address. He remarked that such moderate leaders were hopeless in national politics. Different political meetings were arranged. In *Varhad* provincial conference, moderates opposed *Vande Mataram.* Thousands of people gathered to listen to speeches on national education, boycott, *Swadeshi* and *Swarajya.* Most of the provinces were supporting the rising nationalist party.[155]

In the 1906 general election of Britain, the conservative party was defeated. Sir Henry Campbell of the liberal party formed the government. Liberals had won 397 seats. The rise of the liberal party in England delighted many people, especially moderates, in Bharat. Morley was appointed as secretary of state to India. Moderates were expecting the rollback of the Bengal partition by Morley. But in his maiden speech, Morley defended the Bengal partition and refused to repel it. Moderates became anxious. Tilak wrote that instead of criticising Morley for his behaviour, one should blame moderates for their stupidity and devotion towards Morley. He wrote a beautiful article in *Kesari* titled 'Philosopher and Diplomat'.[156]

Another round of war began between Gokhale and Tilak. Gokhale preached the moderate doctrine of constitutional and legal methods of agitation. Tilak wrote an excellent article in *Kesari* on 5th March 1907. In that article, he exposed faults in Gokhale's arguments. The aggressive rationalist approach of Tilak was irrefutable for Gokhale. The title of the article was 'Constitutional and legal'.

The 1906 Kolkata Congress session was highly polarising. Ideological differences that surfaced in the movement became sharp and clear in that session. Moderates were unhappy as the resolutions of *Swadeshi* and the boycott were passed. Some of the nationalists were having thoughts of starting a new congress. Tilak strongly opposed the idea. Both camps were eagerly waiting for the next session of Congress. He was preparing for the democratic capture of Congress.[157]

---

155 केळकरकृत लो. टिळक यांचे चरित्र, खंड क्र. २, भाग 5,पृ.क्र.29-31.

156 उपरोक्त पृ.क्र.32-33.

157 केळकरकृत लो. टिळक यांचे चरित्र, खंड क्र. २, भाग 5,पृ.क्र.39.

The nationalist party was in the majority but did not have a two-thirds majority. It was possible that the nationalist party could establish their president. Moderates sought the reconstruction of the executive council. They called an assembly on 22nd October. But the debate took place about the legality of organising such meetings, and moderates were forced to confess that the meeting was illegal. First, it was decided that the congress should be held in Lahore. But moderates knew that if a congress session were held at Lahore, nationalists would dominate it, and Tilak would become president. So, they choose Nagpur. But even the public opinion of Nagpur was with Tilak. Tilak was contemplating the moderate's strategies. Still, he argued against the split in congress in the 8th October issue of *Kesari*. He further said that the ideology was essential and not personal conflicts.[158] But moderates were not ready to tolerate the rise of the nationalist party.

After deliberations and discussions, *Surendranath Banerji's* name emerged for the presidency. Nagpur people suggested the name Tilak. The prospectus of Tilak becoming the congress president sent waves of terror in the moderate camp. One meeting was arranged at Mehta's bungalow to resolve the conflict. It went in vain. Finally, the All India Congress Committee (AICC) meeting was organised on 10th November to settle the issue again in Mehta's bungalow. Many people were absent, but they favoured holding the congress session at Nagpur. Along with Tilak, thirteen people were present. Proceedings of the meeting started. Various compromises were suggested. However, Mehta and Gokhale had planned a conspiracy. They had arranged a secret deputation from Surat. That deputation from Surat suddenly came forward and submitted an invitation to hold a congress at Surat on behalf of the people of Surat. After that, the voting was nominal. Tilak refused to vote, and the congress session was shifted to Surat.[159] Surat was chosen because nationalists were not in the majority in Surat. Nagpur was not treated fairly.

---

158 उपरोक्त पृ.क्र.40.
159 केळकरकृत लो. टिळक यांचे चरित्र, खंड क्र. २, भाग 5,पृ.क्र.41-42.

Tilak was in an extreme state of anger due to the autocratic nature and monarchical behaviour of Mehta and Gokhale. Still, he kept calm and maintained the peace.

Lala Lajpatrai was released on 11th November. The whole of Bharat celebrated his release. Letters and telegrams were sent to the reception committee to appoint Lala Lajpatrai as president of the Surat congress session. Moderates received another shock. Mehta sent Gokhale and other moderates to Surat to 'take care' of preparations for the congress session. Gokhale persuaded the people of Surat to veto the name of Lala Lajpatrai for president. Finally, *Ambalal Sakarlal* made it explicitly clear that the moderates were holding the All India Congress Committee in their hands, and the name of Rash Behari Ghosh was declared for presidentship as the nationalist party had already left the meeting.[160] Tilak sarcastically remarked in the 3rd December issue of *Kesari* that the upcoming session was not the twenty-third session but the session of 'Mehta and company'. He further stated that Mehta had abused public opinion, and there was no difference between tyrannical British rule and the arrogant behaviour of Mehta. Public opinion was against Mehta and others. Letters and telegrams were sent to elect Lala Lajpatarai as president. But moderates were acting as deaf to the demands of the people. It was a battle between AICC bureaucrats and public opinion. Tilak advised nationalists to go to the Surat session and warned them to maintain their behaviour.[161]

The 1907 Surat session was one of the stormiest sessions in the history of congress. From the beginning, signs were clear that the session would be stormy. There was only one reason. Many provinces supported the resolutions of *Swadeshi, Swarajya,* Boycott and National Education. But Mehta, Gokhale and other moderates were anxious to repel those four pillars. That is why they had moved the venue of Congress from Nagpur to Surat to accomplish their sinister plan of

---

160 उपरोक्त पृ.क्र.43-44.
161 केळकरकृत लो. टिळक यांचे चरित्र, खंड क्र. २, भाग 5, पृ.क्र.44-45.

rolling back of four-pillar resolutions passed in the Kolkata session of congress.[162]

Gokhale was a member of the reception committee. The reception committee's draft of resolutions was unavailable until the congress met.[163] Tilak reached Surat on 23rd December. The reception committee did not receive him. But the nationalist party offered him a grand welcome. He gave a speech in front of four to five thousand people. He explicitly stated that his intentions were not splitting the congress but that the nationalist party would oppose the moderate's agenda to subdue Kolkata resolutions. Fake news was circulated that Tilak wrote terrible things about the Gujrati people in *Kesari*.[164]

On 24th December, a conference of the nationalist party was arranged. Shri Aravind Ghosh chaired it. Nationalists discussed their strategy. It was decided that the truce would only occur if moderates agreed to keep Kolkata resolutions. Lala Lajpatrai reached Surat on 24th December. The reception committee did not welcome him. But the people of Surat offered him a grand welcome. The irony was that the president and Mehta received a mild reception. The reception received by Tilak and Lala Lajpatrai overshadowed Mehta and the president.[165] Winds were blowing. Both camps were anxious. The war was set to begin.

The session started on 27th December. Malvi was the chairman of the reception committee. He gave a long speech, and the name of Rash Behari Ghosh was proposed as president. Shouts and noises erupted. Surendranath Banerji seconded the proposal. The screams and noises became more intense. People from both camps were shouting. Finally, proceedings were adjourned to the next day. Tilak was trying hard to find the middle ground. But moderates were not responding. Moderates tried to defame Tilak. They asked the people

---

162 केळकरकृत लो. टिळक यांचे चरित्र, खंड क्र. २, भाग 6,पृ.क्र.2-3.

163 Sitaramayya, Pattabhi. *History of the Indian National Congress, Vol. 1*. 1935. p.96.

164 केळकरकृत लो. टिळक यांचे चरित्र, खंड क्र. २, भाग 6,पृ.क्र.7.

165 उपरोक्त,पृ.क्र.8-9.

of Surat to stand against Tilak. Moderates even arranged bouncers and prohibited some people from the nationalist party from entering the session. Proceedings began on the next day. Banerji continued his speech. Tilak had handed a slip to Malvi informing him that he wished to address delegates on the proposal of the president's election when it is seconded. Also, he wanted to move an amendment with a constructive proposal. Tilak did not receive any response from Malvi. The slip sent by Tilak was not attended to despite the warning given by him. As the proposal was seconded, Tilak proceeded to the platform to address delegates and began his talk.[166] Rash Behari Ghosh immediately started his speech, assuming he had been elected. Tilak stopped him and said that he was about to oppose the proposal. Shouts and noises began. Swear words and abusive language were used against Tilak. One person even attempted to throw a chair at Tilak. People gathered by the moderate party started moving toward the platform. Supporters of the nationalist party also ran towards the platform. A shoe was thrown towards the platform, and Mehta and Banerji got hit.[167] Moderate hooligans attacked nationalist people, and some of them got seriously injured.[168] Melancholy and cacophony loomed over the congress session. Finally, the police came, peace was restored, and the blame game began.

The reception committee published the 'true' account of that day. They accused nationalists of planning the squabble. They put all the blame on Tilak. The Nationalist party also published their report in which the arrogant and autocratic behaviour of moderates was exposed.[169] (Henry Nevinson also reported the account of the Surat session in his book.[170] He also described the personality of Tilak in the same book.[171])

---

166 Sitaramayya, Pattabhi. *History of the Indian National Congress, Vol. 1.* 1935. p.97.

167 केळकरकृत लो. टिळक यांचे चरित्र, खंड क्र. २, भाग 6,पृ.क्र.12-13.

168 बापटकृत लोकमान्य टिळक यांच्या आठवणी व आख्यायिका खंड 1 पृ. क्र.152-154,160-161.

169 केळकरकृत लो. टिळक यांचे चरित्र, खंड क्र. २, भाग 6 पृ.क्र.14-15.

170 Nevinson, H. W. (1908). *The new spirit in India.* London and New York, Harper & brothers. pp.233-262.

171 Ibid, pp.62-77.

Mehta and other moderates were anxious to form a new party. Some attempts to restore peace and continuation of proceedings were made. On the 27th of December, Tilak said nationalists would accept Ghosh as president, but Kolkata resolutions should not be touched. Moderates declined all the attempts at a truce and started their new convention.

Tilak gave his account: "Both sides were pertinacious about their demands. The pertinacity is not the problem; even *Pandavas* were also pertinacious. The only question is whose demands are genuine. To whom should we listen, Maharshi from Kolkata or Aurangzeb from Mumbai? Why does it take one month for someone like Gokhale to prepare a draft? These facts indicate that moderates did not favour revealing the draft proposals. If moderates are happy with schism, then it would not be wrong to say that they are responsible for schism."[172]

Tilak was anxious to spread the nationalist party. He invited Shri Aravind to Pune. Shri Aravind was also a great nationalist leader. It would not be wrong to say that he was an extreme extremist! Aravind gave an energetic and enthusiastic lecture in Pune. In that lecture, he explained how old leaders in Bengal opposed boycott movements and the national education movement. Still, they were obliged to support those movements due to strong public opinion and the participation of the younger generation. He further said that "We should not discuss the true or false evils in our nation all the time. Instead of that, we should induce sentiments of pride, belief, and power in the people's minds and should guide people towards the path of the reawakening of the nation. This principle was preached by the Swami Vivekananda and is at the root of the movement against the Bengal partition."[173] He gave further lectures in Nashik and Dhule and returned to Bengal to attend the provincial conference.

In February 1908, in Mumbai, the National Publishing Company was instituted. Tilak was among the founder directors. The company

---

172 केळकरकृत लो. टिळक यांचे चरित्र, खंड क्र. २, भाग 6,पृ.क्र.27-28.
173 केळकरकृत लो. टिळक यांचे चरित्र, खंड क्र. २, भाग 7,पृ.क्र.1-2.

launched a new Marathi daily named *Rashtramat.* The ideology of *Rashtramat* was based on four pillars: *Swadesh, Swadharma, Swarajya* and self-reliance. Also, it was proposed to shift the *Samartha Vidyalaya* of Satara to Talegaon.[174] Tilak continued his work of spreading the nationalist party. His party got significant success in the Pune municipality elections. When schism took place in Surat, moderates thought Tilak would be finished. They were proven wrong. Public opinion was with Tilak. Even Times took notice of the rise of Tilak.[175]

In March 1908, Tilak appeared before the decentralisation commission. He opposed the increase in the powers of collectors. He said the rights should be given to the people rather than bureaucrats. He also took part in the anti-drink campaign.[176]

The schism was reality, and there was no sign of compromise. In February 1908, Tilak wrote one article in *Kesari* titled 'How is truce possible?'. He again highlighted the need for a joint congress. He also discussed the root cause of schism in congress. He declared that the root cause was the intention of moderates to establish the moderate party as the only party of congress controlling its narratives and prohibit another party from joining it. He continued, "Moderates like Mehta were astonished when they witnessed the rise of the nationalist party. The government started questioning the loyalty of moderates and asked them to condemn the new party. Moderates were trapped in the crisis. Nationalists were gaining public support, and moderates were preaching their old methods of petition and prayer. To counter the crisis, moderates planned the conspiracy at Surat."[177]

Tilak faced the second sedition case in 1908. A Series of bomb blasts in Bengal in 1908 stunned the British government. British were anxious to crush the revolutionaries and those who induced unrest in the Bharatiya people. Tilak was the most suitable candidate!

---

174 उपरोक्त पृ.क्र.2-3.
175 उपरोक्त पृ.क्र.6-7.
176 उपरोक्त पृ.क्र.7-15.
177 केळकरकृत लो. टिळक यांचे चरित्र, खंड क्र. २, भाग 7,पृ.क्र.21-23.

After all, he was the father of Bharatiya unrest. On 23rd June 1908, the provincial government of Bombay filed a suit against Tilak. The case was filed based on articles on 12th May 1908 in which Tilak had criticised the government. Warrants were issued, and Tilak was arrested. He was fearless and careless about the ultimate result of the case. Tilak's house and office of *Kesari* were searched. After almost two and half hours of search, a piece of paper was found in which some information related to bombs was written. Also, Tilak had written articles in which sympathy was shown to revolutionaries. Police were happy as they had found 'substantive' evidence. As usual, Tilak was not released on bail by Justice Davar. Ironically, Davar was the barrister defending Tilak in the first sedition case, and Tilak was released on bail![178]

A special jury was appointed. There were nine juries, of which seven juries were European. Branson was the advocate general. Hearing commenced. Again, in that case, the question was whether the articles written were seditious and whether there was even a deliberate attempt from Tilak to induce emotion of sedition against the government in the minds of the people. Articles were written in Marathi, and most juries were European who did not know Marathi. The same play was repeated. Only barristers, judges and juries were changed, and the accused was the same person! Tilak gave a marvellous speech. He said: "Every article written by me is represented as having seditious nature. So, I must discuss every word and the semantics and linguistics governing it. Every language has its style. Words uttered in language can have different meanings other than dictionary meanings. The meaning attached to the word is relative to the reason behind the use of the word, the situation and the context in which the word is used. The translations are in front of you and not the original articles. The question is not whether words induced sedition, but the real question is whether the actual sedition was attempted or not. There is absolutely

---

178 केळकरकृत लो. टिळक यांचे चरित्र, खंड क्र. २, भाग 8,पृ.क्र.7-10.

no evidence that proves that articles written by me are responsible for sedition. If opium is found at someone's house, then the crime will be illegally holding the opium and not of will be of attempting murder or suicide using the opium.

If I say there is unrest in people, it does not mean I am attempting sedition. I have spoken the truth. All of the political reforms were the results of political agitation. There is a difference between speech and action. If I want to be a billionaire, does it mean I am attempting burglary? An article is invariant, but its effect and meaning are subject to change. It's my duty as an editor to write articles. An editor is an independent person. When revolutionary activities erupted in Bengal, my duty was, to tell the truth to the government. I know that the government hates the truth and those who speak it. Newspapers are there to advise the government. If some issue surfaces today, editors are obliged to write on that issue. We have to take a side; the conflict is inevitable when the opposite narrative emerges. When Pioneer sided with the government and condemned bomb blasts, I asked them to analyse the reason behind those bomb blasts. Both newspapers were sad about the bomb blasts, but their positions differed. I have spoken the public opinion. Why do we need newspapers if I cannot express a public opinion? Why is freedom not granted to us when given to Anglo-Indian newspapers?

The government never explicitly expressed its view. It was the job of Anglo-Indian newspapers to propagate the opinions of the government. I told my opinion, which favours political reform. Suppose the government does political reforms and gives more power in the hands of the people. In that case, the unrest spread will dilute, and revolutionary activities will calm down. Pioneer says the same things about the Russian Tsar and the revolution. It said that the revolution in Russia was the direct effect of the misdoings of the Tsar. Now would you say that the Pioneer is behind the revolution in Russia? Then, what is the problem with the statement that the unrest in India is due to the oppressive policies advocated by the government? I only questioned the government and bureaucracy and advised them to learn from bomb blasts.

If you do not want to grant the freedom of expression to the native press, close down all the existing newspapers. Bureaucracy is not identical to the government. *Swarajya* is nothing but the transfer of power from the bureaucracy to the people. The incumbent system is corrupt and not working, and that is why there is a demand for *Swarajya,* and if we demand it, it becomes sedition. Then, how should we express the need for *Swarajya*? You should not keep anarchist and politically motivated revolutionaries in the same basket."

Tilak gave a long speech for five days. This speech highlights his astute diplomatic abilities and command of law and language. Kelkar has reported his entire speech in his biography.[179] His magnificent defence proved useless. He was declared guilty. When asked about the punishment, he calmly said, 'Even though the jury had convicted me, I think it is a divine wish that I should face conviction so that the work undertaken would move forward.' He was sentenced to six years imprisonment and fined one thousand rupees. He was sent to Mandalay. His imprisonment days are captured by Kelkar, in which there is a testimony of Tilak about his imprisonment.[180] Tilak wrote his famous commentary on Gita titled *Gitarahasya* in prison. Kelkar sketches a concise account of the literary career of Tilak in the third volume of his biography.[181] Interested readers should read that account.

Tilak was released in the last week of June. India was delighted. Letters started flying towards Pune. On 20th June, Tilak received a grand welcome from the citizens of Pune. People from Nagpur, Belgaum, *Varhad,* and Solapur had come. The mob was estimated to be about five to six thousand in number. Tilak gave a speech. It was his first speech after his release. He thanked people for welcoming him.[182] Tilak

---

179 केळकरकृत लो. टिळक यांचे चरित्र, खंड क्र. २, भाग 8,पृ.क्र.14-31.
180 केळकरकृत लो. टिळक यांचे चरित्र, खंड क्र. २, भाग 8, पृ.क्र.51-58.
181 केळकरकृत लो. टिळक यांचे चरित्र, खंड क्र. 3, भाग 7, पृ.क्र.1-76.
182 केळकरकृत लो. टिळक यांचे चरित्र, खंड क्र. 3, भाग 1, पृ.क्र.4-5.

remained popular, and his popularity was increasing day by day. Hence, the government kept him under house arrest on 25th June 1914. But government orders were fruitless. Despite the constraints imposed on Tilak, people used to visit his house. The government used some comic tactics to suppress the popularity of Tilak.[183]

The geopolitical situation was changing rapidly. The period was of enormous transformation in world politics. The liberals who got the majority in the 1906 United Kingdom general election were reduced to the minority in the 1910 general election. They had to form a coalition government with Irish nationalists. In 1912, the Irish home rule bill was introduced, and it became law in 1914. Tensions were rising in the Balkans, and the first world war began in 1914. It was a difficult time for Britain. Tilak knew that in the difficulty of Britain, an opportunity for Bharat was hidden! He had two options before him. One was to go for armed revolt. But the groundwork was not laid, and hence the option was impractical. Tilak was not opposed to the idea of arm rebellion. He had said that he would have begun a revolution if conditions were favourable.[184] He considered even armed rebellion constitutional![185] The second option was diplomatically helping the government and obtaining political reforms. Tilak was obliged to choose the diplomatic way. He published his declaration on 1st September of *Kesari,* which was in favour of the government. He asked people to help the government in difficult times. The government sighed in relief and relaxed all the constraints on Tilak's movements. Tilak became free to restart his political career.[186]

Tilak started rewriting in *Kesari.* He advised the young generation to obtain military education. Tilak was keen to end the war with moderates and began resolving conflict. It resulted in another set of battles between Tilak and Gokhale. Unfortunately, Gokhale died on

---

183 उपरोक्त पृ.क्र.8-9.

184 बापटकृत लोकमान्य टिळक यांच्या आठवणी व आख्यायिका खंड 1 पृ. क्र.206.

185 उपरोक्त पृ.क्र.24.

186 केळकरकृत लो. टिळक यांचे चरित्र, खंड क्र. 3, भाग 1, पृ.क्र.10-13.

19th February 1915. Tilak wrote an obituary article in *Kesari* on 23rd February 1915. He wholeheartedly praised Gokhale and highlighted his patriotism and other excellent qualities. Unfortunately, Tilak and Gokhale were on opposite sides of the political spectrum. It was not a personal conflict. Both battled with each other based on principles. Tilak was nine years older than Gokhale. He knew that his days were also getting over.

Tilak started restabilising the nationalist party. The conference of the nationalist party was arranged in Pune. Barrister Baptista was the head. He stressed the need for a home-rule league to attain the *Swarajya*.[187] The conference was successful. Moderates envied the re-emergence of the nationalist party. They arranged their conference. But it failed. Only a few people and the governor attended that conference. The reception committee chairman said that the moderates were in the minority but had an important place in politics![188]

There were two options in front of Tilak. One was to form a new party, and the second was to join Congress by compromising with moderates. He chose the second option. It resulted in the re-entry of Tilak into Congress and Lucknow pact. Tilak and Baptista were contemplating the idea of a home-rule league. Tilak wanted an instrument to carry forward the nationalist movement towards *Swarajya*. Annie Beasant, on 25th September 1915, in New India, declared the establishment of the home-rule league. She said that the league was not established to oppose Congress, and the only intention of the home-rule league was to spread awareness among the people about the idealism of *Swarajya*. Tilak supported the home-rule league and started writing editorials on *Swarajya,* in *Kesari,* in December 1915. Tilak started a separate home-rule league. The reason for the two home-rule leagues was that some of the followers of Tilak disliked Mrs. Beasant, and some of the followers of Mrs. Beasant disliked Tilak.[189] On 18th January 1916 issue of *Kesari*

---

187 उपरोक्त पृ.क्र.27.
188 उपरोक्त पृ.क्र.28-29.
189 बापटकृत लोकमान्य टिळक यांच्या आठवणी व आख्यायिका खंड 1 पृ. क्र.450.

Tilak wrote: "One should praise his own country. There should be a feeling of love towards the country. This is evident if you look at each country in the world. But some people in our own country talk badly about our country. They think that the Bharatiya people are not worthy of attaining *Swarajya*. It hurts when our people assist foreigners."[190]

From 1908 to 1915, the nationalist party was not attending the sessions of Congress. A provincial conference was arranged at Belgaum. *Khaparde* was president. Tilak received a grand welcome at the Belgaum. At the conference, a resolution of peace was passed. The home rule movement was gaining momentum. Tilak and Mrs. Beasant further spread the movement by giving speeches in various parts of the country and consolidating public opinion favouring home rule. The nationalist sentiment was rising, and the government attempted to curb the rising nationalist sentiments. The government was furious with Tilak. In Belgaum, Tilak gave a speech in which he said:

"There is a misconception in the mind of some people about the *Swarajya*. The idea is quite old. Our country has a government, but it is not our government. Hence, we need a home rule. The question is not whether British rule benefits us or not. It is a foreign rule, and this fact must be remembered. There are two parts of government. One is the advisory council, and the other is the executive council. The question of *Swarajya* is about the executive council. Even in England, the executive council can be changed as public opinion changes in the election. In India, we want to change the executive council. This is the aim of the home rule league. East India Company first ruled India. After that, the British imperial government took charge. Now parliament is controlling our interests. But still, the taxation is in the hands of the secretary of state. Legislative councils and municipalities were established. But we have only the power to give speeches in the council and not the real power. The only difference between speech

---

190　केळकरकृत लो. टिळक यांचे चरित्र, खंड क्र. 3, भाग 2, पृ.क्र.2-3.

in council and speech given in public is that the former appears in a gazette published by the government, whereas the latter appears in the newspaper! We know better about the taxation of our country. We do understand our interests. We don't want bureaucracy to decide our interest."[191]

In May, Tilak visited Nagar. He again received a grand welcome. Tilak gave a speech on 31st May. He said:

"I am here to talk about political interests. We do not have the political freedom to carry out political reforms that benefit us. This is because our government is foreign. They understand only trade and profit. When the British came, people thought British rule would benefit our country. But soon, the reality of the British government was exposed. We are being controlled by rigid bureaucracy. The *Swarajya* movement aims to drastically reduce the authority of bureaucracy and obtain the right to pass (our) legislations. We are not planning to drop British rule but want control over the executive council. There are some native officers in the administration, but it is hard to point out any difference between native and British officers. There is no significant spending on education but the collector, governor, and viceroy receives fat salaries. The root cause of our problems is if we do not have home rule rights. We need to raise our voices in support of the home rule. The war has opened a new door of opportunity. Fight until we get *Swarajya*. If we die, the next generation will continue our work."[192]

People were unsatisfied with just one speech, so another lecture was arranged at Nagar. Tilak said in that lecture, "The demand for *Swarajya* is self-explanatory. To carry out all sorts of reforms, we need *Swarajya*. Government do not want to give us *Swarajya*. That is why other reforms are highlighted. Some prestigious people are raising objections over the movement of home rule. The government carries

---

191 केळकरकृत लो. टिळक यांचे चरित्र, खंड क्र. 3, भाग 2, पृ.क्र. 30-33.
192 उपरोक्त पृ.क्र.34-37.

out some insignificant reforms, but they will never lead to *Swarajya*. The authority of the monarchy in Britain is minimal. British citizens have the right to run their government. We also want to enjoy similar rights as those British citizens. Try to take at least a percentage of power in your hand. Government should bring a second amendment to the Government of India act passed in 1858.[193]

When Tilak was busy giving speeches, the government sent journalists to record his speeches. It appears that after the speeches given at Belgaum, the government began planning the sedition case. On the 22nd of July, a case was filed against Tilak in front of the Pune Magistrate. He was accused of sedition under 124A, and the basis was speeches given to him in Belgaum and Nagar. After the proceedings, the verdict was declared on 12th August. He was not jailed but was released on bail. Tilak appealed to the high court, and a favourable ruling was issued. Tilak continued his work of consolidation of the home-rule movement. Baptista created the draft explaining the philosophy behind the home-rule movement. Slowly, differences between moderates and extremists began to wane, and they united in the Lucknow Congress in 1916.

The 1916 Lucknow Congress session is one of the most famous sessions held in the history of Congress. It was basically a grand political ensemble! *Ambikacharan Mujumdar* was the president. Tilak received an incredible welcome. Congress was split in the 1907 Surat session, and in the 1916 Lucknow Congress session, Congress got united, and the goal in front of Congress and the nation became clear. The goal was *Swarajya*.

Tilak had attained the pinnacle point of his public life and political career. After the Lucknow Congress session, Tilak visited Kanpur on 1st January 1917. After Kanpur, he visited Kolkata to meet Motilal Ghosh. After that, he returned to Nagpur. Then, he visited *Yavatmal*, and Akola. He was one of the most popular and tallest leaders of his time.

---

193 केळकरकृत लो. टिळक यांचे चरित्र, खंड क्र. 3, भाग 2, पृ.क्र.37-38.

In February 1917, a special conference was arranged. Tilak advised the young generation to obtain military education. He also advised them to enter the military and get higher positions.

All India Congress Committee was in the process of sending a delegation to London. As a representative of the home-rule league, Tilak sent Baptista to London. On 20th October 1917, Montagu declared that the British government favoured granting home rule to Indians. He also proclaimed the reforms and amendments which were about to come. Montagu, then secretary of state, was coming to Bharat and was scheduled to meet Chelmsford, then viceroy of India. He was also designed to meet several delegations. The home rule league also sent their delegation. Montagu personally interacted with Tilak and Mrs. Beasant.

Tilak toured Maharashtra from 5th February 1918 to 20th February 1918. Kelkar gives an account of the tour.[194] The government had banned Tilak from travelling to London. Newspapers protested against the ban on the passport of Tilak. A war conference was arranged in Delhi on the 27th of May. Tilak was not called on. An additional Congress session was organised in Mumbai. After that session, Motilal Ghosh, *Chittaranjan Das*, Bipin Chandra Pal, *Vasantkumar Ghosh*, etc. people were invited to Pune. A meeting was arranged, and guests gave speeches. Tilak was banned from speaking in public. Kelkar acted as his deputy. Motilal Ghosh gave the last lecture. He was pretty old. He got emotional when he saw a massive gathering of Maharashtrian people. He recalled his association with G V Joshi, M G Ranade, and *Namjoshi*. He called Tilak his younger brother. Ghosh recalled one incident, "Tilak suddenly entered one conference in Kolkata. Thousands of people stood up and cheered for Tilak. Justice Sir John Woodroof, who attended the meeting, said to me that he could drop his 'Sir' title to receive such a grand and thundering welcome!"[195]

---

194 केळकरकृत लो. टिळक यांचे चरित्र, खंड क्र. 3, भाग 3,पृ.क्र.29-41
195 केळकरकृत लो. टिळक यांचे चरित्र, खंड क्र. 3, भाग 3,पृ.क्र.58-59.

In 1918, a Congress session was held in Delhi. Madan Mohan Malviya was president. In 1919, Tilak was in the London case. He had lodged a defamation suit against Valentine Chirol. Kelkar gives the details of the case.[196] As the nature of the case was private, I will not go into the details of the case. Interested readers should read cited material. I will only present the diplomatic activities of Tilak in London. Tilak reached London on 30th October 1918 and left London on 6th November 1919. During the 13 months of his stay, Tilak never visited any tourist place. He always left his home in London to do some important work. Tilak had visited London for two reasons: the Chirol case and the other was to push diplomatic activities in London.

In December 1918, the general election of Britain took place. The liberal coalition won the election. Llyod George remained the prime minister. The noted fact about the 1918 general election was the rise of the labour party as the opposition party. There exists a letter written by Tilak in which the political situation in Britain was explained. It shows remarkable political acumen. Tilak said, "Llyod George has consolidated position as prime minister. Reforms that will be closer to Montague – Chelmsford reforms in nature are out of sight. We have to send a small delegation. It appears that Mrs. Beasant will send her a separate delegation. There should not be any miscommunication between the two delegations."[197] Tilak also thought about the constitution of delegation and wrote a letter on 6th March 1919. He advised sending four to five small delegations. He suggested sending one delegation, which should include a person like Tagore (who would speak confidently in front of the elite class in England) and *Chittaranjan Das* or Baptista (who would speak in front of the parliamentary committee); the other delegation should include Kelkar and other (who would provide secretarial assistance to Tilak), another delegation should consist of Mrs. Beasant (who would carry forward movement in Labour party and females), and another delegation should include Malviya and *Khaparde*

---

196 केळकरकृत लो. टिळक यांचे चरित्र, खंड क्र. 3, भाग 4,पृ.क्र.9-114.

197 केळकरकृत लो. टिळक यांचे चरित्र, खंड क्र. 3, भाग 5, पृ.क्र.26.

as they were councillors.[198] Tilak also gave some lectures on the home-rule movement in London. Kelkar had reprinted the letters written by Tilak during his stay in London.[199] Also, Kelkar had reprinted the report given by a delegation sent by Congress in London to Amritsar Congress.[200] Tilak tried to establish diplomatic ties with the Labour party. In the past, moderates had established a strong association with the liberal party, which favoured constitutional movement in Bharat. The liberal party had lost its place in British politics, and the Labour party had filled the political vacuum. Tilak tried to weave his network by establishing contact with George Lansbury, Wedgwood, Spur, etc.

When Tilak was in London, The Anarchical and Revolutionary Crimes Act of 1919, popularly known as the Rowlett Act, was passed by the imperial legislative council in Delhi. Sir William Vincent introduced two bills to curb 'anarchical' tendencies. If passed, they were supposed to give infinite and ultimate authority in the hand of the government to arrest anyone. When introduced, those bills became controversial. The government wished to destroy revolutionaries at any cost. Finally, the Rowlett Act was passed on 18th March 1918, and protests started all over Bharat. The act was one of the most oppressive acts passed in history and gave enormous power to the state to arrest anyone without trial and judicial review. Another era of oppression and despotism began in India. It reached its height, and the Jallianwala Bagh massacre, which took place on 13th April 1919, was the epitome of British arrogance. It displayed the heinous, despotic, autocratic and barbarous character of the British people.

Tilak reached Bharat on 26th November 1919. He came back to Pune on 1st December. He received a grand welcome. Pune Municipality felicitated him. Tilak was the first non-governmental person to receive an award from Pune Municipality. Tilak was about to visit the Amritsar Congress session. But he first visited Madras. While going to

---

198   उपरोक्त पृ.क्र.27.
199   उपरोक्त पृ.क्र.10-69.
200   उपरोक्त पृ.क्र.70-72.

Amritsar, Tilak got the news of royal amnesty. Tilak sent a telegram with the assurance of 'responsive cooperation'.[201] Tilak received a grand welcome. In the Amritsar Congress session, the Jallianwala Bagh massacre was discussed. After the Congress session, Tilak took part in various provincial conferences which followed the Congress session. Tilak published the manifesto of the Congress Democratic party in the *Kesari* dated 20th April 1920.

Tilak knew that his days were getting over. His health was deteriorating sharply. In July, the final judgement of the Tai Maharaj case was delivered. The decision was given in favour of Tilak. He was in Mumbai. He got favour, and after diagnosis, it was found that he was caught pneumonia. He left the world on 1st August 1920, at 12.40 am. The news spread like a fire, and it was a deadly blow to the *Bharatvarsha*. Pune people were anxious to attend the funeral rites. Special trains were launched from Pune to Mumbai. A huge mob gathered in Mumbai. At 2 pm, *smashanyatra* started. Thousands of people attended it. Rain was pouring. Still, nobody cared. His *asthi* were brought to Pune. Even those *asthi* also received a grand welcome in Pune.

Pune witnessed an unprecedented gathering of people. *Asthi* were taken to *Prayagraj* for the *asthivisarjan*. The physical life of Tilak was over. It was not just the death of a person but an end of an era. But, his thoughts, his philosophy, his life, his devotion to the nation, his unconditional love towards his motherland, his relentless efforts towards the rejuvenation of the nation, his striving for the betterment of country and countrymen, his adherence to the *dharma* and *niti*, his spotless character, his fighting spirit, his love towards people, people's love towards him, his sacrifice, his intellect, his editorials, his passion for *Sanskrit*, his love for *Marathi*, his contribution to the Marathi literature, his roar of *Swarajya,* his efforts for *Swadeshi,* his advocacy of national education, his passion for *Swabhasha, and* his adherence to *Swadharma* will guide future generations.

---

201 केळकरकृत लो. टिळक यांचे चरित्र, खंड क्र. 3, भाग 6,पृ.क्र.38.

Part Three

In the previous two parts, I have sketched the life and times of Tilak. The death of Tilak was not only the death of the person but also the end of an era. Tilak and his thoughts have become immortal in Bharatiya history.

British were consolidating their power when Tilak was born. They had consolidated the power and were ruling ruthlessly when Tilak made his first appearance in public life. When Tilak was gone, the freedom struggle had picked up a pace. The ideas of freedom, *Swaraj*, and *Swadeshi* had swept the entire course of public discussion, and Tilak was the principal reason behind that.

The real British domination started when the Marathas were defeated in 1818. After that, they began to assert their position as rulers. Bharat became an enslaved nation. Slavery is not unidimensional. It manifests itself in various forms across various dimensions. When the British started controlling the political affairs of this country, the autonomy of the Bharatiya people to safeguard their interests was gone. It is precisely what we call political slavery. To rule Bharat, the British needed administrators. So, they began educating Bharatiya people to create loyal clerks. This education produced 'loyal clerks' who became bureaucrats, judges, professors, and journalists. They formed the intelligentsia. This whole intelligentsia was a loyal subject of the British empire. This was the existence of slavery in the domain of education.

The economic subjugation was obvious. British had arrived in Bharat for trade. As they became the political masters of India, they began the systematic destruction of Bharat on the economic front. The raw material was looted from India and supplied to Britain. Bharatiya goods were restricted from entering western markets due to high import duties. British goods started flooding Bharatiya markets, and the Bharatiya people became consumers. Bharat became the importer of British goods, consumer of British goods, and supplier of raw materials to Britain. British rule was nothing but the heinous looting of the wealth of Bharat. Bharat became a beggar in the streets of London. This was the economic dimension of slavery.

Through education, seeds of hatred of Bharat, its culture, traditions, and *dharma* were sown. Hence, students receiving such education were uprooted from Bharatiya culture. The education system produced Anglophilic Indians devoid of *dharma* and *niti*. They started the mockery of Hindu *dharma* and culture. They had blind faith in the west. Missionaries also increased the anti-*dharma* fervour. The philosophy was also borrowed from the west. This was cultural slavery.

The same case was with language. British imposed the English language. They started administrating Bharat, and English became the official language. So, the English language became the de-facto medium of instruction. Bharatiya languages were thrown into the dustbin. Language is the medium of culture. Hence, people who received English education were staunch critics of Bharat and were constantly thriving for the betterment of the British people. This was the linguistic dimension of slavery.

Political, economic, educational, cultural, and linguistic slavery are five dimensions of slavery to which the Bharatiya people were exposed during British rule. Political and economic dominations are clearly evident. But cultural domination is subtle and has far-reaching consequences. K C Bhattacharya says:

"If self is evident in man, he can oppose cultural domination or keep it as a necessary evil and remain free at the philosophical level. Slavery is when cultural domination is not felt and reaches its peak when foreign culture is accepted as good."[202]

Tilak was born in the days of British consolidation and spent his entire life under British domination. Even though he had received an English education, his 'self' was not fallen to its low like his contemporaries. He accepted British power and western education as

---

202 *Swaraj* in Ideas by K C Bhattacharya.

necessary evils and remained free at the philosophical level. His whole life was spent responding to British domination in various spheres of national life.

Tilak, throughout his life, resisted British domination. Tilak bravely fought against every dimension of slavery. His blazing editorials and fiery speeches kept the fire of 'self' burning in the hearts of the Bharatiya people. He fought against political, economic, intellectual, cultural, and linguistic domination. To gain political freedom, he exclaimed the slogan of *Swarajya* and spread it into the brains and hearts of the Bharatiya people. He also vigorously preached the doctrine of *Swadeshi* and supported the boycott movement to fight against the evils of economic domination. His response to educational domination was also dynamic. He formulated and spread the doctrine of national education. His public life began in the field of education, and he was among the founders of the New English School.

He also fought against the cultural domination of Bharat. He heavily stressed *dharma* and *niti*. He was a staunch follower of *Vedanta*. He was greatly influenced by the Bharatiya philosophy. He had great reverence for *Gita* and has written a majestic commentary on Gita (*Gitarahasya*). All of his responses had seeds sown into his philosophical understanding. His alignment with *dharma* and study of philosophy kept the fire of 'self' blazing in his heart. He also stressed the use of the mother tongue and advised the young generation to keep English as a necessary evil and use it for professional purposes and otherwise use the mother tongue. He primarily wrote in Marathi, even though he also had an excellent command of the English language. He knew that language was the medium for the spread of culture. Hence, he opposed education in English. He carried and successfully forwarded the battle against the domination of Bharatiya languages from *Chiplunkar*.

The response of Tilak can be reduced into five keywords: *Swarajya, Swadeshi, Swabhasha, Swadharma* and national education.

These keywords were extensively used by Tilak while countering British domination in respective spheres. These five keywords form the basic tenets of the concept of self-reliance in the freedom movement. They represent forms of self-reliance during the freedom movement.

Chapter 3

Swarajya

The word 'Swarajya' is historically associated with two magnificent personalities, *Chhatrapati Shivaji Maharaj* and Lokmanya Tilak and both are from Maharashtra! The idea behind *Swarajya* of *Chhatrapati Shivaji Maharaj* and Lokmanya Tilak is the same, but the context is different. The times of *Chhatrapati* Shivaji Maharaj and Lokmanya Tilak were highly different. Hence, both personalities responded differently to their times. Every leader has to submit a response to political, social or economic situations prevalent at his time. Depending on the era in which the leader lives, the dynamics of political, social, or economic conditions change, leader's responses to those situations also change. Positions are variant, but the principal remains invariant! Thus, we find a continuum from *Chhatrapati Shivaji Maharaj* to Lokmanya Tilak through this invariance of the basic principle of *Swarajya*. *Chhatrapati Shivaji Maharaj* was the inspiration or role model in front of Tilak when he was expounding on the philosophy and practical aspects of *Swarajya*. *Chhatrapati Shivaji Maharaj* fought against the Mughals and Lokmanya Tilak against the British; the British and Mughal were foreign oppressors. Their vision was not limited to political freedom but also covered other dimensions. The battle of *Swarajya,* as fought by Tilak, was long stretched. I shall first analyse the progression of the political spectra of the Bharatiya political movement, and then I shall elaborate on Tilak's concept of *Swarajya*.

British came to Bharat as traders, but destiny led them to the throne of Bharat. British operated in Bharat, first through the East India Company and then by parliament. The British were not acting in the interest of the Bharatiya people but for Britain's mercantile, economic, military, etc., interests. To plunder more wealth, state and military control of Bharat was necessary. That is why the British created the government in Bharat. The primary aim of state and state officials was to serve British interests, whether political, economic, cultural, etc.

Britain needed good administrators from the Indigenous population to administer a vast country like Bharat. Hence, they established the education system, infamously known as Macaulay's education system. The system had clear goals. It was supposed to impart the skills required to create administrative clerks loyal to British interests. Macaulay's education was supposed to be a factory for producing loyal servants. The system worked fantastically and supplied the army of educated Indians, the majority of whom were Indian in blood but British in tests!

The system served its purpose. The generations of Bharatiya people educated in Western education dominated Bharat's intellectual and public domain. They can be divided into five classes. Each class had a different outlook on Bharat and its future. Those five classes are:

1. Anglophiles = Those were people serving in the innermost circles of power. They received western education and got administrative, judicial, and academic posts. Their outlook was western, and a western lifestyle also dominated their private life. They were sheer copycats and serious bootlickers! They got blind by the splendour of the British. They exercised enormous power over the rest of the Bharatiya people. This class hated everything that was Bharatiya.

2. 'Enlightened' Anglophiles = This class was also Anglophilic in nature. They looked at the west with sincere devotion (The devotion of the first and second class was so intense that if they had worshipped god with the same devotion, they would have attained liberation!). The difference between this class and the previous class is that the people of this class used to analyse the condition of Bharat from the point of view of western (critical) rationalism which they had learnt. After critically analysing the condition of Bharat, those people were led to the conclusion

that Bharat was an absolutely backward country with no culture and the reason for its backwardness was its culture, societal structure and Hindu *dharma*. According to those people, the reasons for our degradation were social rather than political. They started criticising Bharatiya culture, traditions, society, and Hindu *dharma*. It was not self-criticism but self-hate. The best representative for this class is Gopal Ganesh Agarkar. This class favoured social reforms more than political reforms. They were social crusaders and radical liberals!

3. Moderates and liberals = This class was also Anglophilic. But it was more politically conscious than the previous one. This class demanded political rights as well as preached social reforms. Through this class, moderates and liberals sprung out. They were moderates in the sense that to achieve political reforms, they preferred constitutional methods and not radical methods. They were liberals because they supported the ideas of social reforms. Mahadev Govind Ranade and Gopal Krishna Gokhale are the two best representatives of this class. Ranade and Gokhale were the first who assign labels like moderates and liberals to themselves to separate themselves from Tilak.

4. Nationalists = This class was not Anglophilic. According to them, the British were responsible for the degradation of Bharat. They were not ready to accept western structures without any scrutiny. They fiercely criticised the British government and vigorously demanded political rights. Lokmanya Tilak is the best representative of this class.

5. Revolutionary Nationalists = This class used revolutionary methods to fight the British. They operated through secret organisations and favoured violent methods to end British rule. The best representatives of this class are Shri Aravind and *Swatantryaveer* Vinayak Damodar Savarkar.

Social reformers like Agarkar or moderates and liberals like Ranade and Gokhale agreed with one thing. The agreement was on the inferiority of Bharatiya culture vis-à-vis western culture. Western ideas shaped their outlook toward Bharatiya society and culture. Tilak opposed this outlook. As visioned by Agarkar, Ranade or Gokhale, the concept of freedom was not multidimensional but unidirectional or two-dimensional. Those differences were philosophical and, today, require more contemplation.

As I have previously discussed, slavery has multiple dimensions. When people like Ranade or Agarkar received British education, they approached Bharatiya culture and traditions with a western outlook created by western scholars. They argued that British education was a blessing in disguise. They were mere consumers of Western ideas and culture and did not even try to compare them with Bharatiya traditions. They lack original thinking. Their state of mind can be explained in the words of K C Bhattacharya:

"In the field of learning, how many of us have had Indian estimates of Western literature and thought? A foreigner can appreciate the country's literature, but it is only expected that his mind would react to it differently from the mind of a native of the country. A Frenchmen, for example, would not, I imagine, appreciate Shakespeare just as an Englishmen would do. Our education has been largely imparted to us through English literature. The Indian mind is much further removed by tradition and history than the French or the German mind from the spirit of English literature. Yet, no Indian, so far as I am aware, has passed judgements on English literature that reflect his Indian mentality. His judgements do not differ materially from the judgement of an English critic, and that raises suspicion whether it is his judgement at all, whether it is not merely the mechanical thinking of the galvanic mind induced in us through our western education."[203]

The above paragraph (especially the last line) perfectly captures the principle behind the operation of 'enlightened' Anglophiles and liberals. Their ideals were deeply rooted in the west. Agarkar was not

---

203 *Swaraj* in Ideas by K C Bhattacharya.

even ready to compare these ideals with Bharatiya ideals. Ranade tried to compare both cultures critically, but even after that, his outlook appears to be western and not Bharatiya. Tilak was not like Ranade or Agarkar. He never accepted western ideals without critical examination. Bharatiya philosophical traditions, especially Vedanta, profoundly influenced his method of critical examination. He also tried to compare Bharatiya and western concepts of culture and philosophy. Still, we can trace a degree of coloniality in the approach taken by Tilak. But the order of magnitude, if compared to Agarkar and Ranade, is much less and can be satisfactorily ignored. This was the fundamental difference between Tilak and Agarkar, and Ranade. This ideological difference is the root cause of various socio-political conflicts precursor to the *Swaraj* movement.

Tilak vs Agarkar was a fierce dispute in the public life of Maharashtra. Initially, both were friends and were busy managing *Kesari* and Maratha. The ideological differences between Tilak and Agarkar became sharp in the second last quarter of the Nineteenth Century. Differences were on two basic issues, one was about the precedence of political or social reforms, and the second was about the use of British administered state to carry out social reforms. Tilak was not against the idea of social reforms, but he supported the precedence of political reforms over social reforms. He was against using the British-administered state to implement social reforms. He was aware of the divisive politics played by the British. Agarkar took the position in favour of precedence of social reforms and was even ready to take the help of foreign power like the British to impose reforms on society. The majority of New Education Society members were with Tilak. Hence, Agarkar submitted his resignation and started another newspaper, 'Sudharak'. The debate continued till Agarkar's death. Tilak emerged victorious. It means political reforms preceded social reforms. This was achieved in the last decade of the Nineteenth Century.

Between 1885 to 1899, Tilak was involved in various social controversies. There is an editorial in *Kesari* that clearly defines the position of Tilak toward social reforms. The editorial was written in 1886. The title was: 'Who should precede, political reforms or social reforms?' (आधी कोण? राजकीय की सामाजिक?) The editorial was the commentary on the speech given by *Kashinath Telang* with the same title in Mumbai in front of 'Students Literary and Scientific Society'. The article was divided into two parts. In the first part, Tilak gave an abstract of the speech given by *Telang*, and in the second part, he commented on the views expressed by *Telang*. Following is the translation of relevant portions of that article:

"There are some people who say that social reforms must precede political reforms. According to them, without achieving considerable progress in the social sphere, no progress is possible in front of political reforms. This assumption is flawed. It is because the exact point of difference between social and political reforms is difficult to show. Both are interwoven with complexity that can only be compared to a spider's net! It is extremely difficult to discern between the two. Pick up any subject such as public education, tourism, etc. Labelling a particular subject as absolutely social or political is impossible. Even if we suppose that some topics are absolutely political or social, how does it prove the precedence of social reforms over political reforms?

The dependency of political reforms on specific social reforms is not true. There are no historical records which prove this assumption. The contemporary social condition in the times of Shivaji Maharaj was not (drastically) different from the current social condition. Still, he was able to build a kingdom. Later, the Maratha kingdom expanded to Atak (i.e., up to the banks of *Sindhu*). The same logic can be applied to King *Harshavardhan* and the kings of the *Pulakeshi* dynasty in the seventh century. Some people doubt the authenticity of Bharatiya history. For a moment, let us accept it and try to analyse the history of England (which has a 'true' history). Even English history does not support the assumption that only specific social conditions lead to better political conditions. British people were not as good as today in politics in the seventeenth century. People began demanding their political rights and tried to put constitutional checks and balances over tyrannical monarchy. To maintain their rights, the British people had to murder one king. They also impeached one king and appointed a king of foreign origin. At the end of the seventeenth century, Britain became a (politically) advanced nation.

But the social conditions in England were not good, and the critical point is that social conditions were not responsible for political reforms. Even today, England does have social problems. Every society, may it be Bharatiya or British, have social problems. Social conditions in Britain are indeed better than their Bharatiya counterparts, but they are not the best. Hence, it is not wise to compare social and political conditions."

In the second part of the speech, Tilak further reported the speech and then commented on it. Following is the translation of relevant portions of that article:

"In the previous lecture, specific examples were given to show that the assumption that the existence of particular social conditions implies the presence of specific political situations is not true. It is recommended to follow a route that is well built, with no potholes on the road, no fear of burglary, and decent traffic to reach the desired destination. Implementing reforms in a huge semi-continental country like Bharat is extremely difficult. Historically, several kings ruled different parts of Bharat. Now we have only one central power. Hence, as they have the same enemy, different provinces should agree on political affairs. This is obvious as Britain is enslaving all provinces. All wish to get out of this slavery, and it is possible to bring them to the table. The successful organisation of Congress has proved this fact. This is one step forward. Reformers in our country want to capture two forts, the first of political reforms and the second of social reforms. Today these forts appear invincible. But after contemplating this, it appears that the capture of political reforms is easy to capture than the fort of social reforms. Therefore, capturing the fort of political reforms is better and more practical. It takes fewer attempts, and the success rate is high. But this is not the case with social reforms. There is a unity to carry out political reforms, while in the case of social reforms, the unity disappears. If political reforms take place, they also bring some changes to society. There are some anecdotes in the Maratha empire which prove this fact. There is another factor also which needs to be considered. The political debate is rational. Intellect loses its strength in debates concerning social conflicts or religious affairs. In political debates, the intellect suffers the attack inflicted by the opposition. At the same time, in the case of social or religious conflicts, it is an emotion exposed to the attack inflicted by opponents. The nature of intellect is calm, but the nature of emotion is stubborn. Intellect can discern and understands fundamental principles. This is not the case with emotions. They get inflamed during debates and become blind with anger. So, it is wise to avoid playing with the emotions of the masses and should allow them to cool down. As they cool down, their power dissipates. If one wants to carry out social reforms, then the best way is to educate people. Newspapers are great instruments for building public opinion. They are of great help in the process of implementation of political reforms. But I think newspapers should stay away from social and religious controversies. If social and religious issues are constantly debated in the public domain and swing to an extreme point, the process of social reforms receives a setback. This is not the case with political reforms. At least in current times, we all are under one ruler due to British rule. Our collective fate depends on the British government. Hence, Marathi, Gujrati, Bengali, etc., can have identical political opinions. The British government is astonished by this fact and is making nonsense arguments against it.

I do not oppose social reforms. We need a group of people to carry out reforms in the social sector. Such reforms are happening on the ground. These efforts are bearing fruits. But it is not correct to say that all educated people should carry out social reform only. It is not the need of our times. Very few personalities like M G Ranade can work in both (political and social) sectors. Intellectual calibre in society is minimal. Hence, it should be spent wisely. After analysing the socio-political condition of our country, I have formed a firm opinion. The opinion is that most educated people should work for political reforms, and few should work for social reforms.[204] ”

This article, written by Tilak, perfectly captures his attitude towards social reforms. He was not against the idea of social reforms. The core issue in the debate between Tilak and Agarkar was the precedence of particular reform. Tilak's position was crystal clear. He thought that political reforms should precede social reforms. He debated with Agarkar and emerged victorious in the last decade of the Nineteenth century. This debate and Tilak's aggressive position cleared doubts about the final goal and direction. It became clear that political reforms were to be persuaded. The people like Dadabhai Naoroji had already taken the steps. M G Ranade was active in the field of political reforms as well as social reforms. Gopal Krishna Gokhale was also emerging as the successor of M G Ranade. Now Tilak was ready to fight the second battle. This battle was not about the goal. It was clear. Now the battle was about the method of achieving that goal.

People like Pherozeshah Merwanjee Mehta and Mahadev Govind Ranade were political activists. Ranade and Gokhale used words like 'moderates' and 'liberals' to distinguish themselves from Tilak. Tilak had already crushed (self-claimed) 'liberal' reformers, and now he was all set to battle with moderates. Ranade and Gokhale used the word 'moderate' to assert that they believed 'only' in constitutional methods of agitation. Constitutional methods of agitation involve prayer and petition. Moderates would become angry even with the idea of fighting with the British! They believed in the liberal values of the British. They were loyalists. But those constitutional methods never bore any fruits. Methods and leaders appeared hopeless. Moderate leaders were hopelessly pro-British, and this fact was disturbing to people.

---

204 "सध्यांच्या आमच्या देशस्थितींत विद्वान लोकांच्या बुद्धिसामर्थ्यचा बराच भाग राजकीय सुधारणे कडे व काही मात्र सामाजिक सुधारणे कडे लागला पाहिजे, असा माझा एकंदरींत ग्रह झाला आहे." This is original statement of Tilak in Marathi.

Tilak was extremely angry with the approach taken by moderates. He was searching for new methods of agitation. Those methods were realised during the Bengal partition. Let us consider one article written by Tilak which elaborates his views. The article was dated 5th March 1907, and the title was 'Constitutional and legal'.[205] Following is the translation of the article:

"Gokhale had used the words 'constitutional' and 'legal' incorrectly. He has unconsciously mixed up the two words. The meaning of words needs more contemplation. There is another reason to write on this issue as well. In the history of England, the word 'constitutional' has appeared thousands of times. Hence, young people (either learning in schools or colleges or graduating) tend to be fascinated with using the word 'constitutional'. This article aims to declutter the fascination and make clear that the agitation, called 'constitutional agitation' in England, does not have the same meaning in our country (and it can only mean a 'legal' form of agitation).

The original meaning of the word 'constitution' is structure. Political power can be in one person's hands or a group of persons. If it is in the hand of only one person, then it is called a monarchy. If power is in the hands of a group of persons, then that group can be aristocrats, bureaucrats, or people's representatives. Republic is the epitome of political power. But whoever may be in charge of power, some rules and regulations exist governing the distribution and regulation of power. Such a set of rules (i.e., structure) is called a constitution. Generally, it is in written format. If something is according to the constitution, then it becomes constitutional. The word 'constitutional' is an adjective. The meaning (as described above) is grammatically correct. But the meaning of the word 'constitutional' according to history and political science is slightly different.

When we say that the political power in England is constitutional, it means that the form of government in England is not tyrannical. The

---

205 सनदशीर व कायदेशीर, ५ मार्च १९०७.

ability of the monarch to exercise his power is severely limited due to checks and balances imposed upon the use of power. The people of England have earned their right to regulate tyrannical power by the imposition of constitutional checks and balances. Traditionally, the word 'constitutional' is not used to describe tyrannical polity. This is because there are no rights in the hands of people in the tyrannical form of government. British people have constrained their political power to such an extent that they can even impeach (and sometimes murder) monarchs. The word 'constitutional' should only be used vis-a-vis that polity where people somehow have the right to regulate political power. Otherwise, if only grammatical definition is considered, then even a tyrannical government (like one in Russia or Mughal rule in the past) can also be termed constitutional!

I do not think that unregulated power in the hands of the king always produces terrible results. If the king is good and kind, his reign becomes popular, good, and prosperous. But if he is tyrannical, then his rule becomes oppressive. It is not always possible for good and excellent kings to succeed on the throne. Hence, European nations have severely restrained their political power. European people had to struggle a lot to earn and exercise their rights. But today, it is established that the polity where people regulate the political power can only be called constitutional. Such polity exists in the west and not in Bharat.

In 1858, the Queen of England issued a proclamation, and we call it the constitution of India. But it is wrong to refer to the proclamation as a constitution as a political power in Bharat has not been regulated by any means. After the mutiny of 1857, Queen proclaimed to cater for the anger prevalent in the minds of the Bharatiya people at that time. We may refer to it as a 'promise', but we do not have the authority to hold political power accountable for fulfilling it. Queen's proclamation is like a mirage seen in the desert. The proclamation is not the constitution. We do not have rights (which Europeans do have) to control government; hence we are compelled to remain satisfied with Queen's proclamation. The proclamation is not milk, but just the white flour mixed with the water! People should not forget that the 'milk' (i.e., the constitution) is different, and our goal is to obtain those constitutional rights to regulate the government. We got sweet but false promises in the name of proclamation, not the constitution; hence, the British Indian polity cannot be termed constitutional as the constitutional polity in England.

British monarch and parliament are constitutional for British citizens, but in the eyes of the people of Bharat, the same monarch and parliament of tyrannical. They are tyrannical because the government of India do not act according to the will of the people or by the will of the people's representatives. One can raise a doubt that if the British people control the monarch and parliament, then how can they be termed tyrannical? The answer is simple. The use of the word 'tyrannical' is relative. Please pick up the country, its monarch and its people and check whether people can regulate the political power in the hands of the monarch. In the past, we have faced tyrannical Mughal rule, and at present, we are facing the rule of the British monarch and parliament. British rule is constitutional in Britain for the British people, but as British power is ruling Bharat also, the British government in Bharat is not constitutional for Bhartiya people. It is as tyrannical as a Mughal rule. The conclusion is that the government of India is not constitutional but tyrannical.

The way of petition and prayer (towards the British people and parliament) is not constitutional. The monarch (or parliament) may listen to our prayers or may not. No constitutional rights are required to pray to someone! Anybody can praise anyone. It is in the hands of the British polity to listen to or ignore our prayers or demands. Our prayers do not put a constraint on the government! Hence, even though the parliament and monarch are constitutional, it is wrong to say that the British government in India is constitutional. Parliament has created a power structure in India by creating posts such as governor, governor-general, etc. This power structure is a set of rules regulating these posts. We can use the word 'constitutional' in a grammatical sense (as argued in a previous case about Russian Tsar or Mughal rule). But the use of the word would not be in accordance with the meaning of the word 'constitutional' presented by history (or by political science).

It has been proved that British rule is constitutional in England but tyrannical in Bharat. Hence, it is not difficult to prove that the word 'constitutional' is not appropriate if you want to describe the methods adopted by the Bhartiya people. We, the people of Bharat, are fighting to constitutionalise the power which is not constitutional. It means we are fighting to regulate (control) the government of Bharat (which is not acting according to our will). The political movements in the west are different (if compared to movements in Bharat). In the west, the monarch's power is already limited by the power of the people. If public opinion changes, it can change the incumbent government and even alter the government structure, and western people have all the right to do that. The people of Bharat do not enjoy these rights.

Some say that if we successfully change the minds of the people running the parliament, it is possible to carry out reforms in our country. But the assumption is false. The people of Bharat do not elect those who are running Bharat. Hence, they are not accountable to the people of Bharat. In the west, if one wishes to change the political system or carry out political reforms, it is enough to change public opinion. As he has the right to change public opinion, guaranteed by the constitution, the movement he initiated can be termed constitutional. No constitution restricts the polity governing Bharat. Hence, it is pointless to refer to our movement as constitutional.

We wish to achieve two things. The first is to change public opinion. The second is to regulate political power. In the west, political activists do not need to fight for the second thing. They already have constitutional checks and balances on the monarch's tyrannical power, and their efforts to change public opinion are thus constitutional. In short, the constitution guarantees the regulation of public opinion over the monarch; therefore, change (or efforts to bring out changes) in public opinion becomes constitutional.

We, the people of Bharat, are not facing the same situation. Political power controlling us is tyrannical. There are no constitutional checks and balances. It is not driven by public opinion. The main question in front of us is how to regulate (i.e., place constitutional checks and balances) the tyrannical power. It is wrong to label our movement as constitutional in such a situation. Our movement can be legal as per provisions in the penal code. But the legality of our movement is another matter, and its constitutionality is different. Those who do not want to receive penalties from the government should carry out their efforts according to the law. This principle is accepted by both (moderates and nationalists). Sedition law and its implementation in our country are stringent (if compared with others). But unless the people (or representatives) do not gain the right to bring out legislation, two words, 'constitutional' and 'legal', will have different meanings. If Gokhale says that current efforts taken by both parties (moderates and nationalists) are legal, then I do not have any objection. But if he wants to say they are constitutional, he is wrong. Our movements are not constitutional as political movements carried out by Bright and Cobden in England. It is not correct to refer particular movement in our country as constitutional or non-constitutional. There is no context for using the word 'constitutional' in the present polity. It is present in western polity, as the constitution guarantees rights of agitation and rules of regime change. These rules do not apply to agitations in our country.

I do not think that Gokhale does not know this subtle difference. His opinion is different. According to Gokhale, the meaning of the word 'constitutional' should not be taken as 'according to the constitution', but it should be done as 'constituted' (i.e. (constitutional) civil servants from whom we want to carry out reforms). The agitation that we want to do in our country has a specific goal. It is to obtain political rights from (constituted) civil servants who exercise tyrannical power. Hence, according to Gokhale, we should call our movement constitutional. I do not know the source from which Gokhale obtained such a definition.

The definition given by Gokhale is wrong and baseless. The meaning of the word 'constitutional' is 'as per the constitution and not as 'constituted' (i.e. (constitutional) civil servants from whom we want to carry out reforms). Gokhale's definition is problematic since it forces us to refer to every legal agitation as constitutional agitation!

My opinion is that all movements (carried out by moderates or nationalists) are legal but not constitutional. This is because we do not have a constitution. All our movements are directed to obtain these constitutional rights, and such movements can be termed legal but not constitutional. This is not just a semantic difference, as it appears to many. Some people think the movement started by Congress was constitutional, but the new party (nationalists) is making it unconstitutional and thus inviting the government's wrath. To support their views, these people give the examples of Cobden and Chamberlain, who tried to create public opinion. These examples are wrong and do not apply to our current political context. To understand this, it is necessary to understand the true meaning of the word constitutional. Hence, contemplation on the meaning of 'constitutional' is necessary. It intends to declutter the meaning of the word 'constitutional' (and not to create semantic contretemps!).

After reading the history of England, some people in our country start clamouring that we should also have a constitutional movement. The word 'constitutional' appears magical to such people. Many people feel proud when they declare their movement constitutional. These people say that movements in the west never included the principle of boycott, and by accepting the principle of boycott, our leaders are making our political movement unconstitutional. They are not ready to accept such unconstitutional methods of agitation. But their argument does not hold water (as explained above). Such flawed arguments are put forward by those who do not know the meaning of the words they use. The semantic analysis of words is the only way to declutter their minds. I hope that the hopeless discernment of a particular movement is constitutional or not will end in future, and by using useful and appropriate methods, we will move forward towards our destination.

The conclusion is: Even though it appears that the polity governing Bharat has a definite political structure, it cannot be termed as constitutional according to the historically proven meaning of the word 'constitutional'. Even though the parliament regulates the powers of the governor or governor-general, the same parliament is not regulated by public opinion. Hence, the word 'constitutional' is out of context in the description of British Indian polity. We are making efforts to obtain these constitutional rights. It is wrong to label our movement as 'constitutional'.

Now, the only question that remains is whether our movement is legal or illegal. Under present circumstances, we cannot pass our laws. So, even though our efforts are within the principles of natural justice and historical traditions, the question of whether our efforts are legal or illegal remains in the hands of the government. Appropriate methods can be termed illegal if the government passes such a law. In that case, it is better to call the law tyrannical rather than declare our methods illegal.

In short, we should not contemplate using the words 'constitutional' or 'legal' in our movements. It is sufficient to check whether we have a basis of morality, history, and principles of natural justice. If these factors are with us, we should not care about determining the nature of our movement as legal or illegal. This is because the law-making instrument is in the hands of foreigners. It is true that if we break the law, then we are obliged to face punishment. But if the rule itself is tyrannical, we should oppose it by facing punishment. There is no other option. The current situation is because of the divorce between morality and justice!"

This brilliant article written by Tilak exemplifies his mastery and control over language and intellect and his magnificent legal acumen. This article perfectly conveys the views of Tilak. It was a dynamic and powerful attack on the moderate ideology. Congress had become an instrument of power in the hands of old moderates like Mehta or new moderate leaders like Gokhale. Moderates were the dominant power in Congress and only preferred constitutional methods of agitation.

When the Twentieth century began, Tilak was hopeless about the ideology of moderates. He did not think that we should altogether drop constitutional methods of agitation. But he had understood that the ineffective methods adopted by moderates would never succeed. He was searching for new methods of agitation. It was a divine coincidence that at the same time the Bengal partition was announced, the whole of Bengal roared in one voice against it. New programs like *Swadeshi*, National Education and boycott come out. This was the opportunity Tilak was waiting for. In the 1906 Kolkata session, Dadabhai Naoroji unequivocally proclaimed the idea of *Swaraj* as the ultimatum aim of the Congress party. Kolkata Congress resolutions were the win of the nationalist camp led by Tilak and the beginning of the defeat of moderates.

One can witness the gradual progression in the political viewpoints of Tilak. In the first phase of his career, he faced the question of the precedence of political or social reforms. He stoutly favoured political reforms. His advocacy was not limited to editorials. He openly debated with Agarkar and others about the importance of political reforms. After the death of Agarkar, the question of precedence became pointless. In the second phase, Tilak faced another dilemma. It was not about the precedence of particular reforms but the way to carry them out. Moderates were in favour of constitutional methods of agitation. Tilak thought of reaching out to the masses. His aim was *Swarajya* and national education, *Swadeshi* and boycott were instruments to achieve the aim. Moderates had serious concerns about the resolutions of *Swadeshi* and the boycott. They plotted the coup and tried to throw away those resolutions and nationalists in the 1907 Surat session (as elaborated in the second chapter). After coming out of prison in 1914, Tilak participated in the unification process, and two factions united in the 1916 Lucknow Congress session. After 1916, the issue with

Swadeshi and the boycott became less relevant, and the schism between moderates and nationalists waned. It was the democratic capture of Congress by Tilak. The third phase of Tilak's political career was the *Swarajya* (home rule) movement.

After the formation of the Home Rule League, Tilak started spreading the message of *Swarajya*. He was trying to build public opinion. He was trying to educate the public and make them conscious of their political rights. He preached the doctrine of *Swadeshi*, boycott, and national education between 1916 to 1920. He wrote several articles and gave speeches. First, I will recollect his views about *Swarajya* by arranging them in a particular order.

The first use of the word 'Swarajya' on the Congress platform was done by Dadabhai Naoroji in the twenty-second session of Congress held at Kolkata in 1906. Tilak had started preaching those doctrines.[206] In Kolkata Congress, Dadabhai Naoroji stated that Congress aims to establish the *Swarajya*. Tilak gave one speech in Kolkata square where he declared that the real problem is the absence of *Swarajya*, and we should try to get it.[207]

On 8th June 1907, he wrote a lengthy editorial in *Kesari*. The title was: 'What was exceptional in the previous Congress session?'. In that editorial, he commented on moderates and Anglo-Indian newspapers and tried sketching his idea of *Swarajya*. Following are the translated extracts from the editorial:

"Anglo-Indian journalists are in great despair. They had predicted two months ago the end of Congress or the expulsion of the new party (nationalists party). The year 1906 has ended, and the new year has begun. Still, Congress is functioning and will function in the future and even rise further. Anglo-Indian newspapers like Times from Mumbai, Englishman from Kolkata and English papers like London Times have

---

206 केळकरकृत लो. टिळक यांचे चरित्र, खंड क्र.२, भाग 4, पृ.क्र.72-73. N C Kelkar has reported the abstract of lectures given by Tilak at Belgaum.

207 उपरोक्त,पृ.क्र.81.

attacked due to the roar of *Swarajya*. When our moderate leaders were busy making futile demands, the same Anglo-Indian newspapers praised them. But as the demand for *Swarajya* is stated, Anglo-Indian journalists have become angry. To understand the real reason behind their anger, it is important to understand what exactly happened in Kolkata Congress.

The first important thing about the 1906 Congress session was that leaders from both parties (nationalists and moderates) attended it. The number of representatives increased to 1800. Moderates used their tactics and tried to calm down the sentiments of leaders in Bengal, Madras and the united province. They prepared well under the leadership of the lion of Bombay (Phirozshah Mehta)! Mehta, Malviya and Gokhale attended the session. I have written this (specifically) because I want to highlight that resolution passed was not due to moderate's decreased strength. Both parties were present. No party stretched the debate to the breaking point.

The difference between old and new (moderates and nationalists) is clear. The old methods used by Congress were the petition. That is to find out faults and shortcomings in different departments, file a petition in front of the government to resolve those faults, and pray for reforms. But Congress or its presidents never gave any advice to the Bhartiya people or motivated the general public. Dadabhai Naoroji has broken the old tradition.

Congress has an ideal person in the form of Dadabhai to proclaim that Bharat demands *Swarajya,* and Congress must attain the *Swarajya.* If some less calibre person had uttered such words, moderates would not have accepted it. I had suspected that Dadbhai would make such bold statements. But moderates never anticipated that Dadabhai would make such bold remarks. Dadabhai used not only the English words 'self-government' or 'home-rule' but also the word '*Swarajya*', a familiar word in Maharashtra (due to *Chhatrapati* Shivaji Maharaj). Dadabhai advised the young generation to attain the motive of *Swarajya.* *Swarajya,* the self-rule or the rule of people, is the only way to end all our miseries. Now I hope that no doubt will remain in the minds of the young generation about the final aim of a political movement. Thus, it has been firmly established that the ultimate aim of Congress is to attain the *Swarajya*.

The second question tackled in Congress was the method of achieving the *Swarajya*. The old method adopted by Dadabhai was prayer and petition directed toward foreign people. But Dadabhai confessed that he was hopeless about the method of prayer and petition. After listening to the remarks of Dadabhai, I do not think the young generation would have any doubts about the uselessness of methods adopted by moderates. It is true that Dadabhai still has hope from the liberal party in England. But the young generation should concentrate on the experience gained by Dadabhai and not on his hope!

The difference between moderates and extremists (nationalists) is on this issue. The nationalist party says we should follow the path of self-reliance by following *Swadeshi*, boycott, and national education. The moderate party, however, is stuck to its old methods of prayer and petition. Congress has not entirely dropped the methods of moderates. But it has adopted three ways of achieving self-reliance. The resolution of the boycott arose during the Bengal partition movement. It was discussed in the session, and Bipin Chandra Pal generalised it. Gokhale and a few people opposed it, but nobody cared about their views! A majority passed the resolution. Therefore, even the secretary of Congress or the president of Congress does not have the right to determine the meaning of the resolution.

Indeed, Congress has not forced anyone to adopt the boycott method. It has just expressed its opinion that the boycott method is perfectly legal due to the situation in Bengal. But the situation in other provinces is similar to Bengal (as government do not listen to the demands made by the public). It means if other provinces adopt the boycott method, their stand would also be legal according to the opinion of Congress. It is one step forward, and if it continues, the resolution of a total boycott will also be passed.

The second resolution is of *Swadeshi*. In the previous session, a fiery debate broke out on whether to prefer goods manufactured in Bharat at some sacrifice. Mehta was not in favour. But the *Swadeshi* resolution was passed. Fortunately, there were no differences in the third resolution of national education. Congress has agreed on the importance, necessity, and applicability of national education.

The 1906 Congress session is a turning point in the history of Congress. Congress has learnt the first lesson of self-reliance. Action leads to the conclusion only when the executive possesses stable and clear thoughts about the goal and means to achieve that goal. The consciousness of Congress has become clear due to the guidance of proud nationalist Dadabhai Naoroji. *Swarajya* is our goal, and *Swadeshi*, boycott, and national education are our means to achieve that goal. Differences between old and new parties have disappeared. Both parties should use three instruments of self-reliance to achieve the *Swarajya*. We will achieve our goal with God's blessings if we continue our path of self-reliance."

This article by tilak is one of the most important articles. This is because it comments on the most important event in the history of the freedom movement. The ambiguity about the end goal in front of Congress was cleared, and the means to achieve the goal were also precisely stated. It was the path towards self-reliance.

Tilak stated his idea of *Swarajya* in one of his articles in *Kesari*, which appeared on 9th April 1907. It was a continuation of the approach he took in the article in *Kesari* dated 5th March 1907 on the issue of the use of words 'constitutional' and 'legal'. In the April article, Tilak contemplated the meaning of two words, '*Swarajya*' and '*Surajya*'. Below is the short version of the article:

"There exists a relation between thoughts in mind and our verbal expressions. If our thoughts are not deep or lack contemplation, verbal expressions will also have ambiguity, opacity, obscurity, and confusion. We can say that those with ambiguity in their thoughts also have issues with their verbal expressions. The relation between verbal expression and meaning is extremely important. It reflects in our verbal expressions when we have definite assurance and clarity about our goal. It is a common experience that the thought process which takes place at the psychological level also happens in the form of words. Sometimes it happens that we read or hear some word or sentence and that particular word or sentence leaves an impression on our mind. But we do not contemplate the meaning of that word or sentence. The result of such neglect is that along with the real established meaning, collateral or ancillary meanings ascribed to the word also leave their impressions on the mind. It creates an illusion about the meaning of the words or sentences. It creates ambiguity about the meaning of the word, leading to the wrong thoughts. A recent example of such ambiguity is the definition of the words 'constitutional' and 'legal'. In this article, we are going to define *Swarajya* and *Surajya*.

In the 1906 Congress session, Dadabhai used both words. Dadabhai said at the beginning of his lecture that good rule could not substitute for home rule. Dadabhai wanted to say that our political thirst would not satisfy the good rule, but it could be satisfied only with home rule. The question of achieving home rule is different. First, there is a need to define *Swarajya*. Recently, the provincial conference of Bengal was held at Burhanpur, and a debate took place between stalwarts like Surendranath Banerjee, Bipin Chandra Pal, etc. That is why it is important to analyse the semantics behind the word *Swarajya*. Its explanation is also important since we are using it to express the final goal of Congress.

When we say *Swarajya*, several ideas emerge to mind. *Swarajya* and *Svārājya* are used in *Vedas*. Also, 'swa' in *Swarajya* means the self. Hence, according to ordinary people, the simple meaning of Swarajya is self-rule. The answer is simple, but it cannot satisfy a person with a critical mind. Several questions can be raised on the above definition, such as: What do you mean by the self? What are the borders within which you define 'self'? Is self-rule implies the rule of a nobleman and family, or does it include the whole population?

When the king (monarch) and his subjects share the same culture, agree on the same set of values, and strive to look after each other's interests, people think that the rule is *swarajya*. *Ramrajya* was *Swarajya*. But when kings become despotic and start oppressing, people get fed up with the rule even though the king and people belong to the same culture. At the end of the rule of *Peshwas*, melancholy was spread, and the administration collapsed. Hence, when the British began their rule, there was no outcry.

The meaning of word *Swarajya* degenerates into two different meanings. The first is the well-administered rule, and the second is the congenial or pleasant rule. Let us take another example of the Russian Tsar. Tsar is a Russian national and orthodox Christian like the Russian people. The rule of the Tsar is also well-administered. But his rule is autocratic. People in Russia lack freedom. Several constraints have been placed on their liberty. The voice of the Russian people is left unheard in Russian polity. Hence, Tsar rule is not congenial to the Russian people. Tsar is a native ruler of Russia, and his rule is well-administered. If one defines *Swarajya* as the rule of the native ruler, then Russian rule is *Swarajya*, and if one defines a good rule as a well-administered rule, then Tsar's rule is *Surajya* as well. But if viewed from the point of view of the Russian people, then the same well-administered rule is not congenial or pleasant. In one way, the rule of the Tsar is *Swarajya* and *Surajya*. But it is not being administered according to the will of the people. If we define *Swarajya* as the polity which functions as per the will of the people, then the rule of the Tsar is not *Swarajya*. Russian people do not feel that their rule is *Swarajya* because it is not functioning according to their will. They are fighting to get this type of *Swarajya*. Hence, it is important to understand the meanings of words like *Swarajya*, *Surajya*, etc. The conclusion is that in present times, the word home rule or *Swarajya* is generally applied to the constitutional polity.

The polity which functions according to the will of the people is *Swarajya*. According to some people, the word 'self' (*Swa*) in self-rule (*Swarajya*) does not just mean the native ruler, but 'self' means people, and self-rule is the polity which functions as per the will of people. If this definition is considered, then not only the Russian polity but native states in our country also do not represent *Swarajya*. The 'nativeness' of the ruler is not sufficient. Monarchical government can be well-administered or bad-administered, but it may not be congenial. If a polity is disciplined, it does not mean it is pleasant. Even though the internal prison system is disciplined, it is not pleasant for prisoners. Most people want freedom, and the rule in which freedom is constrained cannot be congenial to people, however disciplined and well-administered it might be. The same conditions are there in Germany. German monarch is also not a foreigner. His rule is also well-administered, but still, people are not happy. Similar conditions are there in various nations. As education spreads further, people will not remain happy with the native monarch and well-administered state. The epitome will be the republican system. In future, people will say that the republic is real *Swarajya*. Republic is the ultimate synchronisation between *Swarajya* and *Surajya*. It will happen in future, but for practical purposes, we should focus on the present situation.

If we define a good rule as a well-administered and disciplined rule or the rule of law, it can be said that British rule is good. But it functions according to policies framed by British bureaucracy. Bureaucracy does not care about the Bhartiya people. It cares only about the interests of Britain. That is why British rule is not profitable or congenial to us, and if the current system continues (without reform), it will not be pleasant in the future. Discipline under British rule can only be compared to discipline in prison. British rule is oppressive. British laws, discipline and rules are oppressing people. Bharatiya trade and manufacturing have finished due to the policies adopted by the government to favour British merchants. Higher posts in government are reserved only for British people. Military expenditure is rising. To offset the expenditure, new taxes are being imposed. Treasury is eating public money. In such a situation, the well-administered good rule cannot be the good rule in the view of people. It is not *Swarajya*.

The British monarch and his religion are not native to this country. Hence, their interests are the interests of Britain and not of Bharat. Such a rule will become congenial only when its government starts being run by the people's representatives. I do not deny the benefits of a disciplined and well-administered state. But disciplined polity does not mean that the rule is congenial. The state should be run to maintain the interests of the people. If people will drive the rule, it serves their interests. If democratic principles gain momentum and the government starts functioning according to the people's will, British rule will not inflict much damage even though it is foreign. We would have to pay salaries to a foreign official. In such a way, even though the king and some officers are foreigners, we would achieve the fortune of simultaneous existence of *Swarajya* and *Surajya* up to a certain extent. The next step is minimum the presence of foreigners in the polity; if no foreigner is present in the system, it is excellent. It is a '*Purna Swarajya*' Even though it is hard to achieve this *Purna Swarajya*, we should fight at least for the *Swarajya* under the empire. It is not right to maintain the status quo because the rule is well-administered. We should think about the increased participation of the public in policy formation and the execution of policy by the government. As there is no fear of public pressure on the government, our efforts are to generate one. The real meaning of Dadabhai's teaching is as explained above.

There should be a fight for *Swarajay* not only in provinces but also in native states. This is because today, the question of the nationality of the ruler (whether he is foreign or native) has become irrelevant, and the only question that is important is how much power is in the hands of the people. This is a fundamental difference between ancient polity and present polity. My opinion is that just the well-administered state or native king cannot become a substitute for *Swarajya*. The absence of *Swarajya* would not benefit people. I have given examples of Russia and Germany. There are also examples from the Asian continent, such as China, Iran, and Japan. Efforts are being taken (worldwide) to regulate the government by public opinion. They are gaining success to some extent. We also want the same thing. I use the word 'Swarajya' with the same meaning as explained above when I ask people to make efforts for *Swarajya*. 'Swa' means people, and the state being run according to the people's will is *Swarajya*. If the king is native, it is good, but even if he is a foreigner, it does not do much harm. Even if discipline is less, it cannot be more valuable than freedom. *Surajya* cannot become a substitute for *Swarajya*. The real *Swarajya* is where people have the right to run the government in a way that would serve their interests."

This article captures the conception of *Swarajya*. He joined the home-rule league movement after his release from prison. He wanted to turn the home-rule movement into a mass movement. He wrote articles, made speeches, created a network of volunteers, and spread the message of *Swarajya* and self-reliance. He was trying to make people conscious of their political rights. His speeches were plain and simple. His sincerity won the hearts of people. He gave one speech in Belgaum that elaborated on the concept of *Swarajya* in the most straightforward manner. The speech in condensed format is:

"There is a misconception among people about the nature of *Swarajya*. Some people know the real meaning of *Swarajya*. Still, they spread lies about it. Some people even deny the right of *Swarajya*. That is why it is important to understand the meaning of *Swarajya and* need to raise your voice for it. The demand for *Swarajya* is not just due to my efforts. The concept of *Swarajya* is ancient. There is a government in our country, but it is not our government. It does not matter whether the government is good or bad. It is foreign. I am not here to tell you how the British took over the ancient *Hindu Rajya*. There is a king in England. But he does not have any power. British officers rule us. They run the government. In our country, there is no anarchy. The existence of government is necessary.

There are two wings of political power. One is the advisory council, and the other is the executive council. We do not want to change the king, but we want to change the executives. *Swarajya* is used for the executive council. Even in England, the cabinet changes after the election. If I ask to change one officer and appoint another, it does not mean I am attempting sedition. There are rules and regulations according to which bureaucracy works. But officers are serving the interests of foreign rulers and not the interests of the people of this country. They are arrogant and do not know the ground reality. That is why it is important to change the bureaucracy. Our problem is with bureaucracy.

After the abolition of company rule in Bharat, the queen took over the administration. The company was gone, and it was replaced by parliament. But still, the taxation structure in Bharat is decided by the state secretary. He is the real master; even governors are his slaves. Legislative councils were formed, and municipalities were opened, but apart from the power of giving a speech, real power is vested in the hands of the people. The only difference between speeches given in the council and speeches delivered in public is that speeches given in public appear in newspapers, and those given in the council appear in the government gazette! We know our interests. We know that the military expenditure is not decided by the king but by the prime minister, and if something wrong happens, the prime minister resigns. If someone demands the resignation of an executive, then it is not sedition. If home rule is given to us, it does not mean that British rule is gone. Bureaucracy is blocking our path toward home rule. We have to kick out these bureaucrats. I know I will not be there when our country gets *Swarajya*."[208]

After Belgaum, he gave another speech in Ahmednagar. It is also plain and simple speech. The speech in the short format is:

"The subject of public importance should be debated openly. The question which surfaces through such debates is the absence of *Swarajya*. We know that alcohol is not good for health. But we cannot ban it as we do not have the power to ban it. The same case is with famine relief works. Our trade should have been in our hands. But our government is in the

---

208 केळकरकृत लो. टिळक यांचे चरित्र, खंड क्र.3, २, भाग 2, पृ.क्र.29-33.

hands of foreigners. Foreigners do not only include those who are born in a foreign land. Those who have a nationalistic aspiration of making Bharat prosperous are not foreigners. Just because a person is of foreign religion does not make him foreign. First, people thought that British rule was good. Now, this misconception is cleared. The government have responsibilities. We pay taxes to the government. There are some things which the government has done. We are debating about things which have not been done yet. Bureaucracy is acting like a middleman. We have to take the function of the executive into our hands. We are not suggesting the overthrow of British rule. Our soldiers are fighting for the British. There is no significant expenditure on public education. But collector, viceroy, etc., officers are drawing heavy salaries. War has changed the situation. It has become favourable to us. We should take advantage of the situation. Do not stop the movement till we achieve *Swarajya*."[209]

Tilak spread the doctrine of *Swarajya* through his writings and speeches. He went on a long and stormy tour in 1918.[210] His speeches were straightforward and pointed. There were no lofty words, no display of literary skills. Still, it appealed to the masses because of Tilak's sincerity, devotion, character, and endurance. The articles written by Tilak collectively form a river flow that carries rationale! Aggressive and argumentative reasoning is typical characteristics of Tilak's writing. It continues to inspire generations of freedom fighters.

Tilak wrote one article in *Kesari* on 9th October 1917.[211] In that article, he categorised enemies of *Swarajya* and the tricks played by them. Below is the translation of the relevant extracts from the article:

"The people who oppose *Swarajya* can be categorised into three classes. The first class consists of retired bureaucrats who have gone back to London. These bureaucrats had looted our country and became reach. Even after that, they plot against our country. Retired

---

209 उपरोक्त,पृ.क्र. 33-40.

210 It is described in the previous chapter.

211 निकराने एकमुखी मागणी करा

governors like Curzon and Sydenham also help them. The second class which opposes the *Swarajya* is Anglo-Indians. These people tried hard to suppress the home rule movement. They even issued threats to the state secretary. They asked the parliament to take care of their interests if the parliament was serious about the demand of *Swarajya*. The third class is bureaucrats. *Swarajya* is a real threat to bureaucrats. But these bureaucrats are just officials. They are bound by rules. They have to implement policies adopted by the British cabinet. Hence, it is not possible for bureaucrats to openly revolt against *Swarajya*. Still, they continue their mischiefs through secret reports and their mouthpieces. But these 'natural' enemies of *Swarajya* are obliged to go on the defensive mode. Irresponsible bureaucracy must be regulated by public opinion. The future of 31 crore people depends on *Swarajya*. We all should come forward and shout in one voice, '*Swarajya* is our birthright, and we shall get it'.

Congress represents the nation. Hence, the demand of *Swarajya* should go through the platform of Congress. We should not show signs of disunity. Bureaucracy will pick up the differences and try to resist the policy of *Swarajya*. Therefore, no alternate policies that oppose the policy adopted by Congress should be adopted. If there are specific provincial problems, they should be brought to notice by respective provincial representatives.

Nobody says that the Congress-league scheme is perfect. There are many parties within Congress. The current scheme does not fully coincide with the vision of each party. Still, after looking at the larger interests of the nation by resolving differences, all have agreed on one scheme. Old and new, moderates and radicals, loyalists and nationalists, and home rulers should consider that we all are under one platform of Congress. We all should respect the collective decision of Congress rather than pushing our opinion.

We should raise our demand for *Swarajya* with greater force. We should not satisfy with smaller achievements. This is our golden chance. A world war is going on, and favourable winds blowing for

Swarajya will also stop once it ends. The British parliament is ultra-conservative. They will approve a small set of our demands and will give us the promise to approve other demands next time with the fulfilment of certain conditions. After some time, they will raise questions over demands with reasons that the conditions remain unfulfilled. Hence, it is important to state our demands precisely. This is not just the question of Bharat but is of humanity."

The diplomatic and strategic abilities of Tilak are evident in this article. He had perfectly understood the bureaucracy. He also knew their tactics of obfuscation and manipulation. He was not merely a philosopher but a practical statesman.

The government announced constitutional reforms in July 1918. They were called Montague-Chelmsford reform. Tilak wrote one article in *Kesari* dated 20th April 1920. The title was: New age and New rule.[212] Below is the (translated) abstract of the article:

"Montague-Chelmsford reform signifies the beginning of new age. The power in the hands of bureaucracy will become less, and the number of people's representatives will increase. In the past, power was concentrated in the hands of bureaucracy. We had become servants of bureaucracy. We chose the moderate way of prayer and petition. Bureaucratic despotism had crushed the morale of our leaders. When a new generation of leaders arrived on the political horizon, such senile leaders called them extremists and immature. But now fortunes are turning.

I am not saying that moderates lacked wisdom. My only point is that the time of moderates had gone. Their method and policies are useless for us and further can be detrimental towards our goal. We want new leaders (from the young generation) to fight bureaucracy. Times have changed. Hence, we also have to adapt to the situation. We have to adopt new policies as prescribed in the proclamation of the Congress Democratic Party. We will fight with legal methods and

---

212 नवी विटी, नवे राज्य!

not with the 'moderate method'. Moderates are incapable of fighting as they have received titles and honours; hence, their behaviour is moderate with bureaucracy. We want brave, courageous, and unselfish leaders. I do not want to insult anyone. Fight for *Swarajya* with new methods and new people, and one day, we will achieve *Swarajya*."

In *Kesari,* dated 20th April 1920, the policy of the Congress Democratic Party was published. It goes like this:

"The basic principle of the Congress Democratic Party is the faith in Congress and strong belief in democracy. Democratic principles are powerful enough to resolve the questions in front of the nation, and the spread of education and an increased voter base are important tools to achieve it. There should be religious tolerance, and there should not be any interference with religion.

Montague act is not satisfying, and with the help of the labour party or other favouring people, this party will try to amend the incumbent act so that we will get the total *Swarajya,* i.e., absolute control over the military, economic affairs, and the declaration of legislative guarantee of protection of natural rights of citizens. Our motto is education, agitation, and organisation.

Reforms to be done in the legislative council:

1. To repel oppressive acts like the Rowlett act, the press act, the arms act, etc. In case of a criminal offence, especially political offences, proceedings should be under a native jury, hard labour punishment to political prisoners to be abolished, reforming prison systems, etc.

2. To decide fair wages and hours of work for labourers in farms and industry to create residential amenities for labourers and to create tribunals to solve disputes between labourers and factory owners.

3. To control retail and other forms of inflation by a method like banning exports.

4. To provide financial assistance from the state or impose tariffs on foreign goods or other measures to boost local industry and trade.

5. To nationalise the railway, decide proper fares, and end all discrimination and privileges in the railway.

6. To cut the budget (especially military expenditure) and apply new taxes only when necessary, and taxation should be progressive.

7. To create an army of Bhartiya people, develop an institutional framework of military education in the army, navy and air force, and end all types of discrimination in military postings.

8. To start the civil services recruitment exam to recruit competent candidates as government officials.

9. To achieve national unity, one language should be promoted, and religious tolerance should be maintained.

10. To organise provinces based on language.

Reforms to be done at the provincial level:

1. To give provincial autonomy to all provinces without any delay.

2. To decide the rightful taxation structure for farmers.

3. *Grampanchayat* should control reserve and protected forests.

4. To end privileges and all types of human trafficking and forced labour.

5. To provide education in the mother tongue up to the highest standard possible.

6. To provide free and compulsory education to both boys and girls and to carry out the work faster, the municipality and local boards should provide grants and aid through provincial funds.

7. To rejuvenate *Grampanchayat* and empower them with judicial powers within their jurisdiction.

8. To ban alcohol completely.

9. To increase the number of votes without discrimination between males and females.

10. To appoint a health minister and under his supervision, the health condition of the nation should be improved by scientific method.

11. To carry out all the reforms suggested by people, such as farming reforms, migration reforms, cooperative movements, provision of technical and professional education as per the need of the nation, to provide medical treatment and give a boost to traditional medicines (*Ayurveda*).

This proclamation is the epitome of the political thinking of Tilak. Before the conclusion, it is important to understand views of Tilak about the structure of *Swarajya*. The vision of Tilak was of the federal Bharat. In his articles, he described the structural, i.e., constitutional form of *Swarajya*. He also elaborated his stand in front of the Montague commission about decentralisation. He explained the democratic, federal form of parliamentary government, provincial autonomy, village bodies, etc. It is conceptually and historically important.[213] Below is the extract of his views:

"We demand the rights of *Swarajya* as we are part of the British empire. The British empire is composed of various nations, provinces, and colonies, and there is no uniformity in the political structure of those political entities. In some places, people have a significant share in government and run the government by electing their representatives, while in some places, it is governed by bureaucrats. There are certain specific reasons behind the division of such polity. But these reasons are not important, and as empire further prosper, different parts of empire should get rights to run their government and Bharat demand that right."[214]

At the least, Tilak was demanding provincial autonomy. According to him:

---

213 B K Kelkar has given an account of the views of Tilak.
214 टिळक विचार पृ.क्र. 340-341.

"Internal government should be in the hands of people. Bureaucratic officials should not be allowed to intervene in it. In this way, the political structure in Bharat gets split into two parts: 1) Imperial and 2) Provincial. An Imperial is one government in which a common system of governance is needed to govern the country and deals with foreign policy. Regional sentiments should not drive it. But the internal matters of the state should be decided by public opinion. It will not hurt the imperial council."[215]

"The basic principle behind the demand of *Swarajya* is about the structure and rights of provincial governments. Hence, I will discuss the polity structure of the provincial government and then the constitution of the government of Bharat. First, we have to decide the extent to which autonomy can be given to the public in matters of the provincial government. Then, it will be easy to determine the extent to which public participation is allowed in the imperial government.

First, let us see the jurisdiction of the provincial government. The provincial government is entitled to receive a percentage of the gross revenue generated. The provincial government have adequate powers to direct the generated revenue towards various departments under its jurisdiction for expenditure. They have the right to introduce and pass the legislation (which is applicable within their area of jurisdiction). But the imperial government is the ultimate authority. In conclusion, we can say that the provincial government is (a political structural) monopoly operating within the jurisdiction of the imperial government (and draws power from it). The imperial list gives the provincial government the right to run some governments with absolute autonomy, splits revenue with them, and provides grants for expenditure. But absolute control (monopoly) should be provided to people and not to the government, at least in the case of the provincial government. The current political system is suitable and profitable for government with no regulation of public opinion."[216]

---

215 टिळक विचार पृ.क्र. 341-342.
216 उपरोक्त,पृ.क्र. 342-343.

Now I will present Tilak's views regarding Bharat's imperial government. The translated extract is given below:

"Wedderburn and Gupta had suggested (reforms) policy for excellent functioning of the council of secretary of state. Now it has been decided that the council of secretary of state is to be dismantled. I think the reforms suggested by Wedderburn and Gupta should be applied to the Imperial legislative council, which will take the place of the imperial legislative council. Suppose those reforms are applied, and the structure is constituted. In that case, the imperial council will get representatives of the department of military, ICS, and separate representatives of the opinion of the British parliament. Thus, it gives the required stability to the government and also gives the rights required to be within the control of the government will remain within the control of the government. The members of the imperial legislative council (other than the above-mentioned members) must be elected by the people, and these members should administer departments allotted to provincial governments. If such division (separation) of powers happens, the probability of conflict between imperial and provincial governments will be less. If a conflict arises, then the responsibility of the conflict cannot be tied on the shoulders of the governor-general or other members in imperial councils (who are bureaucrats)."[217]

Tilak has also commented on the federal parliament. Below is the extract of his views:

"Imperial legislative council is the root of the future parliament of Bharat. When the provincial government governing different provinces of Bharat becomes autonomous and democratic, then the polity of Bharat will resemble, to some degree, the polity of the USA. There is a resemblance because in the USA, each state is autonomous in some matters (departments), and the rule of the US Congress is general (all over the USA). In Bharat also, provincial matters will be in the hands of

---

217 उपरोक्त,पृ.क्र. 343-344.

the provincial government, and all the matters concerning the nation (as a whole) will remain in the hands of the imperial government. There can be differences in the question of which matters are provincial and which are imperial. But the suggestions put forward have explicitly separated the matters into the hands of the provisional and general government. Home-rule league thinks that provincial governments should become truly democratic governing provinces, and the imperial legislative council should govern matters related to the nation as a whole. It would not be wrong to say that the same imperial legislative council will become the parliament of Bharat. Hence, the people to be appointed must represent the people of Bharat and people from all socio-religious and financial backgrounds should be included in the council."[218]

Now I will present the views of Tilak about the rejuvenation of village bodies. The abstract is:

"We are demanding *Swarajya* to create a polity such that the representatives of the people will get independent rights to govern and the government would function as per public opinion and not with the opinion of bureaucracy. If the government wants to give us *Swarajya*, then at least the provincial government should be handed over to the public representatives. Village affairs should be in the hands of rural bodies; Taluka-level affairs should be in the hands of Taluka-level bodies, district-level matters should be in the hands of district-level bodies, and provincial-level matters should be in the provincial bodies. Many people think that the start of *Swarajya* should be from a village-level (bottom to up) approach. In a way, it is true, but when we believe in the constitution adopted by an assembly, it makes no sense to start from the village level. Village-level bodies functioning in the past have disappeared. But they have not disappeared due to the government of India act (passed by the council). They disappeared because of the powers exercised by the provincial government,

---

218 टिळक विचार पृ.क्र. 344-345.

which were drawn from the law passed by the state council. Hence, if we want to rejuvenate village-level institutions, the powers in the provincial government's hands should be transferred to the public. If such powers are transferred from the provincial government to the people, people can create institutions at the district or Taluka level. The demand for *Swarajya* should not be limited to village level only but should also include provincial *Swarajya,* which will automatically include base."[219]

This was the long and exhaustive account of Tilak's views about *Swarajya.* I have shown that there were three phases in the evolution of political thought of Tilak. In the first phase, he dealt with the question of precedence of reforms. He preferred political reforms over social reforms and fought with Agarkar and others. In the second phase, he fought hard with senile moderate leaders and opposed their reliance on constitutional agitation methods. The third phase was the phase of *Swarajya.* It began with the Bengal partition movement. Three methods of agitation and self-reliance surfaced during that movement. Those methods were *Swadeshi,* boycott, and national education. In 1905, Dadabhai Naoroji declared *Swarajya* as the ultimate goal of Congress, and the three methods to achieve the *Swarajya* were three methods of self-reliance. Tilak started making people aware of their rights. He became the voice of the people. He successfully created a mass base for the freedom movement. Congress split on the issue of boycott and *Swadeshi* in the 1907 Surat session, and Tilak went to jail in 1908. After an interlude of six years, he returned from prison in 1914 and again continued preaching the doctrine of *Swarajya.* He was the co-founder of the home-rule league. He also published his views about the structure of the polity of Bharat.

Tilak built his idea of *Swarajya* on two levels. One was theoretical, and the other level was practical. At the theoretical level, he tried to assert that the concept of *Swarajya* is ancient by referencing ancient

---

219 उपरोक्त,पृ.क्र. 345-346.

Bharat. Also, he discussed the legality of the movement. He also discussed different polities and wrote extensively on the constitution, parliamentary, and federal republican systems. He also bitterly criticised bureaucracy. Hence, he provided an intellectual, legal, and philosophical basis for the demand of *Swarajya*. He was not a mere philosopher, lawyer, professor, or editor but also a practical diplomat and pragmatic politician. He was a gifted statesman of ingenious strategic intellect.[220] He knew the theoretical foundation is useless if it is not reflected in the ground reality. Hence, he created a network of volunteers, built a nationalist party from scratch, and formed an alliance with leaders from other parts of Bharat like Lala Lajpatray, Bipin Chandra Pal, Yogi Aravind, or Annie Beasant. He created a mass base for the freedom movement. He tried to educate them about their rights. He ignited the flame of nationalism and patriotism in the people of Bharat. He built public opinion through articles and speeches. His articles in *Kesari* are monumental proof of contemporary political life in Bharat, the evolution of the concept of *Swarajya* and the freedom movement. They are national treasures. Tilak expounded and explicated the political dimension of the concept of self-reliance (*Aatmanirbharta*).

---

220 The proof of his strategic intellect is his attempts of establishing diplomatic relations with the labour party during his stay in London.

Chapter 4

Swadeshi

The *Swadeshi* movement began as a response to the Bengal partition. In Maharashtra, the doctrine of *Swadeshi* was already there. Opposition to the Bengal partition provided nationwide context. In the 1906 Kolkata Congress session, a resolution of *Swadeshi* was passed. But there was a schism in Congress on the issue of *Swadeshi*. In the second chapter, I have given a detailed history of *Swadeshi* and boycott movements and the opposition of moderates to them.

When Tilak began his career on *Kesari*, initially, he used to write on political and legal issues and *dharmashastra*. But as time passed, new issues arose, opening new horizons for Tilak to explore. He wrote several articles on issues like farmers' problems, irrigation, labour problems, trade, manufacturing, professional education, self-reliance, self-sufficiency, revenue collection, expenditure (especially military expenditure), poverty, its causes and ways to abolish it, political economy, etc. The economic views of Tilak are thus scattered in his intellectual universe. In this chapter, I have tried to put them constructively.

British rule in Bharat was one of the most oppressive regimes in the history of the world. Oppression need not be just political. It manifests itself in multiple forms. They were ruling this country with ruthless power concentrated in their hands. Hence, it was difficult to expose the true nature of British rule in public life. Tilak was among those few people who ferociously exposed the oppression of Bharat.

Tilak was not the originator of the economic analysis of the poverty of Bharat. The economic analysis was started by M G Ranade, Dadabhai Naoroji and Rameshchandra Datta. Tilak began expressing his views on economic issues in the last decade of the nineteenth century. The first economic issue on which Tilak wrote articles was the pathetic condition of farmers and their distress. In the second chapter, I have already described the pathetic condition of Maharashtra due to famines. I have also described the work done by M G Ranade through *Sarvajanik Sabha* during famines and the continuation of the legacy of Ranade by Tilak. He wrote several articles on the issues faced by farmers. Those articles are proof of the brutality and callousness of British rule. Those articles appeared in *Kesari* in the year 1892.

Tilak wrote one article in *Kesari* on 2nd February 1892 titled 'Law of farmers'. In this article, one finds the description of the horrible condition of farmers. Relevant translated extracts are given below:

"Almost 95% of people in Bharat depend directly or indirectly on land for their livelihood. But the condition of a farmer who cultivates the land is pathetic. He is deeply embedded in poverty and debt. His house and animals are kept as a guarantee. He has to pay taxes and, if not paid, faces the confiscation of the property. In such hardships, he faces natural disasters like famines. He waits for eight months before the rainy season, and suppose rain does not arrive; then, he is obliged to visit the moneylender's house. In the past, there were instances when moneylenders used to help, and even kings also used to provide support to farmers. Now the government is being run by traders. Hence, there is not even a chance of waiver. Whether rain falls or not, whether the crop is generated, whether the farmer and his family die due to hunger or go to jail, the tax must be paid within the given time constraint. The condition of farmers has worsened to such an extent that in Solapur, people are selling cows and bullocks for two paise and the government dues are 23 paise. According to the government, this situation is due to moneylenders who oppress farmers. Hence, the government brought a law to save farmers from the clutches of moneylenders. But instead of being helpful, it worsened the condition of farmers.

To rescue farmers from the oppressive moneylenders, the government set up (state-owned) financial institutions (to provide credit to farmers) and became moneylenders! Still, the weight of the debt on farmers' shoulders is increasing daily. Now people say that the law, framed for the welfare of farmers, has become oppressive. Hence, the government has appointed a commission. When discontent arises on a particular issue, the government sets an inquiry commission to silence critics. It is a legitimate practice in the government business, and our government has mastered the art of appointing an inquiry commission!

The commission is visiting different places to understand the ground-level situation. I am not saying that the efforts taken by the commission are useless. But we have a long history of hundreds of inquiry commissions. It provides no reason to be hopeful of this commission. As the commission's work is in process, I do not want to comment on it. But if people want to gain substantially from the work of the commission, then it is the responsibility of the people living in taluka level or rural areas to show the ground-level situation to the commissioner. It is possible that the commission would neglect the fact that the assumption of the government that moneylenders are responsible for the pathetic condition of the farmers is wrong. The government wants to pass on the sin of problems faced by farmers on the shoulders of moneylenders. I hope the commission will read articles written in Kolkata's newspaper 'Statesman'. People should be aware of these articles. I shall give the abstract of these articles.

The real cause of the loan issue is not the moneylender but the oppressive government. The stringent government control is the root cause of the poverty of farmers, and due to such laws, farmers are not getting small credit guarantees (used to be given by the moneylenders). Statesmen have beautifully narrated these facts and also have put forward their suggestions.

Last November, the government issued one ordinance. According to that ordinance, when southern Bharat became part of the British empire, people bore the loan on their shoulders and were obliged to depend on moneylenders. But the statesman has proved that the statement given by the government is incorrect. The total amount of loan in a region compromising several villages appears to be high. But the loan was collective and not individual. The responsibility of clearing the loan was on the village (as a single unit) and not an individual. Moneylenders used to give loan to *Peshwe* with the revenue collection from villages as a guarantee. Patil was the revenue collection officer. There has been no progress in the state of farmers after the reforms by the British government. There are reports written by Grant, Elphinstone, Chaplin, etc., kept in the Bombay secretariat, and they are being neglected. In 1875, farmers revolted against oppressive moneylenders. Hence, the government appointed a commission, and it published the report. In that report, instead of focusing on the root cause, ancillary causes were discussed in depth. Farm laws introduced by the government are also similar. These half-wit laws do not tackle the original cause of the poverty of farmers. The only relief to the farmers was the temporary relief from the oppression of moneylenders. According to the law, a moneylender cannot confiscate a farmer's land but can sell cattle or farming instruments. Hence, if a moneylender is selling farming instruments, then the farmer has to again visit the moneylender for the purchase of farming instruments and to purchase the farming instruments, he has to mortgage his land or house! So, again farmer loses everything. There are also other minor flaws in the law, but I will not discuss those flaws. The revenue collection system of the government is the root cause of the pathetic condition of the farmers. Hence, the commission has advised in a smooth tone (so as not to face the government's wrath!) that the government should adopt a flexible and progressive taxation structure instead of fixing the revenue valuation. It is obvious that the Bombay government did not like the recommendation and bluntly denied its implementation. Even though the Bombay government has impeded the implementation, the imperial government should implement it after testing it in a particular region. This advice given by the stateman is correct.

Farm laws are worsening the situation of farmers of southern Bharat day by day. If the situation continues in the same manner, it will be repeated in other provinces and become a national crisis. Hence, immediate action is needed. There are three stakeholders in the system. They are government, farmers, and moneylenders. The system which guarantees the interests of each party is best. But the present system is causing harm to each party. Farmers are the most oppressed class. The myth has spread that the moneylenders are oppressing farmers. Hence, moneylenders are deprived of sympathy. The moneylender provides necessary credit to the farmer, and even the credit given by him is not of his own, but he borrows it from another bigger credit society. Hence, if a loan defaults, then the moneylender bears a loss. There is a dim ray of hope for farmers in the form of a waiver, but it is not possible in the case of moneylenders. Hence, most of the offenders in non-criminal disputes are moneylenders. Sir Raymond West records this fact.

Even the government do not get benefited from this system. It must spend more on public infrastructure (capital expenditure), but the revenue is constant. If the waiver is issued during famines, then the revenue falls. Hence, the current system creates problems for all three stakeholders. People have to battle for one day meal. They lack the power, money, and incentive to reform their agriculture methods or increase the soil's productivity. In the southern province, the conditions are highly volatile. If one good season is recorded in three years, it is considered good fortune. Instead of collecting revenue in the form of money, it is better to collect it in the form of production. It will solve many problems which are the product of the present system. Wedderburn also has approved this method. When no crop is generated in famine, farmers would automatically get a waiver (as they would not have any production of a crop), and when a good amount of crop is produced, then the revenue collection of the government would be increased. This is beneficial for each stakeholder. These are the views expressed by the Statesman. These views are important, and I hope the commission will pay attention towards these views."

In December 1892, Tilak wrote explosive articles on the farmers' discontent. The title itself was explosive. It was: Are farmers being forced to carry out a revolution? The relevant translated extracts are:

"The conditions of America and Hindusthan are drastically different. In America, the land is abundant, and the population is small. Hence, economic opportunities are ample for the American people. There is no shortage of land, and the land is abundant for cultivation. Hence, the American people are constantly and swiftly acquiring wealth. But the condition of Bharat, which has a history of at least five to six thousand years, is drastically different, and the incumbent British government is worsening it. As the land has been under cultivation for thousands of years, its quality is decaying day by day. Natural fertilisers are also becoming rare. There is no option of migration to a foreign land. There would have been an opportunity in the trade. But even in trade, there is the dominance of foreigners. The wealth has decayed. If famine comes, one cannot find even a single farmer who can sustain famine for fifteen consecutive days. The peace under British rule is amazing, but we are paying the price of that peace, and the price is such that crores of Bharatiya people are facing the danger of eating for only a day.

In 1891, the census was conducted. It was found that the population increased by an average of 20 miles per square from 1880-1881. But the land under cultivation has not increased proportionately. But the burden of tax is increasing day by day. Increasing population, fallen trade, heavy government expenditure, and decaying land quality are ominous signs. If a large quantity of material is being exported from Bharat, it is not satisfying. It would have been good if profit had fallen in the hands of the Bharatiya people. But the compensation we are getting for exporting the material is the employment under the foreigners. For how many days are we going to starve like this? The answer to this question is uncertain.

The commission appointed for farm reforms has recommended some reforms. But those reforms are temporary, and even collectors have said it. The poverty of farmers is a sign of poverty in the nation. We are not self-sufficient in food production, and our business also has lost an opportunity to export. Crores of farmers in this country will not happily embrace death with the arrival of famine just because there is extreme peace under British rule. Also, government do not dare to kill crores of farmers. So, what should farmers do?

If farmers revolted, then you could not control them with your bayonets. Melancholy will prevail, and all big and small trees will fall in this storm. Our government is free from the threat of Russia, native rulers have been crushed, and British education is producing obedient servants. Still, even though these things favour British rule, they are not solutions to the pathetic conditions of farmers. The pathetic condition of farmers is the biggest problem in front of the government. I do not think the robust fortification in the northwest province, well-equipped European military, and railway system can annihilate the crisis. Even though the government and administration are smooth, people who are dying due to starvation will think that the system itself is the root of all problems.

Sir Louis Mallet says that temporary reforms will not cure the problems in Bharat. It would hurt the foundation of the empire. The root cause of the problem should be inspected and annihilated if found. There is no other option. The report dated 24th October 1888, published by the imperial government, depicts a similar picture. Bengal farmers feel satisfied even if they eat two meals a day. In Bihar province, 40% of farmers do not get adequate food. One-third of the population of the southern province lives under the constant threat of starvation. In Ratnagiri district, 90% of people are left with mango, jackfruit, and vegetables for months with no other available option. The collector of Madras also reported the same situation in his province. In the Madars province, labourers have said that their annual income barely meets annual expenditure.

The conclusion is that farmers are dying everywhere in Hindusthan. If annual expenditure barely meets the annual income, it is considered bliss. If famine arrives, one-third or half of the population gets severely affected and dies."

This fierce article written by Tilak is a sketch of the horrible condition of farmers. There are two articles written on the commission and its report. The first article appeared on 20th December 1892. The title was: What work commission did? The abstract is given below:

"In southern Bharat, farmers were subjected to extreme conditions and thus revolted in 1878, burning houses of moneylenders. After that, the government woke up. And decided to roll out reforms. Human nature is arrogant. He thinks the whole world is wrong. This human nature is evident in government. Due to the taxation system, governance, and trade policy, the Bharatiya people suffer. But the government do not hold the same opinion. Government think that it is doing a favour to the people. This attitude is reflected in the behaviour, articles, and speech of every officer. Hence, it is natural for a 'caring' government to think that moneylenders are responsible for the problems faced by farmers.

The main problem is loans. Indeed, farmers have not revolted after 1878, and the misunderstanding between moneylenders and farmers is reduced to some extent. Oppressive tactics practised by moneylenders are banned by the law, which was a necessary step. If farmers revolted against moneylenders for oppressive tactics, then the reasons why farmers revolted are addressed. If farmers are still suffering from poverty, then farmers should revisit the cause of the problem other than the moneylender. When such poor and malnourished farmers look for the cause of their suffering, one cannot predict their target. Now let us examine whether such revolt is possible or not.

The main reason for the farmer's revolt is poverty. The family has expanded, no alternative option for business (due to government policies), decaying quality of land and unpredictable monsoon are some of the conditions which result in farmers' poverty in any nation. Hence, the important questions must be raised: 1) Does the farm act reduce poverty? 2) Does it reduce the burden of a loan? Even commissioners tried to answer these questions, but their answers were vague. Farm acts will not annihilate the root cause of poverty. Bombay government have accepted and stated in one resolution that now the moneylenders will give loan according to rules prescribed by the act, and the proportion of loan in four districts will reach the normal level. *Krushnaji Lakshman Noolkar* has also verified this fact.

It means that after 14 years of the act, the burden of the loan on the shoulders of farmers is not decreased. Hence, it was obvious for the commissioner to question the usefulness of the act. He says at the end of his report that such laws are hopeless in the eradication of poverty of farmers, and he also stresses that the reasons behind the poverty of farmers are different at different places and to reduce poverty, political and social upliftment of farmers is necessary. This remark shows the usefulness of the 1879 act passed by the government. To implement the law, the government appointed special judges and other officers with an annual expenditure of 57-58 thousand rupees. It means that the government have spent at least 80 lakh rupees in 14 years in four districts. But still, the burden of loan has remained as it was."

Tilak wrote another article on 27th December 1792 in which he explained the solutions suggested by the commission. The title is 'The recommendations of the commission'. Below is the translated extract:

"Commissioner does not think that the changes in the law will annihilate poverty. There are social reasons behind poverty. Commissioners think that the problems will get annihilated with the spread of primary education. It is the responsibility of the government to impart primary education. Hence, it is responsible for the situation of farmers. It is the government's responsibility to make farmers literate and financially literate and create a network of financial institutions so that farmers can invest their money rather than spend it on unnecessary things. The population in our country has increased, and hence it is the government's responsibility to increase the country's employment opportunities."

These articles written by Tilak show his sincerity and empathy towards farmers. He also wrote articles on irrigation. Below is the translated extract of his views on irrigation:

"It is possible to save farmers catastrophe of famine to a certain extent. The government needs to spend more money. The major step to be taken is in the field of irrigation. By increasing the field of irrigation, we can reduce the dependence of farmers on rain. But the government is not spending enough on irrigation works. Most of the money spent on public works is on railway infrastructure. In the past three years (1898, 1899 and 1900), the spending on railway lines was twenty-six crores. But only 2.25 crore was spent on the irrigation works."[221]

The economic views of Tilak have a particular rhythm associated with the socio-political environment of his times, just like his political views. In the first decade of his writing career, his economic analysis was mainly confined to farmers' problems and issues they faced. At the beginning of the twentieth century, he wrote articles about western imperialism and the rule of the East India Company. In those articles, he discussed the origin of imperialism and its relation to the economic policies of the British empire. The translated abstract is given below:

"Europe was the epicentre of the war between different political powers, religions, and sects. But soon, Europe got fed up with religious tensions and sectarian divide, shifting towards materialism. Physical pleasures attained the highest status, and European ideals were recalibrated and centred on achieving physical pleasures by any means. The polity and its structure were used to achieve the target. In modern Europe, material progress and republicanism have coincided. This is because people shifted towards materialism. Hence, they felt the importance of political power and thus slowly established control over it. In this way, the unification of material progress and democracy has been achieved, and England naturally leads the world in this race.

---

221 टिळक विचार पृ.क्र. 149-150.

But this radical shift in thinking also altered the ideals of England. Dacoits like Hastings and Clive are regarded as top nationalists. The trinity of material progress, political power (in synchronisation with material progress) and the change of ideals marked the contours of modern England. This trinity is the root of the imperialist hunger of the British. If England captures a particular (region or country), then the whole of England (as a nation) starts plundering resources from that nation to satisfy their material hunger. When England conquered a nation, financial institutions in England established their foothold in conquered land and started plundering profit from helpless native people. This is the nature of the transformation of England."[222]

This article captures the soul of the British imperialistic hunger. Now I will explain the actual economic analysis done by Tilak about the economic oppression of Bharat. British rule is divided into two parts, company rule and imperial rule. Tilak has written articles about both rules. An abstract of his views is given below:

"At the beginning of the eighteenth century, plundering, trade and slavery were used to plunder the wealth out of Bharat. At the end of the eighteenth century, laws were framed to subdue the Bhartiya trade. Export duty of 62.2% was placed on goods going out of Bharat, and hence traders, manufacturers and artisans in Bharat were systematically destroyed. But the real aim of the company directors was not just to destroy the trade of Bharat. They were anxious to make Bharatiya people consumers of western goods. They have achieved their goal.

In 1830, approximately 50000 pounds of foreign goods were imported to Bharat. In 1900, the import of goods was 6,11,13584 pounds. Also, about 92 crore rupee export of Bharatiya goods to foreign is almost finished. Only raw materials are being exported. This was done systematically by company directors. At the end of the nineteenth century, we do not have much to say about the Bharatiya trade. It is finished. Only foreign traders are controlling trade and becoming rich.

---

222 टिळक विचार पृ.क्र. 126-128.

In 1830, Montgomery Martin estimated the plundering of the wealth of the Bharat by the East India Company. He assumed an outflow of 30 lakh rupees with a 12% interest rate. He estimated 72 crores 39 lakh pounds were plundered by East India Company in the past thirty years. Today, the base value of plundering is increased from 30 lakh pounds to 3 crore pounds (3 crore rupee to 45 crore rupee)."[223]

This eye-opening article by Tilak exposes the systematic destruction of the Bhartiya trade. Also, it shows how Bharat was reduced to a state of dependency on the west. Bhartiya people became not only consumers of western goods but also consumers of western culture, language, philosophy, etc. Farmers were destroyed, traders lost their position, intellectuals became loyalists, English replaced the Bhartiya languages, and the proselytising activities of missionaries were in full swing.

Dadabhai Naoroji and William Digby have written excellent books that scientifically explain poverty's causes. Tilak wrote three articles in *Kesari* and reviewed those books. The first article appeared on 10th December 1901. The title is 'Two good Books'. The relevant translated extracts from the report are given below:

"Those who want to see the effects of the movement of the past twenty-five to thirty years should read two books written by Dadabhai Naoroji and Mr. William Digby. Dadabhai Naoroji is a devoted nationalist, working hard to alleviate the nation's condition. In the past fifteen years, he has been searching for the economic reasons behind the poverty of Bharat under British rule. He is trying to pursue western people and working hard to generate favourable opinions about Bharat in the west. He is a great leader.

It is the leader's responsibility to analyse the causes that lead to the nation's pathetic condition and then strive to annihilate those causes. A country where such leaders are not born that country is considered to be a dead country. Leaders are the life of the nation. The nation is not just a piece of land. If the piece of land is a nation, then

---

223 टिळक विचार पृ.क्र.130.

we are obliged to declare the Sahara Desert or North pole as a nation. Similarly, a community of people is also not a nation. A society which lacks *dharmic*, social or political cohesiveness and whose units are not bound together by general constraints or a society which do not have a separate identity cannot be termed as a nation. Further, a society in which leaders are absent who strives to keep the general principles which define the nation is set to die.

There are thousands of people living in the country. All these people do not contemplate the principles which define nationality. It is the job of leaders; unfortunately, such leaders are rare under British rule. Power was shifted from the kings in Bharat to the British. The people who were trained by the British started praising the British. Our ancestors did not know the political system of Europe, the imperial hunger of European nations and the policies adopted by the British to satisfy the imperial hunger. Hence, in the beginning, the Bhartiya people could not recognise the true nature of British rule. With the introduction of the railway, telegram, hospitals, prisons, etc., the new and disciplined rule created a mirage that British rule would benefit Bharat. The illusion lasted for a few years, but soon it disappeared.

Foreign merchants and businessmen started dumping their goods in our country, and artisans, manufacturers and traders in our country were systematically finished in the name of free trade. The new ways of communication, i.e., railways and ships, increased the logistics movement and decreased the time to send the grains and goods out of this country. In the past, there used to be few Europeans, and slowly, their number increased, and their salary, pensions, and profit (and interest) were looted from Bharat to such an extent that we were reduced to poverty.

When we are facing such a situation, some people in our country constantly praise British rule and try hard to impose British superiority on us. The British government has destroyed our nation with three instruments, viz., opium, trade, and political power and from the status of a wealthy nation, we are reduced to a pathetic state. Mr. Digby echoes the same views. Dadabhai Naoroj is among the few who discern the condition of the society and state to which it was subjected in the past 50 to 75 years and its effects which would happen in the future. His intellect was not attracted to the pompous showdown of British rule. But with the help of calm intellect and economic principles, he analysed the new political system. He concluded that we were heading towards catastrophe. Today we are witnessing the truth in his conclusion. Just like the great sailor who can gaze at the arrival of an upcoming typhoon even when the atmosphere is clear, leaders should also be able to predict the future correctly. We do have a significant number of leaders, but they are insignificant!

Bharat has been reduced to the status of poverty, and the condition is worsening further. If only one year goes without rain, thousands of people are forced to join relief works to sustain their lives. Many people accept this fact. But there was a lack of a book which gave a comprehensive summary of the topic. In the past 25 to 30 years, provincial conferences, Congress and other public institutions and newspapers have published different accounts of problems faced by the country. A heated debate occurred between loyalists and nationalists in which various figures, statistics, etc., were cited. At such time it was essential, to tell the truth to the British people and the British government about the pathetic condition and poverty to which Bharat was subjected due to British rule, how the nationality of Bharat was finished and how the political system institutionalised by the British government systematically destroyed the fighting spirit of the people. Dadabhai Naoroji and Mr. Digbi have done this work through their books. The name of the written by Dadabhai Naoroji is 'Poverty and Un-British rule in India', and the name of the book by Mr. Digbi is 'Prosperous India'. The title of the book written by Digby is satirical. Those people who want to understand the views of the leaders of Bharat should read these books. Digby published the letter written to Lord George Hamilton and requested him to disprove his findings based on government records or change the pathetic system of government. The book consists of various figures and is designed in a particular way so that a reader can easily understand the facts about Bharat's poverty. On the front page, a statement is published in golden letters: The per capita income of people in Bharat was two pence in 1850, 1.5 pence in 1880 and 0.75 pence in 1900. There is a scientific explanation of the flow of wealth from Bharat to Britain. These two books should be translated into Marathi. In upcoming articles, I will publish abstracts of both books."

The second article appeared on 17th December 1901. The title is: 'Prosperous British Hindustan'. The translation of the relevant extract is given below:

"Mr. Digby has recently published the book of the same title. It contains an account of poverty in British-ruled Bharat. It has been highlighted that if the challenge of poverty remains unsolved, then at the end of the twentieth century, Bharat will become the prison of beggars. Due to the theft of wealth from Bharat, Bharat is devoid of wealth and values and is reduced to the state of slavery, and if the situation continues, the twenty-crore population will soon remain hungry. The only solution to this problem is that the wealth of Bharat should remain in the hands of the people of Bharat, and it should be used to accelerate the growth of trade and business in this country. Any sensible person will empathise with Bhartiya people after reading Digby's book.

There is no surprise in the fact that the people of Bharat are living in poverty. This is because:

1. The storage of grains at the village level is disappearing.

2. Gold or silver ornaments (savings) are becoming rare.

3. Trades and businesses are closed, and the livelihood of all people depends on farming.

4. Ships are built and operated by the British, controlling the export of goods and grains. Hence, the profit also goes into the hands of foreigners.

5. New consumption ingredients like coffee are traded by foreigners using foreign capital for their profit.

6. Trade, large industries, and all profitable businesses are in the hands of foreigners.

7. Government posts with significant authority are also in the hands of foreigners.

When the twentieth century started, foreign newspapers began publishing articles about the prosperity in England in the nineteenth century. But in the same century, Bharat was thrown into poverty. Mr. Digby has reproduced an extract from the book of Brux Adams that after the three years of the Plassey war of 1757, the idea of the cotton mill originated in England and in 1768, James Watt made the steam engine. But there was no large-scale production. One needs capital to start large-scale production. Today, hundreds of cotton mills are running in Manchester and Lancashire. The capital is obtained from Bharat after the Plassey war. In other words, under the East India Company rule, the flow of wealth was directed towards England through trade, plundering and salary. This flow of capital was instrumental in the foundation of large-scale industries, accelerating England's growth. England prospered, and Bharat suffered. Further, the prosperity of England was due to the systematic degradation of Bharat. Mr. Digby has beautifully proved this cycle of progress and regression between two nations, England and Bharat.

In the past, Bharat was a monopoly in the production of excellent clothes of cotton and silk. If it had been *Swarajya* in the nineteenth century in Bharat, then the Bharatiya people would have mastered the technology of the steam engine just like the Japanese, and the profit generated would have remained in Bharat. But the irony is two events; one is of discovery of mechanical power and new technology, and the second is of theft of wealth from Bharat to the west due to the control of political power coincided. As the political power was in the hands of Englishmen, no constraints were placed on the flow of wealth from

Bharat to the west and policies were formulated to increase the loot from Bharat.

Mr. Digby has given an extract from the report published by Mr. Thackrey. In 1812, there was a dispute about the collection of land revenue. There are two methods of revenue collection. The first method was the collection by native people, which was the traditional way. The second method was direct revenue collection by the government from farmers. If collected by the first method, the native people responsible for the revenue collection receive their share of generated revenue as salary. It increases the number of prosperous and wealthy people. This class of people is an engine of economic growth and sustains society. But Mr. Thackrey commented that the existence of a wealthy and prosperous class was not in Britain's interests; hence, the traditional method of revenue collection should be abolished. From such a prosperous class, diplomats and other officials rose, and British rule never required such people from Bharat. The British government never liked people who were freedom-living and politically ambitious. Hence, they try to curb the freedom, ambition, and self-pride of people. British government required people living in poverty.

It is impossible to expel the ruling class of the previous regime in one stroke. But if the system is placed to restrict the rejuvenation of such a class, then political ambition never arises in the minds of the new generation. Thackrey published his reports in 1812, and we have seen the implementation of those reports in the past thirty years. Those who praise the British rule for the 'peace' and 'prosperity' of telegram and railway must read the reports of Mr. Thackrey. British government tends to subdue the powerful person in Bharat. The power is centralised in the hands of the British officers and their loyalists. The rest of the Bhartiya people should become slaves and embrace poverty. This is the central principle of the operation of the British government. We were pursuing reforms in other sectors because we could not understand the true nature of British rule. After the analysis of the past fifty years, it is clear that the British government is responsible for the decay of the intellect, power and wealth of the Bharatiya people, and even though there is peace, we are devoid of all things which are tenets of freedom. Mr. Digby has logically proven this fact. Those who want to understand the reality of British rule should focus on this."

The third article appeared on 14th January 1902. The title is 'Poverty in Hindusthan'. The abstract is given below:

"In the past twenty-five years, Bharatiya people have debated about the poverty of Bharat. Two hundred years ago, Bharat was the golden bird; hence, British, Dutch, French, Portuguese, etc., and western people came here. But the status of the wealth in Bharat and the speculations about Bharat by foreigners have undergone a drastic change. The epithet of the golden bird has survived, but our status has declined. Digby has printed the per capita income of Bharat in 1850, 1880 and 1900 in golden letters, proving the above statement. He has proved it with the help of the government report.

Generally, newspapers are supposed to criticise the British government for its mistakes. But moderates ask all the time to praise the government for their 'good' intentions. One will know Bharat's ground reality if he reads Digby's book. In 1882, under the reign of lord Rippon, official Sir Baring had estimated the per capita income of Bharat to be twenty-seven rupees. In 1888, Lord Dufferin was governor-general. In his term as a governor-general, provincial governments were asked to prepare secret reports about the real condition of farmers and labourers. These reports have been published, but as they are confidential, nobody can access them. In 1891, Bradleigh stated that the reports should be in front of the parliament. But his demand was rejected. Finally, incomplete reports were tabled in front of the parliament, and one copy was given to Bradleigh, which Digby used. He has written his book based on those reports.

After doing a rigorous analysis of Bengal, Assam, Myanmar, Mumbai, Punjab, and central and north-western provinces with the help of reports mentioned above and other methods, Digby has proved that the annual income of crores of the poor people in Bharat is approximately 9.5 or 10 rupees (if the income of poor is considered less than the unnecessary spending of the wealthy elites in Bharat). Lord Curzon has estimated the per capita income to be forty shillings. But it is not the true estimate. The real estimate per capita is 22-25 shillings. If we cut the income of wealthy people in Bharat, then the rest of the poor people live on barely an annual income of 13 shillings. If one estimates the wealth accumulated in the hands of native princes, then those estimates are wrong. If one sees a small amount of wealth in the hands of a few people in Bharat, then he should not estimate the country's wealth on that basis. Those who want to understand the real economic condition of the nation should study the condition of farmers and labourers. The prosperity of the nation is decided by the conditions of the food, clothes and shelter of the poor people living in that nation.

Spencer has estimated that the poor in southern Bharat must spend fourteen rupees annually to sustain their living. But his income is less than his expenditure. A prisoner in prison needs twenty rupees for his living. It means that the farmer in Bharat does not even get enough food compared to the prisoner. What should people do in such a condition? Their life is hopeless. Farmers cannot earn even twenty shillings if the farming season is good. What should he eat? What should he wear? How should he manage marriages and other ceremonies? How should he repay the debt of the moneylender? All people have been reduced to such a pathetic condition that if for only a season rain does not fall, then lakhs of people would join relief works. There is no surprise in this fact.

If the imperial government was unaware of such conditions, then one could have given the justification for their behaviour. But as per orders issued by the imperial government, officials in different provinces surveyed the actual condition of farmers and labourers and reported facts to the government. Still, in the past twelve years government has been neglecting these reports. Can anyone explain such behaviour? Those reports prove that Bharat has been reduced to a pathetic condition under British rule. Still, shameless Lord George Hamilton, a bureaucrat with high authority, is giving a speech in parliament about the prosperity of Bharat under the British government. This behaviour exposes the selfish and cunning nature of bureaucracy. Bureaucracy knows the pathetic condition of Bharat and tries hard to hide it from the western people. The aim of Dadabhai and Digby behind writing the book is to make western people conscious of the real condition of Bharat, and I think they would successfully achieve their aim to a significant extent.

It is useless to raise our voices in front of the imperial government in this country. They know the fact, and their view is that Bhartiya people should remain in a pathetic condition, and hence they are ready to tell a lie to their countrymen. Therefore, Dadabhai and Digby have written a book, to tell the truth. The state secretary hides the original report. Now the only question is, are western people going to listen? It is an almost impossible task to make imperial and materialistic Britain conscious of their deeds. We do not know the efficacy of this method, and valid questions should be raised about its continuation."

This article proves that the government knows the people's pathetic condition and is neglecting it. The government wishes to keep people in the same situation. Now leaders should decide the next path."

These three articles of Tilak are proof of his devotion towards the nation, sympathy toward farmers and labourers and his ability to understand the root cause of the problem. He was among those few leaders of his contemporary times who had understood the importance of industry, technology, and their role in the development of a self-reliant and robust nation. Tilak wrote one article in *Kesari* dated 25th September 1894 on industrial dependence with the title 'Industrial dependence'. The translation of the relevant extracts is given below:

"The dependency exists in several dimensions. It can be divided into political, social, *dharmic* and industrial dependence. We are debating about political dependence through the platform of Congress, newspapers, and other institutions. *Dharmik* and social dependence are also under discussion. This debate has created a dichotomous division, and both parties debate vigorously. It is a good sign. When intellectual conflicts occur, the analysis of old and new ideologies occurs, and both ideologies' good and bad points come in front of the people. Through such discussions, people learn and understand basic principles and behaviour changes. Industrial dependence is not discussed adequately in the public domain.

We depend on the west because (finished) goods come from the west. We are fighting to achieve rights enjoyed by British citizens. We feel bad because we lack the freedom to carry out our activities, and we agitate against the government. But we are not giving enough attention to the root cause of our dependence and our agony. The root cause is industrial dependence. It will be better if we understand the nature of industrial dependence as early as possible.

In the past, human labour was required to do work. But after the industrial revolution, the value of human labour has fallen. Europe and America have exponentially progressed due to the industrial revolution. We have not gained an advantage from the industrial revolution for several reasons. First is a vast country and fertile land. Second, our approach is spiritual rather than material. The third reason is that we have been fighting for the past 700-800 years to maintain our independence. Four is our weather and our satisfactory nature. The conclusion is that we remained aloof to using natural powers to drive the huge machinery. Europeans have understood and mastered the control of natural powers like heat, steam, electricity, etc., so they are overpowering us. We are facing the machine power with the manpower.

There are two types of goods, viz., handmade and machine-made goods. We produce handmade goods, and Europe produces machine-made goods. It is not possible to compete machine-made goods with hand-made goods. This condition worsened with the consolidation of British power, and we attained the lowest point of industrialisation in 1872. However, after 1875, people realised the importance of machines, and we have made significant progress.

There is a long way to go. But at least our direction is right, and we are on the right path (however slow our speed is).

Still, there is a lack of capital and technical and professional education. What is the point of crying about these facts? Is it possible to get all the above things if we lament their absence? It is impossible to generate capital without establishing industry and industrial education, and it is impossible to start an industry without capital and industrial education. To gather the capital, we should at least create small-scale industries. We can take loans from foreigners and even employ skilled people from the west or train our people. We need two things. First is dedication, and second is honesty. When both combine with business acumen and calculated risk-taking ability, we shall rise quickly. Hence, educated people should come forward to establish and run industries."

Tilak wrote an article in *Kesari* dated 11th February 1896. The title is 'The height of injustice'. Below is the translation of the relevant extracts from the article:

"For what reason is England ruling Bharat? The queen's charter says that the queen took the reign in her hands from the East India Company. For the benefit of the Bhartiya people. But the experience is diametrically opposite. The recent taxation law is the epitome of oppression. It was impossible to dismiss public opinion in any country other than Hindustan. I do not think that government should not impose a tax on the goods produced in our country. But when the government imposes a tax on goods made in Bharat to benefit foreign traders, it cannot be tolerated. Even Englishmen deserted their motherland in America and became independent (due to draconian taxation policy). We have this example in front of us. Still, if we do not fight against them, it would be the height of our weakness. Those who tolerate such injustice will never have political rights. Hence, I appeal to people from all provinces to understand this issue and should come forward to resist the despotic government.

There was no justified reason to tax thick clothes produced by local cotton mills. It was taxed because of the pressure of the lobby of

Manchester cotton mills. It violates the basic principles of economics. The rich should pay more taxes than the poor. But the incumbent law is the precisely opposite. Wealthy people and the middle class wear thin clothes, and they pay 5% tax on the retail price, and now they will pay 3.5% tax, whereas poor people who wear thick clothes (who were paying no tax) are now obliged to pay 3.5% tax. It means the tax burden on the rich has become less, and the tax burden on the poor has increased. The loyal tendencies of moderates are useless. Real loyalty and tolerance of injustice cannot stay united. In the past, it was a king who used to impart justice. Today it is assumed that the person who imparts justice is the king! When a meeting was held in Mumbai on this issue, Mr. Kitriz publicly said that people of any other country would never tolerate such injustice. The dispute between Ireland, America, and Britain is similar. The issue of taxation invokes a furious and tempestuous response. When England imposed the tax a hundred years ago on the tea from America without consulting them, American people threw tea boxes in the ocean but did not pay taxes, and after that, America became independent. Mr. Gosling cited this example in the meeting in Mumbai. These examples teach us what we should do.

I request all people to come forward and protest against such oppressive law. Our government should run the government for our welfare and not for the welfare of Manchester. Those whose minds do not get infuriated due to oppression are animals. Americans, who were originally British, separated from the kingdom. We are at least not planning to do that. But it does not mean that we are going to tolerate such policies. If the law is oppressive, then we should use appropriate tactics to protest against such a law. Many people in America and France are well-educated in economics. They do not find anything wrong in providing an impetus to local goods. So why are our 'middle-class' people deserting local clothes? Poor people do not wear foreign clothes. The real consumer of Manchester goods is the educated class. It is ironic. If Manchester is not considering our interests, then why should we take care of their interests? Hence, I sincerely again request that if you have humanity left in your heart and are against oppression inflicted by the government, please wear local clothes. It will be revenge against Manchester's oppression.

We should not waste time and express our anger not with words but through action. Educated people should act. If all people unite against this law, the government will take it back and, in the future, will not bring such a law. We do not need any special occasion to begin using Bharatiya clothes. All types of local garments are available and are being produced. Hence, I request the people of Maharashtra, if you want to strive for the welfare of this country, if you are angry with the government of Bharat, if you think that the government should maintain the interests of Bharat, if you know the basic principles of politics and economics and if you are not able to tolerate injustice then use Bhartiya clothes without giving any excuses."

Tilak has written extensively about the British's destruction of trade and business in Bharat. Below is the translation of the relevant extracts from the article he wrote in *Kesari* dated 11th November 1902 (Title: How our trade and businesses were destroyed?):

"If the wealth of a country depends entirely on agriculture, then the country's economic condition will not remain stable for a long time. If the people's fortune is linked to the rain, it is not possible that people would live happily. There are only two solutions to relieve this uncertainty, and implementing these solutions depends significantly on the government. The first solution is to give people an impetus to excel in trade, business, and art forms. The second solution is to permanently fix the share of the king so that farmers would be able to survive for years and would be able to store the grain for the future; the amount to be paid should be minimal so that the farmer and his family could sustain for a year and store for the famine year.

From ancient times to East India Company rule, Bharat witnessed various rulers and dynasties. But no Bhartiya (or even foreign rulers) touched basic principles (explained above). According to Manu, land tax should be between 0.0833 (1/12) and 0.166 (1/6). It was raised to 0.25 (1/4) by Islamic rulers. But there was no specific attempt to destroy the Bhartiya trade. Hence, even under Islamic rulers, we did not face many hardships economically. Before Islamic rule, the prowess of art and trade had lured foreigners. Our ancestors knew the importance of trade and business. *Rishi Valmiki* has given an exhaustive and detailed list in *Ramayana* describing various businesses. *Maharshi Vyas* has gone one step ahead and has advised *Dharmaraja Yudhishthira* on the importance of trade and business through the mouth of *Bhishma*. Skills of ancient times are evident even today in the form of caves, edicts, etc. They show how advanced our country was if compared to contemporary nations.

Even before the sixth century, we were trading with China and Iran. We were trading with the Roman empire through the Mediterranean Sea in the tenth century. There was also a robust trade with the other faction of the Roman empire (Byzantine empire), whose capital was Constantinople. The trade received a setback in the eleventh century due Arab uprising and in the thirteenth century due to anarchy. But at the end of the seventeenth century, there was no sign of the destruction of trade or art forms. Foreign travellers like Diluvial, Rey, Termer, and Dr. Frayer visited Bharat at the beginning of the seventeenth century. They had written their accounts which depicted the prosperous trade and business. Even when the rule of East India Company was not established and even after a few years of the establishment of the rule (company officials had confessed that), Bhartiya people were far advanced in various art forms and skill works. But soon, times changed. Local industries became extinct. Artforms and skills also disappeared. I have elaborated on the oppressive policies adopted by East India Company on the issue of land tax collection. In this article, I will explain the systematic destruction of trade and businesses in our country.

East India Company governed Bharat with the instruments of trade and political power. There was a demand for Bhartiya goods in Europe.

Bhartiya garments, especially silk and woollen garments, were popular in Europe. Kashmiri shawls were extremely popular. The textiles manufactured in Bharat were of the highest quality. Thomas Munro had replied in the House of Commons committee that he uses the Kashmiri shawl and would not use any other top-quality shawl manufactured in the west.

Directors of East India Company were upset with the prosperous textile industry. They issued an order to discourage the export of finished goods, and only the export of raw materials was encouraged. They also forced hand weavers to work in the company's factory; if they were not ready, they were punished. Company government used to appoint 'residents' at various places. Those residents were responsible for providing the material demanded by the company. Residents used to make agreements with hand weavers. The trade of the East India Company was going in this way. They wanted to establish a monopoly over the trade. Hence, they issued an order in 1769 to punish those hand weavers who were not ready to work with the East India Company. Further, in 1793, they amended the law, and a provision was introduced to ban hand-weavers from working with other customers and were also forbidden from selling even foods before the completion of an agreement. Through this law, residents gained virtually unlimited powers. They gained the authority to control payments, revenue, etc. They were behaving arrogantly. Their behaviour is explained in previous articles. Such oppression resulted in the gradual decay of the business of textiles. Handweavers lost their art. It was obvious since the progress in skills and artwork was due to increasing trade. Increasing trade was due to the system which placed the least constraints on the movements of goods, which gave manufacturers freedom to sell their goods where they get a good price. The price would fluctuate according to the quality of goods manufactured; hence, workers would automatically be incentivised to work hard and produce the best quality goods. The policy adopted by East India Company was exactly the opposite. Officials of the company established a monopoly over trade.

They forced hand weavers to work. Slowly they lost their art. This was not the only mistake in the rule of the East India Company. There were many others.

The order issued in 1769 was the starting point of the grand policy envisaged by company officials to destroy the export from Bharat. They knew that if Bhartiya goods were incentivised, England would not gain but would lose to Bharat. Hence, they began further extraction of raw materials from Bharat and export of finished goods from Britain to Bharat. The indigenous textile industry was already in miserable condition due to residents' persecution of hand weavers. It did not survive the second shock and finally collapsed completely. Silk materials were banned from exporting, and high duties were levied on cotton textiles. The tables given show different duties imposed on different goods.[224] Heavy taxes were levied on goods manufactured in Bharat, but only a 2.5% duty was placed on the goods manufactured in Britain. Exhibitions of foreign goods were arranged. Eminent personalities like Lord Wellesley organised such exhibitions in Rohilkhand, Haridwar, etc.

Generally, the wishes of rulers get fulfilled! The production of goods in Bharat decreased, and the import of foreign goods increased. Officers did not stop there. They even levied high duties on goods produced and consumed within Bharat. An excise duty of 5% was imposed on raw materials, and an excise duty of 15% to 17 % was levied on finished goods. If the dead animal's skin is to be transported within the country, then the excise duty is 5%. If it is processed, the duty is 10%, and if goods (like shoes) are manufactured from it, then the duty is 15%. To collect taxes, collection centres were set up on roads and at the city's entrance. As officers were strict, traders had to offer heavy gifts to silence their voices! This was the internal state of trade and art-crafts. It resulted in the dramatic flooding of western goods in Bharatiya markets. Meanwhile, the steam engine was discovered in

---

224 Tilak has given two tables in his original articles to show duties on different goods in 1812, 1824 and 1832.

England, and wealth was looted in Bharat, which was used for raising capital. It fueled the industrial revolution. Physical sciences developed. The scientific method was applied in business. Directors of East India Company were busy in lotting Bharat. They were not ready to introduce new technology to Bharat. They did not give any impetus to local industries but murdered local industries by banning exports and imposing draconian duties. However, Indigo was being exported in large quantities. But its trade was in the hands of foreign traders. They had a monopoly in trade.

In this way, trade was destroyed. The destruction of hand weavers has been explained above. Other small-scale industries and businesses were also destroyed. The introduction of the railway also destroyed traditional transportation methods, and many people lost their jobs. In the Ganga River, thirty thousand sailors transported goods in 1780. One can imagine the scale of the destruction of the employment of such people due to the introduction of the railway. Farmers were the biggest customers of bullock carts (transport vehicles). So, farmers lost their key service providers.

We have only seen the past and not the present. The account of the destruction of trade and business in our country is shocking and creates a feeling of anxiety and consternation. If the same laws had been implemented in Britain, or Britain would have become dependent for ten to twenty years, then Britain would have been reduced to the lowest possible state. Unsurprisingly, the trade in Bharat is destroyed, or business has become extinct."

Tilak also criticised the huge military expenditure of the government. Below is the translation of the relevant extracts:

"The imperial hunger of Britain is not going to calm down. England is consuming the resources of Bharat to calm its imperial hunger. Bharat must train soldiers for the interests of Britain! Bharat is obliged to send military assistance to Britain.

Unfortunately, the substantial military expenditure is eating a large share of the revenue collected from poor Bhartiya people. To secure Bharat and British rule in Bharat, approximately sixty thousand British soldiers are deployed. The expenditure of those British soldiers is imposed on poor Bhartiya. After each British soldier, the British government in London exacts 7.5 pounds, i.e., 112 rupees, annually from the government of Bharat. It means the British imperial government in Bharat pays 75 lakh rupee (five lakh pounds) to the British crown.

The plundering of wealth and rising military expenditure are two critical questions in front of the nation. The behaviour of Britain with Bharat, especially in monetary matters, is oppressive. Colonial officers get paid by the British parliament, but state secretary and other officials get paid by the British government in Bharat. British empire extends to all parts of the world. England had to maintain an advanced naval force to secure the empire and the vested interests of Britain. The maintenance of the navy is exacted from Australia, and the amount is 45000 pounds. But no such amount was extracted from Canada when Bharat paid 262502 pounds. When Canadians revolted, British soldiers were sent to destroy the mutiny. British people paid the expenses. When British soldiers in Bharat rebelled, it was crushed with the help of Bhartiya soldiers, and a large section of the Bhartiya people remained neutral. Still, war expenses were levied upon the Bhartiya people. The expenditure on maintaining diplomatic ties with Iran (diplomats, embassy, etc.) was also levied on Bharat.

The large army is kept in Bharat, and we are told it is stationed here to protect Bharat. But in reality, the army is kept to provide security to the British empire extended in Asia. It means that the Bhartiya people pay for this army, and Britain uses it to secure its interests. This is how the division of labour works between Britain and Bharat. If there is a conflict with China or to crush mutiny in Africa or to capture Myanmar then, it has become habitual for Britain to use Bhartiya soldiers. In recent years, however, the British government has paid some amount for war expenses. It does not mean that the Bharatiya people can afford the military expenditure. In 1885, annual military expenditure was 16 crores; in 1890, it was 22 crores, and now it has become 27 crores.

It means that the revenue collected from farmers alone is equal to military expenditure. Constraints must be placed on such huge military expenditure. Educated leaders are crying against such huge military expenditure but have not achieved any success. As famines and poverty continue in Bharat, military expenditure is rising day by day."[225]

We have seen an exhaustive account of Tilak's writings about his time's economic situation. Almost all articles mentioned above were written before 1903. They formed the background (or foundation) of the Bengal revolution. Tilak described the pathetic situation of farmers, traders, manufacturers, and many people working in various occupations. He also went one step further and analysed the causes of their agony, and he found only one reason: the lack of political power in the hands of the Bhartiya people. He also identified ways in which the British plundered Bharat, like export bans, trade monopolies, military expenditure, land taxes, etc. He wrote extensively on each issue and tried to create unrest in the Bhartiya public. This was the foundation of *Swadeshi* and the boycott in the Bengal partition.

East India Company's and Britain's imperial rule destroyed the Bhartiya economy. Most of the people were living in extreme poverty. Bharat was a dependent nation. When the twentieth century began, the baggage of poverty was becoming larger. There was unrest in Bharat. Bharatiya people were angry and searching for a reason to display their anger. Tilak was fed up with useless tactics practised by moderates and their loyalty toward British rule. He was also searching for new methods of agitation. The situation was inflammable, and Curzon declared the partition of Bengal and Bengal uproared in one voice. A flame of nationalism ignited in Bengal and spread all over Bharat. The Bengal partition was the temporary reason. The unrest in the people was desperately searching for an event to manifest itself, and the Bengal partition provided the trigger required for the manifestation. Under the British, all provinces faced the same economic devastation.

---

225 टिळक विचार पृ.क्र. 133-137.

Hence, there was national anger against the British. Consequently, the movement in Bengal against the partition became a national movement. Two new methods of agitation, *Swadeshi* and boycott, came forward. In the second chapter, I have described the history of the Bengal partition and the schism between moderates and nationalists on the issue of boycott and *Swadeshi*.

Tilak knew the importance of *Swadeshi* and boycott. *Swadeshi* was the natural consequence of his economic analysis. The doctrine of *Swadeshi* completed the economic philosophy of Tilak, just like the doctrine of *Swarajya* completed his political thinking. He understood that Bharat's dependency was due to a lack of political power. This dependency reduced Bharatiya people as consumers of foreign goods, and Indigenous manufacturing was destroyed. *Swadeshi* and boycott of foreign goods were perfect solutions to those problems. Tilak vigorously spread the doctrine of *Swadeshi* and boycott. The doctrine of *Swadeshi* was not unknown to Maharashtra. We find the views of Tilak in *Kesari* in 1896 about *Swadeshi* clothes.[226] Tilak wrote multiple articles on Swadeshi. We shall see three articles which clearly explain his position. The first article appeared in *Kesari* on 22nd August 1905. The title is 'National boycott'. Below is the translation of the relevant extracts from the article:

"In the huge public meeting in Kolkata, the boycott resolution was passed. Many people have not understood the importance of that event. Some think that Bengali people have passed the resolution whose implementation is not practical. Some people have doubts about the capacity of Bengali people to implement the resolution. Both views are wrong and immature. These people have not understood the catastrophe of the Bengal partition. If these people had understood the gravity of the situation, they would have understood that the path of the people of Bengal was correct, as their demands were left unheard by the government.

---

226 See: *Kesari,* 17 March 1896.

I have written in the previous article that this is a time of emergency, and the people of Bengal are on the right path. For the past twenty years, Congress has been crying and praying. But our experience is that the government does not pay attention to our prayers. If there is a debate in an intellectual field, it is possible to pursue the opposite party with intellectual methods. But there is a drastic difference between the transformation of people's views about science and the transformation of the government's political views. Our experience is that if self-interests are threatened, then a radical transformation in views occurs (and not just by intellectual debating!). The same principle is applied in politics, especially in the relations between foreign nations and colonised populations.

Bharat is becoming weak day by day. Our government know this. But they are here to plunder our wealth. So why should they consider our situation? There is no threat to rulers' interests if the Bharatiya people lose their self-pride and fighting spirit. It is a blessing in disguise for the stability of the British empire. This is because if self-pride and nationalistic sentiments rise in Bhartiya' the people would object to plundering the nation. Hence, the government is anxious about not raising the Bhartiya people's condition and destroying all possible means of progress. The Bengal partition is one such attempt. Lord Curzon realised that Bengali people were united due to the Bengali language and the same culture, and the Bengali union was becoming strong. Hence, to curb the unifying tendencies of Bengali people, cunning Curzon attempted the partition. Superficial analysis of the Bengal partition can result in the perception that it is a provincial partition and should not be taken seriously. Some people do not understand the ill effects of partition on the nation. Nationalism is not mature in our country. I wholeheartedly congratulate the Bengali people. If the government tries to subdue the nationality of this nation, then we should unite and fight like the people of Bengal.

But the product of this movement is different. The Bengal partition has again proved the autocratic tendencies of the government. The government have always neglected public opinion. In such a situation, a need for different forms of agitation is evident and Bengali people have fulfilled the need. If rulers become autocratic, then people infuriate and even punish the king. The most prominent example of this can be found in the history of England. This method is not possible in Bharat, which is demilitarised and diverse. But there are other ways available, and they should be pursued. Our demands are rational and justified. The only question is how to compel the government to fulfil our demands. We were trying to pursue British people. But the success in such attempts was exposed by Mr. Hindman in a speech at the inauguration ceremony of 'India house' established by *Shyamaji Krushna Verma*. We need extreme methods (not moderate) to force the government to complete our demands. Lord Curzon, Mr. Broadrick or parliament are not ready to listen. If we do not have weapons, then the only option is unity (public opinion), and public opinion should be directed to annihilate the government's autocratic tendencies. We should try to build public opinion (in fact, it is our responsibility). Moderate methods will lead us nowhere.

Mr. Hindman has iterated the same principles. He said that the moderate methods are useless if you want to obtain rights from British rulers; instead, you should build your movement with determination and even use radical ways as there is no other option left. The truth in the preaching of Mr. Hindman is in front of us. It is good that the message delivered by Mr. Hindman is published at the right time.

It has been proved that we need an extreme form of agitation to open the eyes of arrogant bureaucrats, and naturally, the extreme form of agitation is a boycott and *Swadeshi*. It has a historical basis. Sir William Wedderburn has given one speech in front of the 'Greenwich Ireland Society'. In that lecture, he said that when Austrians had conquered Italy, Italians had boycotted the political system and Austrian foreign officers; hence governance became impossible. Wedderburn has said that if the people of Bharat adopt the same method, governance will become impossible. But our leaders are not in favour of boycotting the government. Instead, they demand cooperation with the government to carry out political reforms. Wedderburn has suggested that the British accept these demands as it is in the interests of Britain. The fear of boycott, as expressed by Wedderburn, is real. If the British want to rule us, let them rule, as we do not have weapons or fighting spirit. But at least we should boycott foreign goods so that the outflow of crores of rupee towards the west feeds foreign traders and labourers would stop. Some indigenously manufactured goods match the quality of foreign goods. If we do not get locally manufactured goods that match the quality of foreign goods, then we should buy goods manufactured in countries other than European nations. We should show our anger at British people who neglect our demands by boycotting their goods. We should not co-operate with them, at least in the trade.

Chinese people have adopted a similar technique against arrogant Americans. They boycotted American goods, and now Americans are listening to Chinese demands. Even Americans had boycotted British goods in the past. We have three examples of America, China, and Italy in front of us, and if we do not learn lessons from them, then we will register our name in history as the 'most hopeless people'! It is historically proven that if public opinion is built up with persistence, courage, and faith, it can defeat the oppressive and arrogant government. Bengal, in fact, the whole nation, is going through the same phase.

Let us decide to boycott British goods. If necessary, we shall buy goods from Germany, Japan, or America but not Britain. If we take such a decision, no law can force us to repel it. It is not illegal. Sedition is illegal. I am not against the use of constitutional methods of agitation. But if they are useless, then the method of constitutional agitation should be coupled with an extreme method of the boycott. Bengali people are following this method. People from other provinces should express sympathy towards their efforts and help them. It is our responsibility, and I hope our leaders will not step back in fulfilling their responsibility. This is a time of emergency, and such moments are rare in history, and if we do not take advantage of such moments, then it would be the height of stupidity.

The people of Maharashtra should help the Bengali people. The idea of *Swadeshi* (i.e., the use of Bharatiya clothes instead of foreign clothes) originated in Maharashtra. Few people in Pune had watched the *Swadeshi* attire of G V Joshi (*Sarvajanik* Uncle). Bengali people are using the same concept coupled with the boycott method. Fundamentally, boycott and *Swadeshi* are the same. We should arrange public gatherings to congratulate Bengali people for their firm decision, and we should extend the use of the method of boycott in all provinces. I have heard that such meetings are arranged in Amaravati and Mumbai. I hope that meetings will take place at each taluka place and district place and that people will start adopting the new doctrine. The sympathy of the people is with the new movement. We will encounter some senile leaders unwilling to adopt the *Swadeshi* and boycott. But we should not pay attention, or we should not waste our time pursuing their mind. Young people should come forward and should push the movement forward. The success of the national boycott is in its nationwide implementation. If the young generation led the movement, it would be one step forward in the national movement. If the boycott is to be implemented at the national level, it should be materialised at the provincial level. Different provinces like Maharashtra, Madras, Nagpur, *Varhad*, Bengal, and Punjab agree on the boycott. Today, many goods are being manufactured in our country. If we follow Bengali people, then it will alleviate our country's industrial and political situation."

The second article written by Tilak appeared in *Kesari* dated 5th September 1905. The title is '*Bahishkara Yoga*'. Below are the relevant extracts:

"Boycott is generally considered to be a religious punishment. But it is now also included in the penal code as the life-imprisonment. The meaning of boycott should be expanded and applied to practical matters. I had expressed this view in the article written in *Kesari,* which was about the Ireland land league in 1881. In that article, it was stated that if the boycott is implemented in practice, it can be used to complete our demands which have remained unfulfilled. In previous articles, the same views have been replicated. The only form of agitation available to Bhartiya is the boycott. In the last article, I gave an example of China, where Chinese people had boycotted American goods, which compelled America to send the council to China. Pioneer, an Anglo-Indian newspaper, says the following about the Chinese rebellion: "If Chinese boycott (of American goods) affect economic interests of America then Chinese people would get what they want. Americans will be obliged to retract oppressive laws passed in America." Use the word 'Bharatiya' instead of 'Chinese' and 'England' instead of the word 'America' in the previous sentence. It will clear the nature of our movement, and the irony is that Pioneer best explains the movement's conclusion!

The only problem is that in this movement, elite leaders and middle-class people have not enthusiastically supported the movement, even though poor people and the young generation have enthusiastically supported it. They have doubts, such as even if we have decided to use *Swadeshi* goods, we do not have sufficient production of *Swadeshi* goods. They asked us first to set up the industry (like the textile industry) and let factories start the production of goods, and then they would use it. This is the height of stupidity. When *Shrikrushna* was explaining the 'yoga' to *Arjuna* in Geeta, *Arjuna* asked similar nonsense questions to *Shrikrushna*. He also raised doubts over the applicability of *yoga* to calm the mind, which appears to be uncontrollable. The impotent questions raised by moderates are similar to that of doubts raised by *Arjuna*, and both have approximately identical answers.

We have decided to use the method of boycott (*Bahishkaryoga*) to curb the arrogant and autocratic tendencies of the government. It is not going to achieve its objectives immediately. It will take time. Using Swadeshi goods only after their production becomes sufficient is like learning to swim without entering the water! If the production of all goods becomes abundant in the country, why would people have to make a firm decision to use local goods? The production of all types of goods will rise if demand is generated by people and by the impetus given by the government. The government will not provide a boost to local production. If people also start postponing their decision to use *Swadeshi* goods, as suggested by moderates, then Bhartiya trade and manufacturing, which is a remnant, will also get destroyed. The decision of the *Swadeshi* does not mean immediately starting the production of every good we use. Imbecile critics should note this. *Swadeshi* also does not mean remaining satisfied with low-quality goods. G V Joshi decided to wear *Swadeshi* clothes. Time has passed since then. Today textiles and other goods are being produced in our country. If people firmly support the idea of *Swadeshi,* then the situation will improve immensely in the upcoming years. People criticising the idea of Swadeshi and advising to postpone the idea until the production reaches a sufficient level are deliberately misleading society. Such behaviour is condemnable. It is fatuous to stop the program's activity, whose effects will be seen in the future.

Not all types of goods are indeed produced locally. But it should not hurt our enthusiasm. If something is not happening at the current instant, we should break the task into pieces and start taking efforts. The demand must be generated if we want to produce all types of goods in Bharat. First, start using local goods. If locally manufactured goods are unavailable, use goods manufactured in Asian countries like Japan. Even if some goods manufactured in Japan are unavailable, use goods manufactured in Germany, France, or America. It shall resolve most of the problems. This is because almost all goods manufactured in Britain are manufactured in Germany, France, and America. The attempt of moderates to discourage the young generation without understanding the real motives (behind the *Swadeshi* movement) is cowardly, impolitic, and imbecile.

Some people say that the present movement is only industrial and not political. It is a misconception. Even though it is true that the current movement is not directly political, its indirect aim is to impact the government. I do not want to hide this fact. British rule has become strong enough in Bharat to neglect and brutally suppress public opinion. We had begged in front of the government, but it had not paid any attention to us. Now we are only left with the only option of the boycott. This is because the government has been controlling political power and trade. So at least we should protest in trade issues. Chinese people used this tactic to teach a lesson to Americans. I do not understand why we should not follow the same way. We would indeed have to use some foreign goods as we do not have enough production of some goods. But we should firmly decide to avoid the goods manufactured in autocratic Britain. This decision is indirectly political, and I think it should be. It is not right to postpone *Swadeshi* just because goods are not available. If we use local goods or goods manufactured in countries other than England, then it would hurt Britain. If goods are manufactured in Bharat, then the profit will also remain in Bharat or should go to any other nation other than Britain.

I want to tell the government that we are not in a position to take a political stand against your work, but why should we pay crores annually in taxes? We shall manufacture goods in this country or import from other countries, but we will not use goods manufactured in Britain. Britain has destroyed our trade. We must rejuvenate trade and business. There is no point in postponing the boycott until trade and business flourish in the country. The *Swadeshi,* as practised by G V Joshi, was commercial. Now the same idea has become (indirectly) political and practical. The movement will not immediately achieve its motives. Its effects will be seen in the distant future. If we start slowly but with conviction and continue the same path, we will achieve political and economic success in the distant future. Nobody tells you to use inferior quality goods but at least use daily goods manufactured in our country. More efforts should be focused on the production of goods. This path is right, and we will not be in trouble if we pursue it. We need conviction. This '*yoga*' is practical., indispensable and preferable. I hope people will follow the *Swadeshi*."

The third article written by Tilak appeared in *Kesari* dated 12th December 1905. The title is 'Criticism of *Swadeshi*'. Below is the translation of the relevant extracts:

"*Swadeshi* movement is gaining momentum and manifesting into new forms. Only a few are opposing *Swadeshi* or the politically sensitive boycott movement. Almost all have agreed to use locally made goods wherever possible. This unified view was reiterated in the Benares Congress, and now I have full conviction that this movement will be in practical use and people will adopt it in their daily life. More efforts are being taken to establish the importance and usefulness of *Swadeshi*. Intellectual people are also supporting the movement. Mr. Pandit, a barrister from Rajkot, has said that Swadeshi will reduce the people's dependency on farming with increased trade and business in rural areas, and it will further ease the burden on the agriculture sector, which will eventually help to reduce ill effects of famine. According to Mr. Pandit, the *Swadeshi* movement is a way towards self-reliance and is moral. The conclusion is that if you consider any dimensions like social, industrial, ethical, or economic, then the importance and applicability of *Swadeshi* are self-evident. Also, the history of advanced nations approves the same fact. Still, some articles appear which criticise the boycott movement and *Swadeshi*. This article aims to de-clutter these insensible doubts. In past articles of *Kesari*, I have indirectly answered some doubts, but explicit contemplation is required.

For the past twenty-five to thirty years, an economic theory has been propagated that if locally manufactured goods are brought at higher prices than cheaper foreign goods, it would ultimately decrease the nation's wealth. Current economists reject this theory. Many modern nations have adopted protectionist policies, i.e., levying high import duties on foreign goods to boost local trade and industries. The motive achieved by the political weapon of raising import duty can be achieved by the doctrine of *Swadeshi*, i.e., the use of locally manufactured goods instead of foreign goods. People are doing the duty of the government. Still, some stupid people suddenly start shouting against *Swadeshi*. Critics have said that due to the *Swadeshi* movement, Bengal and other provinces, a collective loss of 1.5 to 2 crore rupees in the past three to four months. They further say that if *Swadeshi* is continued further, it will lead to catastrophe. This is a misconception.

Let us assume that we buy locally manufactured goods at 1.25 rupee and their foreign counterpart is available at one rupee. It means if five crore local goods are consumed, the consumers pay one crore extra (if they would have bought their foreign counterparts). It appears that there is a loss of one crore. But one important point is not discussed in the criticism of *Swadeshi*. When we buy foreign goods, the profit goes to the foreign lands. When we buy local goods, the same money remains in our country. It is true that if people purchase *Swadeshi* goods, then they have to pay more. But as profit remains in our country, the money is used as capital to start new industries, factories, etc. Local trade and manufacturing get a boost by imposing high import duties or people voluntarily buying local goods. When a factory owner (capitalist) earns a profit, he uses it to expand his industry or to start a new industry. In this way, new industries and factories begin operation, and production automatically picks up, ultimately increasing the supply of goods. As the supply of goods accelerates, prices of local goods automatically drop and attain equilibrium. People who criticised *Swadeshi* for apparent loss do not understand economics. Protectionist trade policies and *Swadeshi* are two artificial methods of increasing local trade and business. Their ultimate effect is an increase in demand for local goods, and local industries start earning a profit which they use as capital to create a new business or reform current business, which in turn reduces the price of local goods and becomes equal to foreign goods. This is similar to the demand-supply cycle in economics. If the demand for commodity increases suddenly, then its price suddenly increases. As the price increases, the production of that commodity also increases, and as production picks up, prices attain an equilibrium.

One statistician has claimed that if we want to cut down the import of 25-30 crore foreign textiles, then in ten years, we need an annual capital of 2.5 to 3 crores. He has asked a question how can Bhartiya businessmen raise such capital? He is criticising *Swadeshi*. The answer to the criticism is not difficult. If the supply of local goods is low, then due to a rise in demand, at first, their price will rise. The industrialist will invest the capital to increase production, decreasing the price. If an annual capital of three crores is to be raised, people have to pay an extra 0.50 to 0.75 rupee per person. For the safer side, assume that 30 crore people would pay 0.25 paise extra. It is true that all the thirty-crore people will not support the *Swadeshi* movement. Even though we assume that half of the population remains ignorant, the extra charge of 0.25 rupee per person is reasonable. Even though a nation of thirty crore people is poor, it is perfectly possible to raise a capital of thirty crores in ten years. The government is earning approximately 100-125 crore in revenue through taxes from the same thirty crore people. If the government had raised import duties on foreign goods to protect local trade and business, the burden of high import duty would have been on people's shoulders. They would not have felt that burden as it would have been distributed equally to each person, and now it is being distributed in the form of a surge in prices due to *Swadeshi*. The only difference is that the action is due to the conviction of people (*bahishkaryoga*) and due to the resolution of the government. This is the only viable way in front of our nation to increase trade and business in our country. In such a situation, it is absurd and puerile to cry about loss due to inflated prices of local goods. The principle is that the profit remains in the nation instead of going into the pockets of foreigners. This is in the interest of the country.

Leaders of the *swadeshi* movement should closely monitor the rising prices of local goods. They should not let the price cross the particular value. To regulate prices, chains of stores which specifically sell local goods should be started (required capital should be raised from the people). The production and logistics must be upgraded to mitigate the rising demand. But up to such time, we have to face the inflated price of local goods, and we (consumers) should bear it for the nation's sake. We should do it in the national interest, and the principle behind our movement is to firmly decide and implement the use of *Swadeshi* (and boycott) in our daily life. It is not the path of pleasure. There is an inconvenience, but we should face it.

Some argue that many people cannot afford to buy local goods at higher prices. But those people who lack the financial ability (but want to pursue *Swadeshi*) can buy the same amount of local goods at which they buy foreign goods. The quantity would obviously be less, but they should try to manage their needs. Take the example of textiles. Assume that (on average) a family needs twenty rupees of foreign clothes annually. Now the same family can buy locally made clothes for twenty rupees. The quantity would be less, but a family can manage their expenses and needs as it is well-established that local clothes are more durable than foreign clothes. In this way, without losing huge sums of money, by bearing some cost, each and every person in this country can help *Swadeshi* and boycott. If the government had not been in the hands of foreigners, we would not have had to do these things. There are difficulties, but if we take appropriate actions with firm conviction, we can eliminate those difficulties. I hope people will follow 'bahishkarayoga'. Some selfish people will try to stop the movement, but people should neglect them and continue the same path."

This completes the exhaustive account of the account of writings of Tilak on economic affairs. He was among those few people who understood the root cause of the economic destruction of Bharat. To counter British imperialism and rejuvenate the Bharatiya economy, he formulated and preached the doctrine of *Swadeshi*. He was not an armchair critic. In the second chapter, there is a description of the practical efforts taken by Tilak for *Swadeshi*. He was the pioneer and architect of the notion of self-reliance (*Aatmanirbharata*) in the economic dimension.

Chapter 5

Swabhasha

Language is the most effective medium of communication. But it is not limited to communication. Language is also a medium of culture. It is a medium through which one accesses knowledge. It infuses unity in the people communicating in the same language.

Lokmannya Tilak was conscious of the importance of language. He had magnificent command over his mother tongue (Marathi). He was proficient in English. He also had an exceptional knowledge of the Sanskrit language.[227] He had a majestic understanding of linguistics. But all these personal qualities are not sufficiently important to understand the vociferous endorsement of *Swabhasha* by Tilak. It requires an inquiry into the personal life of Tilak and the public and intellectual life of Maharashtra and Bharat.

Tilak's father, Gangadharpant Tilak, was a primary teacher in a Marathi school. He was a self-educated man and had acquired proficiency in mathematics and Sanskrit.[228] He wrote books on the history of England, arithmetic and grammar. The school education department published a few.[229] Now we shall discuss the evolution of Marathi grammar in which Tilak's father had a little contribution.

When British rule began, the school education department was established. Officers on the education board ordered three *pandits* to write a grammatical book for Marathi. The grammar book was first

---

227 When he was in Mandalay, he tried to learn French and German.

See: केळकरकृत टिळक चरित्र खंड २ भाग ९ पृ. क्र. १७

228 केळकरकृत टिळक चरित्र खंड 1 पृ. क्र. 7.

Kelkar. (1928). *Life and Times of Lokmanya Tilak.* p. 14.

229 उपरोक्त पृ. क्र. 7.

Ibid, p. 14.

written in 1824. Handwritten copies were created and circulated in schools. It was in use for twelve years. The book was extremely small. It was based on Sanskrit grammar. It survived for three to four editions. *Balshastri Jambhekar* (a Marathi journalist from Mumbai) wrote another small book titled '*Balvyakaran*'. It was similar to the first book and had a format of question and answer. It was a beginner's book and was being used in Marathi schools for many years. After that, *Dadoba Pandurang Tarkhadkar* wrote '*Maharashtra Vyakaran*' in 1836. Its revised edition was published in 1850. As *Dadoba* was superintendent of Marathi schools in southern Maharashtra, he was well aware of the grammar format most suitable for pedagogical purposes. He wrote the grammar based on the English language. Maybe, because he was not sound with Sanskrit grammar and lacked historical discretion, he further revised his grammar based on Sanskrit grammar. Still, changing the basic framework based on English grammar was impossible. Hence, even though one cannot doubt the intellect, scholarship and knowledge of *Tarkhadkar*, his grammar was somewhat incomplete and had some mistakes. But without any doubt, *Tarkhadkar* was the first Marathi grammarian.

Tarkhadkar's grammar book was not suitable for pedagogical purposes. Hence, Gangadhar Ramchandra Tilak (father of Lokmanya Tilak) wrote one book titled '*Laghuvyakarana*' in 1860. It was a short version of *Tarkhadkar's* book. It was not an original book, but extremely useful in teaching primary schools. Further, the government asked *Tarkhadkar* to write a short version of his book, and it replaced Tilak's short book. Reverend Varghese, a missionary, also had written an excellent book on Marathi grammar.

Tarkhadkar systematically founded the structure of Marathi grammar. But there was no historical analysis involved in it. When the university was established, the Marathi language was introduced as a subject in higher education. Hence, in those times, intellectual debates were in full swing between brilliant teachers and students like *Mandalik*, Ranade, Pandit, Modak, Kunte, etc. and young people from

Pune Pathshala like *Chiplunkar*, Godbole, *Rajwade, Talekar*, etc. about Marathi grammar. Major Candy was Marathi translator in the school education department.[230] He was associated with multiple Bhartiya *pandits*. Fierce linguistic debates were held in those days, and some discussions were published. Dr. Bhandarkar gave lectures on the origin of the Marathi language. Candy and his associates and Dr. Bhandarkar, *Chiplunkar*, etc., differ fundamentally over the structure and origin of the Marathi language. During such time, *Dakshina Prize Committee* threw a challenge to Marathi intelligentsia to write a grammar which would have systematic exposition and contemplation about the transformation of Sanskrit to Prakrit to Marathi. *Krushnashastri* Godbole completed the challenge. He wrote a book '*Navin Marathi Vyakaran*' published in 1867. In this book, we find a profound contemplation on the historical and etymological aspects. The structure of Godbole's grammar book is based on *Chiplunkar's* essays. *Krushnashshtri Chiplunkar* wrote highly intellectual, academic and erudite essays, which were later compiled into a book titled 'Essays on Marathi grammar' (*Marathi Vyakaranavaril Nibandh*).[231]

This history of Marathi grammar and grammarians is not only interesting but sheds light on the background in which Tilak began his literary career. *Krushnashastri* and *Vishnushastri Chiplunkar*, and Tilak single-handedly transformed Marathi prose in the nineteenth and early decades of the twentieth century. It was a remarkable, incredible and astonishing phenomenon which went unnoticed. Maharashtra has a rich tradition of saints who enriched the Marathi language with poetic works filled with devotion and love towards god. Excellent and unparalleled poetry texts like *Dnyaneshwari* by *Santshrestha Dnyashewara Maharaj*, *Tukaram Gatha* by *Santshrestha Tukaram Maharaj, Dasbodh* by *Samarth*

---

230 Candy served in the military and then as headmaster in *Vishrambag* school. He had an excellent command of the Marathi language.

231 This whole discussion on Marathi grammar and grammarians is based on the following:

कृष्णशास्त्री चिपळूणकरकृत मराठी व्याकरणावर निबंध पृ. क्र. ५-११.

Ramdas Swami, etc. are a few examples. Prose works mostly consist of historical letters and *bakhar*. This Marathi prose lacked sophistication and needed systematisation. Grammarians like *Tarkhadkar* and *Krushnashastri* did this sophistication and systematisation, and it was brought into the application to transform and create a new Marathi prose style by *Vishnushastri* and then by Tilak.

A person learns the mother tongue by imitation. He imitates words and sentences spoken by others. This method of imitation is natural and better than learning through grammar. Grammar generalises rules governing the structure of language. But such general rules do not hold good (in absolute terms) in practice. To learn a new language, a person must communicate regularly with people who have that particular language as their mother tongue and read excellent literature in that language. Hence, it is a must for a person who wishes to learn a new language for general-purpose communication and does not need to learn grammar. However, it does not downgrade the importance of grammar. One who wishes to become an effective orator or prudent author has to learn grammar (even for mother tongue). Grammar is as helpful for authors or orators as musicology for vocal musicians. It is possible that some vocal musicians may lack an understanding of musicology and also that excellent orators lack a grasp of grammar. It can be justified based on natural talents which lie in such people. But for the majority, understanding grammar is essential. There are many other important aspects of grammar. It is a science of language. It expands the analytical and thinking power.[232]

The Constitution of Marathi grammar was a dramatic event in the history of the Marathi language. After this, the dimensions of Marathi prose widened. Marathi prose witnessed significant expansion in two directions. One was studying history (especially of the Maratha empire) by stalwarts like *Rajwade, Parasnis, Vasudevshastri Khare*, etc. The second direction was journalism, philosophy, monographs, and

---

232 कृष्णशास्त्री चिपळूणकरकृत मराठी व्याकरणावर निबंध पृ. क्र. 1-10 Pages are to be read from main text and not from the introduction.

dharmashastra by stalwarts like *Vishnushastri* and Tilak. Instruments used were newspapers, periodicals, monthlies, magazines, etc. These two people transformed and created a new Marathi prose style. *Vishnushastri* had a special place in the life of Tilak. He was among very few people who influenced Tilak. A significant impact of Chiplunkar's views on Tilak's views on education and language is evident. Now I shall represent a brief analysis of *Chiplunkar's* views on language. This is extremely important because *Chiplunkar*, in his initial monographs in *Nibandhamala,* has sketched the real state of the Marathi language, the government policy towards the Marathi language and the linguistic slavery of 'educated' Bhartiya people. His articles are illuminatory, eye-opening and self-explanatory. I have translated relevant portions from his monographs. He wrote his first article in *Nibandhmala* in the year 1874. The title was 'Present state of Marathi language.' Below are relevant extracts from the article:

"This is a phase of transformation for nation and language. In this essay, I am not going to discuss the nature of the transformation of language, but I am going to discuss the transformation of language. This is an important issue because advancement in the language is important for the nation's progress. Also, this essay does not discuss the historical evolution of the Marathi language. The only question discussed is the present state of Marathi and where there exists a scope for progress.

Established intelligentsia in Maharashtra is composed of people who think that Marathi is a qualitatively poor language compared to English; it lacks the quality of comprehension; it is unsophisticated and unable to convey the proper meaning. Many teachers cannot translate English into Marathi, and they blame Marathi for this! Before ten to twenty years, educated people used to write books in Marathi. But now nobody wants to express their thoughts in Marathi. The majority of educated people express their thoughts in English.

I do not find any logic in rejecting Marathi. Marathi people in the past had raised their flag to Delhi and *Atak.* In Marathi, saints like *Tukaram* and *Ramdas* have written poetry texts. Many poets like *Mukteshwar, Moropant,* and *Vaman Pandit* have brought Marathi at par with Sanskrit for prudence with their eloquent and excellent style. Marathi language has many inherent qualities and does not need to import from other languages. Those who doubt this statement should read Molesworth's[233] and Candy's dictionaries preface. Especially, Molesworth's dictionary is excellent for those who wish to understand the exact nature of the Marathi language. But due to shameless neglect towards such dictionaries or egoistic attitudes, Marathi has downgraded to the lowest state.

Some funny remedies are being prescribed, such as reintroducing Marathi at the university level or making Marathi compulsory at the matriculation level. Ironically, after eight to nine years of establishing a university, Marathi was at the university level and also was compulsory for matriculation. How does Marathi benefit? How many books were written in Marathi? Similar questions can be raised for the *Dakshina prize committee.* In the history of the world, no language has ever achieved (a significant level of) prudence due to the introduction of such forceful or greedy measures. A person who achieves remarkable success does not achieve it through such artificial solutions. It needs a natural solution. No solution would be effective till the neglect and contempt for *Swabhasha* continue to present in people's minds. But somehow, if neglect and contempt disappear, then (above mentioned) artificial measures would not be needed.

Critics may point out that the Persian and Arabic languages were in close contact with Marathi. Hence, according to critics, why should we have a problem with English? The impact of the Arabic language over the Marathi language became negligible when the dominance of Islamic rulers vanished in Deccan. Also, the Persian language and its impact on Marathi have become insignificant with the end of *Peshwai.* The content of foreign words in Marathi has shrunk in the past thirty

---

233 Molesworth was a missionary who prepared the English-to-Marathi dictionary.

years, and it appears that this trend will continue in the future. In *Peshwai*, official documentation was also kept in Persian along with Marathi. Hence, Persian words became prevalent in use. But the way the Persian language was being studied was significantly different from the English language study. People used to learn the Persian language for practical purposes only. It means that the use of the Persian language was constrained to official purposes. Today we find several people with excellent command over the English language and its literature. It was not the case with the Persian language.

Today it is necessary for every person to understand the English language. It has become a part of life. Mastery of English has become a status symbol. Young intelligentsia has become intoxicated with this language. They even cannot converse in their mother tongue with their parents, spouse, sisters, or servants. The functions of mind (like deliberation, conceptualisation, etc.) of these people also happen in English. Hence, writing or oration in the mother tongue is expressed after translation! This 'universal' dominance of the English language is threatening the existence of Marathi. As ideas and thoughts originate from the mind and have become British, it is evident that Marathi has gone to rack and ruin. After this analysis of the present state of the Marathi language, I will elaborate on my views on the advancement of Marathi.

The English language is mixed with the Marathi language. If this unprecedented mingling continues with no barrier, Marathi will lose its original identity, and soon we will be unable to separate it from the English language. If we become British and Christian, our identity gets destroyed, and there would be no point in discussing national rejuvenation. Similarly, if Marathi became identical to English, there would be no reason to talk about its rejuvenation. I do not have hatred towards English. We can get benefited from various books in the English language. But to receive these benefits, we have to maintain the 'linguistic independence' of Marathi. Marathi has another benefit. It shows remarkable linguistic affinity with Sanskrit. In the past, most of the sciences were written in Sanskrit. Hence, specific terminology in Sanskrit can be used in Marathi. If we lacked such convenience, we would be compelled to use cacophonic words like Mediterranean, atmosphere, and refraction, which have elegant, beautiful, and dignified counterparts in Marathi. Also, Sanskrit has a treasure of poetry works. In the field of poetry, Sankrit can help us. Those who want to master the Marathi language should have at least introductory knowledge of the Sanskrit language.

In the past fifty years, dictionaries and grammar were created in Marathi, which standardised it (due to an impetus provided by the government). Now let us discuss the work done by journalists and independent authors. Newspapers have sprung up in large numbers. People think this is a sign of an increase in the intellect of our society! I do not think so. There is some truth in the claim that people's general knowledge has increased. But the real reason behind the sudden increase of newspapers is the habit of blind imitation. Blind imitation only reflects a lack of intellect, a confused state of mind, and intellectual slavery. Still, the role of newspapers is extremely critical in the growth and development of the language. Some newspapers, which were excellent in the past, have degraded, while others have excelled in quality. There is obvious room for improvement, and the quality is improving, and I think it will improve further in the future. The same case applies to monthlies.[234]

Now I will take about literary works published in the recent past. When people started reading English literature, they felt the vacuum in Marathi prose. They were eager to fill that vacuum. Most people fill the void with translation. This trend of translation continued. Numerous English and Sanskrit works were translated. Slowly, Marathi's prose

---

234 Vishnushastri used to write in monthly 'shalapatrak' started by his father, *Krushnashastri Chiplunkar*. Other important monthlies were *danbhharak, vividhdyanvistar, stridnyanpradip,* etc. *Ramakrishna Gunjkar* was the founding editor. In it, scholarly articles were published and written by contemporary physical and social sciences scholars.

was improving. But unfortunately, intelligentsia started distancing themselves from Marathi due to rising Anglophobic tendencies. One should not think that all of the current books which are being published are inferior in quality. As there is devoid of scholarly critics, it is obvious that good and bad books are kept in the same place. There is an increase in enthusiasm for writing. Not all the books published may be excellent in quality. There exists an extent of discernment. If we want to evaluate our scholarly work, then the evaluation should be done by a critic who possesses two important qualities: lack of jealousy and another is outspokenness. Critics with these qualities are extremely rare. If such critics are present, the discernment of the quality of literature gets amplified.

Today if the author wants to publish his book, he has three options. First is self-publication, second is appeasement of subordinate officers in the education department, and third is to apply directly to higher authority in the education department. The first method is costly and difficult. The remaining two methods are horrible! The government appoints officers, editors, and critics in the education department. But they even lack a basic understanding of literary criticism. Hence, the newspaper should frankly publish their genuine opinions without fear and enlighten people about good books that have become obsolete."

In this article, Chiplunkar has sketched the contemporary condition of Marathi. In the following article, he talks about the history of books and magazines and discusses the benefits of books and magazines to language and the rejuvenation and growth of language. The title is 'The aim of *Nibandhmala*.' Below are relevant translated extracts from the article:

"In the past ten years, there has been appreciable progress in the quality of content in newspapers. But there is not much progress in periodicals or books. This is astonishing. I think there are three important reasons for the lack of growth of books in Marathi if compared to the growth of newspapers. The first reason is the neglect of intelligentsia towards Marathi. The second reason is the inclination of both old and new generations towards newspapers. The exponential growth of newspapers is due to this tendency. Newspapers set the narrative in public life. They also spread knowledge in society to an appropriate degree. Hence, their exponential growth is commendable. But people think that the epitome of resources of knowledge is newspapers. There is no other way to gain knowledge. Sometimes news about the establishment of libraries, even in villages, surfaces. But it has not translated into the increase in reading habits of society. Hence, instead of reading voluminous books to gain knowledge, people prefer reading newspapers (in which they read irrelevant topics such as entertainment). The third reason is that running a newspaper is easier than publishing books. Newspapers are profitable due to advertisements. There is also scope for editorials and columns for other scholars. There always exists a subject on which an editorial can be written. But the content in newspapers is ephemeral. This is not the case with books. It should always contain a pristine idea. It is not always possible to borrow from other books. Books are not ephemeral like newspapers but are enduring. Hence, books draw criticism for a relatively long duration compared to newspapers. Also, it is important to fill all the pages of the book with our content; it is also critical to give attention to defects in writing! These are three reasons for the lack of growth in books. The first two reasons offer biter resistance to the growth of books. But if somehow they vanish, the third reason would automatically disappear. Now, I will discuss the importance of books in national rejuvenation.

A few years ago, there used to be articles in newspapers on trade, current affairs, language, etc. There used to be articles on literary criticism of books. People also used to send letters to newspapers. In current newspapers, many of the above-mentioned things have completely disappeared. Articles on language have become rare. This is a good thing because the subject of the language does not come under newspaper writers. It is a subject of books and periodicals. Now I will elaborate on a brief history of periodicals in Marathi.

Periodicals were started by *Bal Gangadhar Jambhekar*. He was the founder of the trimonthly periodical *Dnyadarshak*. There were a few monthlies like *Digdarshan*, *Chandrika*, *Dnyaprasarak*, etc., in the early period of British education. In that period, periodicals were the only medium to access a new form of knowledge. The history of periodicals is not so old. Even in England, it started 150 years ago. Addison was the first essayist in England. Johnson, Goldstein, etc., succeeded him. In those days, essays were small, two to three pages. But at the beginning of this century, there was a transformation in prose style, and the number of pages also increased. Macaulay was the famous essayist of his generation. People ran periodicals do not take the history of periodicals into account. In those days, periodical *Dnyadarshak* was the leading periodical. It was based on the model of periodicals like 'Edinboro,' and 'Quarterly'. The aim of the periodical should be that reader should get easily acquainted with various branches of knowledge. If we want to get complete knowledge, then we must read original voluminous books. But such books do not attract common readers. Common people do not find those books interesting. If such periodicals introduce complex subjects interestingly, it becomes easy for people to comprehend the topic, and some may continue reading.

Periodicals were not possible in ancient times or even five hundred years ago in Europe due to a lack of printing. The lack of printing had put obvious constraints on the spread of knowledge. Today most of the barriers to knowledge and trade have disappeared. Today the people who wish to write in Marathi lack mastery over Marathi and literature, and those who do not want to write in Marathi possess the ability to create literature! These people have an insane fascination towards the English language. English has percolated into each and every sphere of life of educated men. They view Marathi with neglect and a contemptuous attitude.

Marathi has attained the lowest state today. If it continues further, it may die out. In public life, many discussions are going on about patriotism, trade, reforms, etc. I cannot understand the neglect towards language. It is our duty to rescue Marathi from such degraded condition and move it on the path of progress and linguistic prosperity. I have written this article to spread awareness about the importance of Marathi. I view this task as a patriotic one. To quote Johnson, 'To an author, nothing is more dangerous than neglect.'. I request my readers to send their opinions even if contrary."

This is an enlightening article written by *Chiplunkar*. It shows a realistic sketch of the degradation of the Marathi language. Now I will elaborate on what exactly degradation means and its process. Degradation of the Marathi language has two components. First is the unnecessary mixing of English words in the Marathi language.[235] The second is the change in the original form of the language, which starts resembling the English language.[236] What are the reasons behind degradation? According to *Chiplunkar*, the reasons behind the degradation of the Marathi language were not the study of the English language but the absence of self-pride, love, and affection towards the mother tongue.[237] When self-pride is absent, it creates a vacuum in a person's mind. Often this vacuum gets filled by contempt and neglect towards language. English education killed self-pride in Bharatiya people. This resulted in contempt and neglect towards the history of Bharat, Bharatiya arts, literature, and mother tongue. Slavery entered into the dimension of the language! *Chiplunkar* has brilliantly connected the concept of 'subsidiary alliance' with the language. We should take the help of foreign languages up to a limit, after which that help starts

---

235 It is important to note that Chiplunkar was not totally against the use of English words. But he was against the 'unnecessary' use.

236 In this type of degradation, the basic character of the language is threatened. In any language, there exists a separation between the figurative and literary meaning; this separation is often a definitive characteristic of the language. Just as each nation has distinctive clothing and traditions, so as language. When this traditional separation breaks down due to an alien language, a new separation is created based on the alien language. It hurts the very soul of the language. Chiplumkar has given a few examples of such change. See: भाषादूषण

237 भाषादूषण

hurting the original language. (That is, any language should not enter into a treaty of 'subsidiary linguistic' alliance with a foreign language (especially English). Otherwise, it would meet the same fate as that of various princely states in Bharat!).[238] There are other essays on the language written by *Vishnushastri*, but the discussion is out of the scope of this book. *Chiplunkar* has covered all the aspects of languages, i.e., script, style, reading, writing, speech, translation, etc. Interested readers should read these articles from *Nibandhmala*.[239]

Chiplunkar and Tilak had similar views about the importance of the mother tongue. One can find subtle marks left by *Chiplunkar's* writing on Tilak's mind, which reflects in his writings on the language. It is important to know about Tilak's own opinion about *Swabhsha* and *Chiplunkar*. There are two articles in *Kesari* dated 19th March 1901 and 2nd April 1901 in which Tilak elaborated on conditions in the time of Chiplunkar and the nature and importance of the work done by *Chiplunkar*. In the second article, while elaborating on work done by *Chiplunkar* in the field of language, Tilak categorically expressed his views on *Swabhasha* and *Chiplunkar*.[240] Below are the relevant translated extracts from the article:

"Language is the only instrument to convey our thought to another person. The people who empower their mother tongue (*Swabhasha*) by expressing their emotions and rationales are equally important as people who first initiated the practical use of language. The growth and progress of *Swabhsaha* are important 'instruments' in the growth and progress of *Swarashtra* (nation), and these 'instruments' were 'perfectly mastered' and brought into use by *Vishnushastri*.[241] If one wants to express his opinions and thoughts to his countrymen, there is no other instrument than *Swabhasha*. This should be remembered by

---

238   भाषादूषण

239   लेखनपद्धति भाषापद्धति वाचन भाषांतर वक्तृत्व

240   The title of the first article is: *Vishnushastri Chiplunkar* and his times.
      The title of the second article is Late *Vishnushastri Chiplunkar*.

241   This sentence perfectly captures the work done by *Chiplunkar*.

the people who have received an English education. Those who do not have any solicitude for the people or do not want to spread knowledge in society cannot contribute to the growth of the language. In the time of *Vishnushastri*, there were contemporary scholars. But those scholars did not use Marathi because of a lack of solicitude. Knowledge of Marathi is necessary to translate English books into Marathi. But one cannot serve his mother tongue if there is a lacuna of ardour and fervour to spread his ideas to people. An actor can effectively express his emotions on the stage. But it is difficult to do the same thing with the help of pen and paper.

Language is a weapon in the hand of the nation. One who makes this weapon has done an immense favour to the nation. One can have differences of opinion with *Vishnushastri*. But for his altruistic work, one should always respect and remember him. An author needs a topic on which he can write and should pick up a topic from his contemporary time. The topic picked up by *Chiplunkar* was the continuation of the work done by his predecessors. Today we are witnessing the growth of patriotism, discipline, morality, etc. *Chiplunkar* was the activator and motivator of these narratives. I sincerely hope that the ripples which surfaced in the minds of people who received English education will fade away; they will recognise the importance of *Swadharma*, *Swabhasha*, and *Swadesha* and their duties towards their fellow countrymen and will perform their duties determinedly with the help of *Niti*."

Chiplunkar and Tilak were co-founders of New English School. The spirit of self-reliance and self-sacrifice shown by the founders and the level of efficiency in education reached and maintained by them were regarded on all hands as remarkable revelations of Bhartiya character and Bharatiya capacity of action.[242] Chiplunkar, in 1880 report had written about three reforms introduced in school. The second reform was about the teaching of vernacular. The teaching of vernacular was closely attended.[243] *Chiplunkar* sowed the seeds of love for the Marathi

---

242 Limaye, P. M. (1935). *The History of the Deccan Education Society*. p.7.
243 Ibid, pp. 12-13.

language. On 1st January 1883, *Nutan Marathi Vidyalaya* (which evolved into *Shikshan Prasarak Mandali* and Sir *Parashurambhau* College of Pune) was established by young Marathi teachers inspired by *Chiplunkar* in memory of *Chiplunkar*. The aim was obvious, i.e., to impart education in the Marathi language from the first standard to the sixth standard.[244]

On 9th September 1882, Apte placed the views of the founders of New English School in front of the Hunter commission. Apte focused on nine points in his evidence. One of the points was the medium of instruction. He stressed the necessity of imparting education in Bharatiya languages.[245] He also criticised vernacular serial reading books as exactly what they should not be![246] The founders of New English School viewed the exaggerated and unnatural importance given to the English language as a serious defect. Apte, in his evidence before Hunter commission, said: "The aim of the whole education appears to be to make the natives speak and write good English, to make them Burkes, Addison or Macaulay in English and not to enable them to be masters of their mother tongue, as if the object of the university was to send forth into the world of Anglicised graduates instead of graduated natives."[247]

Bharatiya languages were neglected, and Apte pointed out this neglect. As English is a foreign language, it becomes hard for a student to grasp the knowledge of the subject; in other words, the high school student's study of the subject means the memorisation of English in which it was presented to him![248] The literary abilities of students cannot be developed as he writes answers to questions which are mere reproductions of selected paragraphs from textbooks. Apte concluded, "Not only is the imparting of a useful and practical knowledge thus

---

244 Ibid, p.18.
245 केळकरकृत टिळक चरित्र खंड 1 पृ. क्र. 165.
246 Limaye, P. M. (1935). *The History of the Deccan Education Society.* p.44.
247 Ibid, pp.73-74.
248 Ibid, p.74.

greatly limited, but the intellectual energies are spent away in learning English first, and then the subjects themselves. More than three-fourths of the time of the student is taken up in mastering the peculiarities of a foreign language."[249] Bharatiya languages were neglected in secondary school and were introduced directly in the degree courses. Hence, there is no surprise in the fact that most of the educated Bhartiya people, in those days, neglected Bhartiya languages. The neglect and contempt of the Bhartiya languages and their degradation resulted from the British education system. Apte highlighted this fact. The views represented by Apte were not of his own but were of all the founders of New English School, and Tilak was one of them.

Tilak wrote numerous articles in *Kesari*. Most of them were about politics. But he also wrote articles on *dharma*, literature, society, education, sciences, history, language, etc. These articles are scattered and lack continuity in time. Tilak wrote one article in *Kesari* titled 'The progress of Marathi language', dated 22nd November 1904. Below are relevant translated extracts from the article:

"Twenty days ago, Mr. G K Beetham delivered a speech on the subject '*Maharashtra Saraswat*' (literature in Marathi) at the hall of National Indian Association, London. Mr. Beetham worked in the forest department in our country. It appears that during his stay, he studied the Marathi language. The effort of Mr. Beetham to introduce Marathi literature to his countrymen is praiseworthy. Former councillor Mr. Birdwood was the president, and many people were present. President Mr. Birdwood, Dr. Pollan, and Mr. *Kolaskar* (associated with the late justice Ranade) also gave speeches. There are many Marathi-speaking people in London. But only Mr. *Kolakskar* attended the lecture. Those who forget *Swadesha* and *Swabhasha* as soon as they touch the foreign land (and try to become Englishman) should view Mr. *Kolakskar* as a role model. I do not have the transcript of the lecture given by Mr. Beetham or criticism of

---

249 Ibid, p.74.

Mr. *Kolaskar*. Birdwood and Pollan, in their speeches, stressed the importance of (cultural) exchange to increase mutual sympathy between the English people and the Bhartiya people. It is hard to find the contribution of Mr. Birdwood or Mr. Pollan in increasing mutual empathy between the English and Bhartiya people when they were in power in Bharat! But it has become a tradition that Anglo-Indian officers give speeches in front of their countrymen and display sympathy and morality towards natives! Still, Mr. Pollan has boldly admitted that he is receiving a pension from farmers' money in Bharat. I congratulate Dr. Pollan for his courageous confession.

In the discussion (after the speech), president Mr. Birdwood proposed a whimsical theory. According to him, the degradation of the Marathi language is due to the growth of Marathi newspapers. Suppose the same principle is applied to England, France, America, etc. European and American nations, then English and French would become the most deteriorated languages. There are many accusations against Bhartiya newspapers, such as being seditious, criticising the government, misleading the public, disturbing communal harmony, etc. But the allegation that Bhartiya newspapers are responsible for the degradation of Bhartiya languages is new. I think Mr. Bridwood wants to say that the language used in Bharatiya newspapers is corrupt and bad, and as the people practice such bad language after reading the newspaper, the language degrades in quality. It is hard to find which Marathi newspapers Birdwood was reading when he was in Bharat and whether he could comprehend the language written in a good newspaper! Maybe Birdwood was familiar with naïve newspapers like *Dnyanodaya, Balbodhmeva*, etc., as he was closely associated with 'Bible text society'.[250] But from such a level of 'familiarity' with Marathi newspapers, Birdwood has no authority to propose a theory on the degradation of the Marathi language. In reality, the elegance, maturity, simplicity, and increased vocabulary gained by the Marathi language in

---

250 To understand the remark made by Tilak please see: अर्वाचीन मराठी साहित्य पृ. क्र. 544.

both practical use and literature are due to newspapers and periodicals like *Nibandhmala*, *Vividhdnyanvistar*, etc. Those who have read articles of *Balshastri Jambhekar*, *Bhau Mahajan*, *Vishnushastri Chiplunkar*, *Gopal Ganesh Agarkar*, *Haripant Pandit*, etc., prominent authors would definitely call Birdwood's theory puerile. Most of the articles in newspapers are indeed ephemeral and incidental. Hence, they will never have perennial existence like independent books. But famous authors like Dr. Johnson, Swift, Addison, Macaulay, etc., first published their articles in newspapers. Here also, authors like Chiplunkar and Agarkar empowered *Swabhasha* by writing articles in newspapers and periodicals. Hence, newspapers and periodicals have substantial importance in the growth of language and literature.

Even though this opinion of Birdwood is absolutely wrong, it is good that some people in the west have warmth towards the Marathi language. We should take lessons from this. If foreigners like Birdwood or Pollan are earnest towards Marathi, why should educated Bhartiya leaders not strive to enhance *Swabhasha*? Beetham, a British, pursued a study of Marathi while working in a forest department and even gave lectures on Marathi literature. But our educated leaders hate Marathi to such an extent that they do not even read in Marathi (forget about writing books). These people have been gaining access to knowledge by means of the English language since childhood. Hence, the English language governs their thoughts, writing, reading, and behaviour. They give excellent speeches and write beautiful essays in English. But they cannot write a small letter or cannot speak for five minutes in *Swbhasha*. This is a pathetic situation. It is due to the current education system or due to the stupidity of our people. Marathi would not be empowered until educated Marathi people think that they must strive for the growth of Marathi. Unfortunately, efforts for the development of language are not even comparable to similar efforts that are being conducted in other provinces.

The Marathi language was once present not only in Maharashtra but also in Mysuru, Karnataka, Hyderabad, Gujrat, Baroda, Malwa, Central provinces, etc. Today it is becoming extinct even in Maharashtra. It is a shame for the Marathi people. When the government constituted the book committee, some people came forward to begin (unnecessary) debates about grammar. Now some people should come forward to talk about the growth and development of the language. In Bengal, the population of Bengali-speaking people is at least 4 to 4.5 crore. Hundreds of books are being published. There are novelists like *Bankimchandra*, modern poets like Tagore, and newspapers like *Hitwadi* (whose collection is 35000-40000 rupee) in Bengal. *Gujrati Dnyaprasarak Mandali* and kings like *Gaikwad* are providing an impetus to the Gujarati language. For the betterment of Urdu, the Nijam government of Hyderabad and Muslims from Aligarh and Lucknow are striving. For the growth of Hindi, an institution named *Nagari Pracharini Sabha* has been established at Benaras, and the founders hope to spread Hindi throughout Hindustan. But no such efforts are being made by Marathi-speaking people. There is no political backing, and people are indifferent. The government book committee is altering our script and words. Missionaries are corrupting (converting) our language like they corrupt (convert) our sons! Educated people have divorced from Marathi! Where should poor Marathi go? Periodicals like *Kaveyatihassangraha* stopped because of the lack of support. Historical papers are taking a rest in the houses of people! The government is not disclosing the diaries of *Peshwas*. *Dakshina Prize Committee* has become moribund due to a lack of active people, and her 'daughter' institution, 'The Deccan Vernacular Translation Society', is also following her parent institution. Debating societies are being closed due to a lack of speakers and activists. Some efforts were made to establish a comprehensive library containing all Marathi books in Mumbai, Thane, etc. But they are not important enough to be counted. Gujrati *sabha* in Ahmedabad and *Sahitya Sabha* in Kolkata are striving for the growth of the language. *Nagari Pracharini Sabha* has established a library and town hall at fifty thousand rupees. Now they have undertaken the task of framing *Vidyan Kosh,* a lexicon which will contain Hindi equivalent words for all scientific words. Marathi people, whose population is 1.5-2 crore, should be ashamed that the number of published books in our mother tongue is limited to one thousand. Similar efforts should be made in Maharashtra. An institution that would work relentlessly for the all-round development of the Marathi language must be established in Maharashtra. People should support such an institution, and its directors should concentrate fully on language growth. The primary duties of a such institution should be to publish ancient and modern texts in the Marathi language, to publish unpublished books, to publish and securely store historical papers, to publish biographies of poets in Maharashtra, to trace the history of Marathi, to research about grammatical and practical aspects of Marathi language, and to provide an impetus to modern writers. These efforts, if undertaken, will alleviate the condition of Marathi. Marathi will spread, and enthusiasm towards language will increase (and 'linguistic aptitude' will be developed in people). The headquarter of such an institution should be located in Mumbai or Pune. In December, leaders from different provinces will come together for Congress. This matter should be discussed in Congress, and if some solution is provided, it will be good for the development of Marathi."

This article summarises his views on language and its role in the nation's development. Tilak wrote a series of articles on the same topic in 1906. The first article appeared in *Kesari* on 29th May 1906. The title is 'The growth of Maharashtra *Bhasha* (Marathi language)'. Below are relevant translated extracts from the first article:

"There is no other resource than language to carry out human activities. There is no other way than language to communicate your thoughts (or emotions) to other person. A few differences separate humans from animals, and language is one of them. As interrelations between humans broaden and become complex, language also expands. The state of language indicates theorize the state of society. If society has progressed and developed, their language has also improved and expanded. In short, the language is a meter which displays the pattern of social interactions of a specific nation. Hence, linguists theorize the state of the society or nation (especially ancient civilisations which have ended) based on the form of language. It is obvious that the language in which abstract nouns are copious or words which convey the meanings of *Atman* and *Ishwar* are ample; the people who use such language would have an excellent understanding of the philosophy. There is a close relationship between thoughts, conduct and the language of society. Hence, a reflection of one can be seen in others. The growth of one implies the growth of another and vice versa. This is the invariant principle!

It is important to remember this invariant principle. The language will not grow if grammarian coins numerous new words from roots. The wealth of nations does not increase if a penurious person amasses crores of rupees and sepulchre in the ground. A similar principle can be applied to the language. Currency is required to carry out (and increase the number of) transactions in an economy. Similarly, words are required to communicate emotions and thoughts mutually. To increase trade, the liquidity of money should be increased. Again, to increase social interactions and communication, words are important. If humans had been speaking one language, then it would have been much easier to develop language. But history tells us that religion and language cannot be the same worldwide. Even if we assume that at the beginning of human life, they were one, and if we further assume that (by magic) it is possible to make them one, these two (religion and language) would acquire different forms due to territorial differences. Today, a single language and single religion have become symbols of nationality. (In other words, it is possible to attribute differences in nationality to differences in language and religion). The aim of the article is not to discuss linguistic and religious differences (and whether it is possible to eliminate them or not). But the article aims to understand reality and how it has evolved since ancient times. Hence, it is important to understand that the relationship between society and the language used by societal elements for the mutual communication of thoughts is perpetual. An analysis of the growth or decay of any language should be based on this principle.

Linguists have proposed a theory for the origin of the Marathi language. Marathi originated in the fifth or sixth century in the region south of *Narmada* and north of *Ghatprabha*.[251] Before that, the *Kannada* language was the prominent language. Aryan people arrived from the north, and the language of the Aryan people (*Prakrit*) and the southern language assimilated to form *Maharashtra Bhasha* (Marathi). In a few years since its origin, it remained in its infancy. *Yadava* kings of *Devgiri* patronised the Marathi, and its sphere of influence slowly increased in the south of *Narmada*. Marathi started governing all societal interactions. Texts like *Dnyaneshwari* were composed in Marathi. Indeed, the origin has yet to be traced, but it is possible to make a general statement based on the available data. Contemporary conditions in Maharashtra were quite strange. Marathi had attained stability due to patronage by the *Yadava* kings. Islamic rulers conquered Maharashtra, and Persian became the official language. Hindus were a minority in the government, and those in the government were compelled to use and study the Persian language. Lingua franca for intellegienceia was Sanskrit. There was no growth of Marathi. In such a situation, the language which grew over the time of *Yadava* kings or at the time of *Dnyaneshwara* or before him would have either become dead or radically transformed in such a way that it would have become impossible to trace the root of the language in *Maharashtri Prakrit* language. In Islamic rule, a form of Marathi changed, and Persian and Arabic words and the Persian and Arabic registers[252] penetrated the Marathi language. It is evident from the language used is *Bakhar* and *Rajvyavaharkosh,* created on the order of *Shivaji Maharaj*. This was a period of the decay of Marathi and it endured such a tough time. There are a few reasons for this endurance.

---

251 It is a tributary of the *Krishna* river.

252 The word 'register' is used for the term *Bhashapaddhati*.

There was indeed severe religious persecution of Hindus under Islamic rule. Most of the Muslims in Deccan were not *Pathan*, Mughal or Turk. But their ancestors were Hindus who were converted forcefully (or by greed). Even though Hindus were exposed to severe religious atrocities, that persecution strengthened the Hindus' faith in Hindu *dharma*. Hindu minds were indeed got affected by the sight of grand and ostentatious mosques, which were raised by brutally demolishing Hindu temples. Still, the persecution by Muslims was physical in nature. The nature of such persecution was to kill (or confiscate the property) if he did not convert to Islam. The faith of the people (who endured brutal torture) in *Swadharma* increased. Under the present rule, people who have received an English education have no faith in the *dharma* (and some are eating beef). This was not the case in the times of Islamic rule. Apart from people who were forcefully converted, faith in the hearts of the remaining people increased against persecution. It resulted in the growth of *Swabhasha*. That is, people, to spread *dharmic* principles, increasingly use *Swabhasha*. This is the reason behind the fact that most medieval Marathi literature is *dharmic*. Higher the persecution, the higher the resistance. The rule in mechanics is that for every action, there exists an equal reaction. A similar principle can be applied in the religious field. When we analyse the works of saints like *Dnyaneshwar* or *Ramadasa*, it is important to understand the historical background.

As the political power was in the hands of foreigners (of a different religion), Persian was the official language. Intellectual subjects like *Nyaya* or *Vyakarana* were taught in *Sanskrit*. In such a situation, if contemporary saints did not attempt to save the *dharma*, then *Dnyaneshwari* would have been Marathi's first and last text. There is another reason also. *Shankaracharya* revived Hindu dharma in the seventh century by defeating non-Vedic sects in debates. But the path shown by *Shankaracharya* towards *moksha* was incomprehensible to the general public. So was the case of *Kumarila Bhat*. If this question remained unsettled before the arrival of Islam, it would have strengthened the spread of Islam. Instigators of *Bhagwat dharma* or

Bhaktimarga saved the nation from this calamity. We should never forget this. *Bhaktimarga* was dominant in those times. It can be said that Islamic persecution, being physical in nature, strengthened the *Bhakti* movement. The existence of 'political saints'[253] under foreign rule is impossible. So, only the *dharmic* sphere was left for people who wished to instigate the movement. In other words, time was not good for political leaders. In such a tough time, contemporary leaders chose the available direction and nurtured the language and *dharma*, which are important aspects of nationality) and contributed to the growth of language. Its effects shall be discussed in the next article."

The second article in the series appeared in *Kesari* dated 5th June 1906 with a similar title. Below are the translated relevant extracts from the article:

"The literature in any nation depends on the conditions of people. As the state changes, there is growth or decay of the language. In the previous article, I described the application of the above principle to the development of the Marathi language before *Swarajya*. As the patient's health can be diagnosed from pulse rate, the nation's condition can be detected from the language. There is no need to give a reason behind the fact that there were no *Powadas* composed before *Shivaji* Maharaj. Before Shivaji Maharaj and after the fall of the *Yadava* dynasty (the last Hindu dynasty), Islamic rulers performed heroic acts. But how could those gallant deeds inspire contemporary Marathi people? But with god's grace, conditions changed, and *Shahirs* from Maharashtra started singing songs of bravery in front of thousands of people in their vigorous and forceful language.

It is not that poet-saints like *Dnyashewara* or *Tuakaram* did not have contempt for Islamic rule or lack pride for *Swarajya*. *Pangarkar* had published two-three poems of saint *Eknath* in *Kesari,* which show patriotism. But contemporary conditions were such that even though

---

253 Tilak uses the word *Rajakiya Maharshi* (or *Sant*). The best example is *Vidyarnya Maharshi.*

flames of patriotism were fuming in minds, precaution needed to be taken to not reflect patriotism in your speech! There is a drastic difference between the time of *Ramadas* and *Eknath*. Those who blame saints before *Ramadas* for preaching doctrine *Nivrutti* than *Pravrutti* should remember this. Today even though we have freedom of expression granted by the British government, there is advice given constantly to write in a 'moderate' tone! Hence, it is not right to blame poet saints for not indulging in political activities. The understanding of *Ramadas* was not different from *Eknath*. The difference in their literature is due to (sociopolitical) conditions prevalent in their times and not because of a lack of patriotism. The conclusion is that all the literature before *Shivaji Maharaj* is *dharmic* in nature, and it is due to conditions in those times.

Nobody should think that *dharmic* literature was not useful in a nationalistic sense. Before the beginning of Islamic rule, Marathi was just patronised by the *Yadava* king. Its dominance in the province was undecided. When this patronage ended with the advent of Islamic rule, there was only a *dharmic* sphere left for any activity. Great men in those tough times kept *dharma* and language alive and retained the *Maharashtrianness* of Maharashtra! *Pandharpur* was the linguistic and *dharmic* capital of Maharashtra. Today, we witness the dominance of Marathi around the *Pandharpur* (i.e., from Aurangabad, Gulbarga to *Vijapur*). It is due to Marathi poet-saints. If those poet saints had not written *dharmic* literature, then the dominance of the *Kannada* language in Maharashtra was possible. Today we talk about the borders of Maharashtra. Poets sketched those borders (in Islamic rule) by contributing to the development of the Marathi language in the direction of *dharma*. The spread of the Marathi language is hugely impacted by *Alandi* and *Padnharpur* (which are just like two focal points of an ellipse, and the ellipse represents the region of influence of Marathi). Current scientists have proposed that Marathi people have mixed ancestry (Aryan and Dravidian). But this principle applies to people living in Bengaluru or Mysuru. But Marathi has not extended to that region. It means the borders of Maharashtra are linguistic and due to common ancestry. In this way, *dharma* is responsible for widening the horizons of language.

There are other reasons also. Before *Dnyashwewar, Mahanubhava Panth* was established in Maharashtra. The original texts of this sect were written in the Marathi language. This sect spread in *Rajputana, Punjab*, etc. Today, their monasteries are present even in *Peshawar* and *Kabul*. Hence, the Marathi language is present, at least in the monasteries of *Mahanubhava Pantha* in *Kabul*. Poet-saints also wrote their texts of *Bhagwat dharma* in Marathi. Compared to the above example, one can realise the importance of such work in the growth of a nation and language. People who were busy with their *Shrautkarma* were not happy with that work. They thought it was unholy to translate (and preach) doctrines of *dharma* in Marathi to ordinary people! They harassed *Eknath* and *Tukaram*. Sanskrit is not foreign to us. In fact, it is the grandmother, if not the mother of Marathi! It is unfortunate for the nation that the lingua franca of the intelligentsia is different from the mother tongue. If the lingua franca of the intelligentsia is foreign, then it is worst. Today, Maharashtra is in the worst state. I just want to tell that before the *Shivaji Maharaj*, in Islamic rule, even though there was no special assistance from Sanskrit intelligentsia, our poet saints, with the help of language in the direction of *dharma,* kept the idea of *Maharashtrianness* alive. Further, they broadened and consolidated the borders of Maharashtra. If they would not accomplish this task, then in 300-400 years, Persian and Arabic languages would have mixed with Marathi to such an extent that *Ramadasa or* Shivaji Maharaj would have faced difficulty with the preaching of *Maharashtra dharma.* Further, they would have proved unsuccessful in carrying out the duties of the Marathi people, which they did historically.

It is not wrong that we make the statement that Shivaji Maharaj's rise implies the Marathi language's growth. Before *Shivaji Maharaj, dharma* was the only reason behind the growth of the language. With the rise of *Shivaji Maharaj,* the Marathi language got political support. The English language also has become dominant due to the mighty British empire. When a person speaking a particular language achieves political power, it is obvious that the prestige of his mother tongue also increases. When the language is honoured, it slowly attains maturity even though it might be weak. Marathi witnessed glorious days for a period of time. As Shivaji Maharaj's efforts to establish *Swarajya* were initially in the region of Pune and first in *Sahyadri* (western ghats), the epicentre of the Marathi language shifted to *Sahyadri* and its surroundings. Soon, rays of the Marathi language reached *Atak* in the north and Tanjore in the south with the javelin of Maratha warriors! The *Peshwai* era was favourable to Marathi. *Shinde, Gaikwad* and *Holkar* spread Marathi in *Gwalior*, Gujrat and Malwa, respectively, by establishing their rule. In the east, it was supported by the *Bhosale* of Nagpur. Belgaum, Dharwad, Mysuru and Tanjore were conquered before. Even though the rule of Nijam was restricted to Deccan, Marathi remained dominant due to the consolidation of the Marathi language by poet-saints and the valour of Marathas. Hence, not only did we take *Chauth* from Nijam, but due to the valour of Marathas, the region, more than the region on which *Chauth* was levied, came under the influence of the Marathi language. Literature of our saints did not constrain Maharashtra but spread with the Maratha empire and occupied one-third of Hindustan. The literature was not limited to the field of *dharma*. Poets came forward to write poetry praising the warriors of Maharashtra who ended the religious harassment of Hindus by Islam. Writers wrote *bakhar*. There was no need to limit their poetic abilities in *dharma*. Historical Marathi prose (and poems) were created and consolidated in this period. When a nation expands, it expands in all directions (and not in just one). People follow not only the behaviour and thoughts but also the language of those in power.

People of Belgaum or *Dharwad* district understand Marathi because, during the Maratha empire's time, people (or leaders) from this district considered the Marathi language a prestige symbol. In those days, it was a shame for the educated person who did not know Marathi.

Women also viewed Marathi as a prestige symbol in the home. There is no exaggeration in the above statements. One can compare the state of the Marathi language under the Maratha empire with the current status of the English language under the British empire. It will resolve all doubts. The time of *Swarajya* was not the only period of the nation's progress but also of language. New prose literature was created, and the direction of poetry was also changed (This can be seen in the works of poets like *Moropant*). If this time had been continued, I do not need to tell the results. Unfortunately, we experienced this glorious period of 100-150 years, and circumstances radically changed. Now we need to think about how to keep the momentum of the growth of language in such circumstances. Without understanding history, it becomes impossible to think about this. In the next article, I will write on this topic."

The last article from this series appeared in *Kesari,* dated 19th June 1906. Below are relevant translated extracts from the article:

"In the previous two articles, the growth of Marathi literature and its influence up to the end of *Peshwai* is briefly discussed. From those articles, readers should have understood how *Swavhasha* is encouraged in *Swarajya*. There is no other reason to answer the questions like why historical *bakhar* or *powade* were not written in the early days of Marathi or why the early Marathi literature is *dharmic* in nature. It is important to understand the historical evolution of the language before we think about the growth of Marathi, its extent and its quality under British rule.

It is not that just calling Marathi our mother tongue will alleviate its condition. As said before, language is an indicator of the nation's state. If the nation is emergent, then its language is also growing. If the trade and commerce of a nation are parochial, then the growth and scope of language are also limited. This is the invariant principle. Further discussion about the growth of the Marathi language is based on this principle.

With the advent of British rule, the political importance of the Marathi language was obviously reduced. At the very beginning of British rule, Bhartiya languages were used for official purposes, and district courts had Bhartiya languages. But as the number of people learning English increased, the number of people understanding the English language also increased. Slowly, the use of the Bhartiya language waned. English became the official language of the polity. Marathi was never the merchant's language like the *Gujarati* language. Hence, Marathi does not have even the advantage that *Gujrati* has to retain its dominance. Due to this reason, three daily newspapers have been running in *Gujrati* for many years. Also, the *Parsi* people accepted the *Gujrati* language, but in the case of Marathi, no community outside Maharashtra accepted it. Hence, as soon as the Maratha empire ended, the official dominance of Marathi waned. Further, its spread outside Maharashtra diminished. In Tanjore, migrated Marathi people speak Marathi at home, which resembles the language in *Dnyasheshwar's* era. But the local language is used in the political affairs of the princely state (or district). Similar is the case of Mysuru. In Belgaum and Dharwad districts, people have established *Karnatak Vidyavardhak Sangh* to counter the Marathi language. In Gwalior and Indore princely states, the Marathi language should have been dominant. But native states are blindly imitating the British empire. Hence, Marathi has withdrawn her presence from these states! (In Gaikwad's rule, Marathi shared position with *Gujrati*). In Nijam's state, even though the language of the *Marathwada* people is Marathi, as the official language is Persian, Marathi do not receive support. Hence, Marathi expanded outside Maharashtra in *Swarajya* and contracted during British rule. *Varhad* province has Marathi dominance. But as this province merged with Nagpur, the provincial government has officially decided to abandon the Modi script. If this policy continues, it will adversely affect the growth of Marathi.

Now we shall see the degradation of Marathi due to the English language. It is unfortunate for any nation that its intelligentsia is gaining knowledge from a foreign language. This principle was stated in the last article. Our educated people have learnt English to express their thoughts (or gain knowledge). Hence, their neglect towards Marathi is obvious. If sciences are learnt and taught in *Swabhasha*, then it will automatically grow due to the efforts of intellectuals. Bharatiya people are devoid of this progress. It would not be wrong that the educated class have become an enemy of *Swabhasha*. It is wrong to assume that by introducing one or two Marathi books at the M.A. examination of the university, Marathi will progress. If *Swabhasha* becomes the lingua franca of all socio-political and economic interactions, it will automatically develop. Higher the degree of interactions higher the growth of language. Tomorrow, if traders start to trade in the Marathi language, the intelligentsia will begin learning and teaching old and new sciences in Marathi, and then Marathi will witness exponential growth. Unfortunately, this is not the condition of the nation. All sciences are taught in English. Once it becomes habitual to read, write and think in English, then it seems easy and more convenient to read scientific literature in English than in Marathi. Some scientific works in English have been translated. But due to the above reasons, they do not gain enough attention. Intellectuals interested in science often read scientific literature in English, and those who do not (because of a lack of knowledge of English) read such literature (most of the time) do not have a liking for such literature. It is not possible for the educated class to strive for the growth of *Swabhasha* as poet-saints like *Dnyashwear* in the time of Islamic rule. This is because their faith in *dharma* is shaken due to English education. The person with no faith in *Swabhasha* cannot sermon in *Swabhasha*. Even if we assume he is an intellectual, how can such a person have as eloquent speech as *Sant Tukaram*? There are attempts by the educated class to establish monotheistic societies like *Pratharna Samaj*. But as such societies lacked the solicitude for *dharma*, they were useless even in the field of language (i.e., they were not able to preach their doctrine in Marathi, which might have benefited Marathi). Missionaries helped in the preparation of dictionaries and grammar. They also publicise the art of printing and newspapers. But the language used in books of Missionaries (often written by British people who have learnt Marathi) is 'eccentric' and hence cannot be compared to the original Marathi. Such adulterated Missionary texts can never become part of Marathi literature. People are demoralised due to foreign rule, and there is no real way left to express your talent. In such a situation, who will have poetic abilities, and if one has, on whom will he write *Powade*? Hence, the time is not good for people to become a poet or to preach *dharma*. The Marathi has become bonsai in British rule. Marathi cannot become the national language of Bharat. If any other language, like Hindi, becomes the national language of Bharat, then it can hurt Marathi.

To achieve growth in language, it is important to increase socio-political and economic interactions. But as stated above, the conditions in Maharashtra are not favourable. Hence, even after eighty years of British rule, Marathi literature has remained parochial. To teach missionaries and labourers Marathi, required books were written in Marathi in the early days of British rule. Few entertainment books were translated into Marathi. Apart from these, there is no significant progress in Marathi literature. The genesis of independent Marathi prose literature can be attributed to *Nibandhmala* of *Vishnushastri*. Before *Vishnushastri*, there were parallel intellectuals or even greater than him. Still, nobody cared about *Swabhasha* and took the responsibility of encouraging people towards a specific goal or discouraging people from certain things with the help of *Swabhasha*. The real reason behind the bold and valorous language of *Vishnushastri* is this. Those who do not bother about addressing people with solicitude cannot serve the *Swabhasha* (and their language would not be bold and valorous). Pick up any prominent writer, and one would witness that they are always eager to convey their thoughts and emotions to people. One should have firm faith in his thoughts and a strong belief that his ideas are good for the country. Without such earnestness, nobody can genuinely perform his duties towards *Swabhsaha*.

As printing technology has improved, books are getting published each year. In Britain, hundreds of novels get published but do not stay in the market after two to three months. In the growth of language, such books play no role. If we discard such books in Marathi, there was minimal language growth in British rule. New literature in Marathi is some entertainment books, revised editions of old books, collections of historical texts and *bakhar*, and translations of general-purpose English books and dictionaries. Newspapers are indeed broadening the horizon of language. This is because editors need to write articles on different subjects; hence he was to coin new words (terms). But this growth is only considered to be temporary growth in language. Real growth in language means growth in socio-political and economic interactions, and also leaders should feel the necessity to change the narrative by conveying their thoughts in *Swabhasha*. *Swabhasha* will progress when intellectuals learn and teach different sciences in *Swabhasha,* when political, social, industrial, and scientific debates will always take place in *Swabhasha,* when *Swabhasha* will be used for the awakening of *dharma* and when *Swabsha* will be used in the government offices, military or university. In British rule, such events have become infrequent, due to which there is resistance to the growth of our language. But educated people should come out of a dreary mindset and impart knowledge to people in *Swabhasha*. If educated people begin such work earnestly, then I am confident that Marathi would develop even more than the development that took place in eighty years. There are indeed some constraints on such growth. But we have not even reached these limits. So, there is no question of pushing limits further! It is useless to hope for the growth of Marathi by introducing *Dnyashweari* in the university. The real solution is to teach all the syllabi in Marathi. If it is not possible, then all other interactions should at least be kept in the mother tongue. People with real solicitude and earnestness for *Swabhasha* should come forward and encourage people and strive to increase interactions with Marathi people. When such interactions increase, language will also develop."

These articles explicitly express his views on *Swabhasha*. Tilak was a firm supporter of education in Bhartiya languages. He wrote one article dated 6th March 1894 in which he described the role of the university in the development of language. The title is 'How should university provide an impetus to *Bharatiya* languages? Below are the relevant translated extracts from the article:

"Many people believe that if Bhartiya languages are included in the university curriculum along with English and Sanskrit, there will be growth in those languages (and also of the nation). This belief has some degree of truth. But there is no significant contemplation on the degree and nature of this reform. It will be great if Bhartiya languages develop and become mature. But to attain such a state, we need some resources, and when I think about the availability of such resources, the mind becomes dreary.

Consider the Marathi language. In 1833, there was a debate on the issue of educating Bharatiya people with western or Bharatiya style. Macaulay ended that debate with a minute in which he advocated western education in the English language. I do not think we would have chosen the English language if we had been experiencing *Swarajya*. A shallow reading of Macaulay's minutes cannot detect the subtle connection between the English language with focused points in the minute. Today, people are certainly more aware and know the importance of ancient Bharatiya arts and sciences (at least in some fields). Even some European people are also of the same opinion. Still, let us assume that western sciences are superior to Bhartiya ones. What was the problem with imparting education in Bharatiya languages? It was not that Marathi (or any other Bhartiya language) was not useful in courts, offices, colleges, and railways. But as our rulers are foreigners, they have made English the official language for the entire Bharat (from the *Himalayas* to *Kanyakumari*) for their convenience. As we were slaves, we had no choice, and slowly, we became accustomed to it. It is true that the interaction of people from different provinces of Bharat has increased, and institutions like Indian National Congress have been established and are running. The English language had a significant role in these events. But with the gain, there is a loss on another side. Bhartiya languages are slowly degrading. As English has dominated all spheres of life, nobody writes or speaks in Bhartiya languages. It is good that many people are taking this problem seriously and are contemplating ways to improve the condition of Bhartiya languages. But I think we forget the important fact that the foreign ruler governs us. Today, this fact requires special attention because readers should get an idea about the degree to which universities, which Europeans are dominating, can provide an impetus to Bhartiya languages. There are very few members of the senate of the university who endorse Marathi.

It requires an unobstructed flow of language in the market, judiciary, government, etc. There is no scope for such an 'unobstructed flow' of Bhartiya languages in the present political situation. At Punjab university, there is an option in which all subjects are taught in Bhartiya languages, and English is taught as a language (like Sanskrit in our university) for a B.A. degree. But the number of students is far less than a B.A. degree with English as the medium of instruction. It is impossible to eliminate obstruction created by the government to the growth of Bhartiya languages. While discussing the ways to improve the condition of Bhartiya languages, we need to remember this.

The knowledge of ancient languages like Sanskrit is important (even if it is less important compared to the practical use of English) in the growth of Bhartiya languages. If one looks at excellent books in Bhartiya languages published in the last twenty-five years, one can witness the high proportion of Sanskrit words and ways in which ancient languages can be used to express new thoughts. Any language needs three things to produce excellent literature: vocabulary, ideas, and the need for literature. A vocabulary can be derived from ancient languages. Ideas can be borrowed from the west. But while borrowing, it is important to make these ideas suitable vis-a-vis the Bhartiya context by synthesising them with our ancient philosophy. I do not think people who do not have command over Sanskrit can perform this task. A movement is going on in the west to discontinue the study of Greek and Latin languages in universities. But the same logic cannot be applied to the Bharatiya context. We can consider such a question of discontinuing the study of ancient languages only when the assistance of Sanskrit to Bhartiya languages reaches the level of assistance of Greek and Latin to English. In the current situation, it is mutilating to discontinue the study of ancient languages.

We are obliged to get knowledge of English as it is the official language and of Sanskrit as Bharatiya languages have not matured enough. Let us examine the possibility of the extent to which the knowledge of Sanskrit and English can help in the improvement of the conditions of Bhartiya languages. It leads to the conclusion that many reforms can be done in the existing curriculum prescribed by universities. It is the opinion of many experienced people that if we teach subjects required for the matriculation examination in the Bhartiya language, and then English is taught for two to three years, then it shall alleviate the exam pressure significantly. But the syllabus for matriculation is set up by the school education department and not by the university; hence, it cannot be blamed for the lack of such a policy. We will also consider only higher education and not school education.

I do not think the knowledge of ancient languages is sufficient to create the required literature in Bhartiya languages. Consider Marathi. The reporter of the native press, *Raosaheb Sathe*, believes that we need books on subjects like economics, chemistry, etc., along with the poetic works of *Moropant* and *Vaman Pandit*. Poetic works of Marathi poets are not inferior vis-à-vis English or Sanskrit poets. But by teaching poetical works of old poets, the aim for which the people demand the entry of the Marathi language in the university would not get accomplished. To achieve this aim, it is important to teach different sciences in Marathi. Sathe has objected to the defect that modern scholars are not creating enough literature in Bharatiya languages and universities also not providing enough impetus for such efforts. This objection is true up to a significant extent. But we should remember that it is also the responsibility of people and institutions other than universities to make efforts to grow the language. If modern scholars determine to write books on the topics mentioned above, then it would not be possible to recover publication costs from the book's sale. The important factor in the production of literature in any language is the demand (or need) for literature and its sales. The principle that demand drives production applies to the publishing business as well. Still, it is true that if at least some subjects are taught in Bhartiya languages, then it provides an impetus to these languages up to a certain extent. When a particular subject is taught in Bhartiya languages in a university, then the sale of books written in Bhartiya languages on that particular subject also increases. Students who are required to write answers in Bhartiya languages also learn the subject in their mother tongue. The English language has become modern not because of Shakespeare or Milton but because it is the language of the British empire and trade which has spread in the entire world, and also because the study of history, sciences, arts, etc., is happening in the English language. Due to this English language has achieved the qualities such as maturity and boldness. Today, Bhartiya languages cannot be used at such a scale. But this should not stop the university from taking exams of various subjects in Bhartiya languages. In our country, at least exams on subjects like the history of Hindustan and Sanskrit should be kept in Bhartiya languages. The current constitution of the university will not allow this policy to be effective from today. But steps should be taken in that direction. There should not be any discrimination between B.A. from Bhartiya languages and B.A. from English language, like in Punjab. We cannot force universities to adopt Bharatiya languages as a medium of instruction. But at least students can write answers to two to three subjects in Bhartiya languages.

Hence, universities should adopt a policy to teach a few subjects in the Bhartiya languages instead of downgrading the quality of education in Sanskrit and English. If universities adopt such a policy, it will give an impetus to the growth f Bhartiya languages."

Articles written by Tilak explicitly express his views on *Swabhsha*. His historical and political analysis of the Marathi language is brilliant. He highlighted the importance of poet-saints in the *dharma* and language. He has an exceptional mixture of a theoretical and practical ways of thinking. He understood that the degraded state of Marathi was due to two factors: one was the lack of political support, and the second was the enslaved mindset of English-educated intelligentsia who viewed Marathi with neglect and contempt. He also suggested practical methods to alleviate the state of language. He also supported the teaching of subjects in Bharatiya languages.

Tilak forwarded the battle for *Swabhsha* after the death of *Chiplunkar*. It will not be wrong to state that Tilak and *Chiplunkar* redefined the Marathi prose and created a new literature. The new literature gets created primarily for three reasons: a new world, a new vision, and new philosophy of life (or conception of life (or satisfaction)).[254] The world is constantly changing. Man lives in the world and experiences different shades of the world. Sometimes these experiences are new, or sometimes old experiences attached to a particular object can appear in a new form. When a person starts narrating these experiences, new literature gets created. When a man watches and explores the new world, he develops a new vision. Sometimes he develops a new insight when looking at old objects (or while analysing old experiences). Such a new vision can recalibrate our sociopolitical interactions. Similarly, conceptions of life and satisfaction can change. These conceptions are not the same for people with a similar set of experiences. The philosophy of life governs the morality and ethics followed by a particular person. It also influences the conception of satisfaction. On the basis of moral and ethical principles, a person takes decisions in life. When the philosophical outlook changes, there are changes in the conception of good and bad, happiness and sorrow, and satisfaction and discontent. Thus, a new world, new vision and new philosophy of

---

254 अर्वाचीन मराठी साहित्य पृ. क्र. 583.

life sketch a new picture on the canvas of the mind. The description of this 'new' picture in words is new literature.[255]

Maharashtra witnessed an unprecedented transformation after the end of the Maratha empire. As the British began consolidating the rule, a new world unfolded. To view a new world, a new vision emerged. It was not uniform. The vision of Ranade was not the same as that of Tilak. The philosophy of life also changed. Western philosophy became the philosophy of life for moderates and liberals. Western philosophers like Mill and Spencer heavily influenced the minds of contemporary intellectuals like Agarkar. With this new vision, those intellectuals developed new thinking, which blinded their discerning abilities! They started viewing Hindu *dharma* and Hindu society with severe contempt. It was not self-criticism but self-hatred. Hinduphobia is reflected in their literature. Ranade was not willing to cross the boundaries of Hindu *dharma*. He was not an atheist. He wished to 'fine tune' Hindu *dharma* with western philosophy. That is, he wanted to 'reform' Hindu *dharma* based on western philosophy. The vision of Tilak was totally different from Ranade and Agarkar. He was not a radical desperado like Agarkar or directionless like Ranade. He developed a new vision which was based on Bharatiya philosophy. He accepted western thoughts only after critical analysis. He always tried to accommodate western notions within the Bhartiya context. He viewed the British as outsiders, and according to him, British rule was disastrous to Bharat. This thinking starkly contrasts with Ranade and Gokhale, who were 'moderate' anglophiles! Reflections of his thinking can be traced in his literature.

With a new vision and *Vedanta* as a philosophy of life, Tilak viewed the new world (British rule). This produced new literature which was nationalistic and *dharmic* in nature. Politically it changed the direction of the freedom movement. He stood for *Swabhasha* in tough times. He coined many new words. Tilak wrote in Marathi and encouraged many

---

255 This discussion is based on an epilogue written by N C Kelkar. The citation is given below.
अर्वाचीन मराठी साहित्य पृ. क्र. 583-592.

young authors to write in *Kesari*. His trusted lieutenants N C Kelkar and *Krushnajipant Khadilkar*, Savarkar, and many others forwarded his thinking on *Swabhasha*. Tilak wrote his *magnum opus* 'Gitarahasya' in Marathi. It is magnificent work. Without any doubt, it is the finest Marathi prose text. Through *Gitarahasya,* he introduced criticism of *Mimansa* in Marathi.

In conclusion, Tilak ended the contempt and neglect of Marathi by educated people. He tried hard to end slavery in the dimension of language and become self-reliant in the field of language. For this stupendous work, he will be remembered forever.

Chapter 6

Swadharma

Dharma is a word that has no equivalent word in the English language.[256] It is a polysemous word. One of the many meanings of *dharma* is duty. Hence, the word *Swadharma* means one's duty. But *Swadharma* is used in a different context in the Maratha empire. In the Maratha empire, the word *Swadharma* was used to convey the distinct identity of Hindus.[257] Tilak used the word *Swadharma* in both contexts. Before discussing the views of Tilak about *dharma*, it is necessary to understand the historical evolution of the conception of *dharma* in Tilak's mind.

Tilak was born on 23rd July 1856. The condition of *dharma* was pathetic in his times. The spirit of Hindu *dharma* was almost dead. It had degraded to its lowest state. Missionaries were attacking Hindu *dharma*. English education had destroyed the faith and devotion towards *dharma* in the minds of educated Bharatiya people. Some educated people like Ranade and Bhandarkar came forward to 'reform' the Hindu *dharma* by establishing *Prararthana Samaj*. But those leaders were blind followers of western philosophy. They wished to 'reform' the Hindu *dharma* on the lines of western philosophy. Apart from followers of *Prarthana Samaj*, no people from the educated class were sympathetic towards *dharma*. There was no *dharmic* education in schools. Missionary schools were preaching Christianity. People who were little educated had secured a job. Due to the lack of *dharmic* education and the bombardment of

---

256 Kane, P. V. (1941). History of Dharmasastra-Vol I, Part I. p.1.

257 The use of the word *Swadharma* as the distinct identity of Hindus was prominent even in the last years of the Maratha empire. It was used by *Yashwantrao Holkar* to unite Marathas to save *Swarajya* and *Swadharma*.

See: मराठी रियासत खंड ८, पृ. क्र. ३११,३२५,३८१.

western education, those people became indifferent towards *dharma*. The rest of the people continued their traditions, culture, and *dharma*. While understanding the evolution of Tilak's conception of *dharma*, it is crucial to understand this background.

Tilak was born into a very *dharmic* family. His mind was heavily influenced by the *samskara* done to him during his childhood. Tilak's mother had done extreme penance and also worshipped the god *Surya* with intense devotion before the birth of Tilak.[258] His home was a typical Hindu home in which the fragrance of *dharma* was wafting in each corner! His father was a self-taught man. *Gangadharpant* had a good understanding of Sanskrit. He began teaching Sanskrit to Tilak in childhood.[259] Tilak acquired a decent knowledge of Sanskrit just at the age of ten years.[260] Due to his study of Sanskrit from a young age, Tilak developed a liking and devotion towards *dharma*. He started reading *dharmic* literature. He first got introduced to *Bhagwat Gita* when he had to read a *Prakrit* commentary on *Gita* called *Bhashavivrutti* to his father during his last illness in 1872.[261] As the impressions made on the mind at a young age were lasting, his liking for *dharmic* literature increased, and he began reading various *dharmic* texts and commentaries. His study of *dharmashastra* was the direct result of the *samskara* he received in his childhood, his marvellous intellect, and astounding diligence. This was the first phase in forming his views on *dharma* and cultivated a liking and devotion towards dharma.

Tilak entered school in 1861. His father was transformed to Pune in 1866 as assistant deputy educational inspector. Since childhood,

---

258 केळकरकृत टिळक चरित्र खंड १ पृ. क्र. २१.
     Kelkar. (1928). *Life and Times of Lokmanya Tilak.* p. 33.
259 केळकरकृत टिळक चरित्र खंड १ पृ. क्र. २१.
     Kelkar. (1928). *Life and Times of Lokmanya Tilak.* p. 34.
260 केळकरकृत टिळक चरित्र खंड १ पृ. क्र. २२.
     Kelkar. (1928). *Life and Times of Lokmanya Tilak.* p. 36.
261 Tilak, B. (1935). *Gita-Rahasya* (B. Sukthankar, Trans.). Tilak Brothers. (original work published 1915). p.xliii.

Tilak has been an independent thinker. He entered Deccan college in 1873. He was not interested in obtaining higher ranks in examinations. He always gave importance to understanding the subject rather than obtaining marks. He was further admitted to an L.L.B. course. Hindu *dharmashastra* was his favourite subject. He read and mastered all the important texts on Hindu *dharma* and commentaries on texts.[262] This period was the second phase in the evolution of Tilak's conception of *dharma.*

In his university years, Tilak got exposed to western philosophy. His generation was influenced by western philosophers like Mill, Spencer, etc. Many educated men in those times were allured by Mill's utilitarianism, Spencer's agnosticism, etc. Tilak was also influenced by western philosophers. He wrote three articles on Spencer's philosophy in *Kesari* in which he compared western philosophy with Bharatiya philosophy and stated the superiority of Bhartiya philosophy.[263] This comparative analysis of both philosophies might have begun after the establishment of the New English School and *Kesari* and Maratha. This was the third phase.

Kesari and Maratha were started in 1880. In the very beginning, Tilak wrote articles on *dharmashastra* and law. Tilak and Agarkar were opposite poles. Agarkar was heavily influenced by western philosophers, and he was critical of Hindu *dharma* and Hindu society. Tilak was influenced by Bharatiya philosophy and was proud of Hindu *dharma,* heritage, and culture. Agarkar was a radical reformer. He wished to throw away *dharma* into a dustbin and transform Hindu society along western lines. Tilak was not opposed to the idea of reforms. But according to him, social reform should not be imposed by throwing

---

262 केळकरकृत टिळक चरित्र खंड १ पृ. क्र. 34.
     Kelkar. (1928). *Life and Times of Lokmanya Tilak.* p. 57.

263 जेयाजेयमीमांसा (पूर्वार्ध) (07/05/1901).
     जेयाजेयमीमांसा (उत्तरार्ध) (14/05/1901).
     अजेयवाद (11/08/1896).
     हर्बर्ट स्पेंसर (15/12/1903).

dharma away but should be based on *Hindutva*.[264] Slowly, the schism between Tilak and Agarkar widened. Between 1884 and 1887, Tilak and Agarkar were involved in a fierce intellectual battle, which resulted in the severance of Agarkar from *Kesari*. He continued his rivalry with Agarkar till his death in 1895. The criticism of Agarkar turned into a bitter hatred of Hindu *dharma*. Between 1890 and 1897, Tilak was involved in various controversies, an account of a few appeared in the second chapter.

This period is extremely important in the life of Tilak. Reformers like Agarkar brutally attacked his faith and devotion towards dharma. He was simultaneously comparing western and Bharatiya philosophies, and it appears that even though he was firm about the importance of the *dharma*, he had yet to attain stability at the philosophical level. He read various commentaries on *Gita*, *Bramhasutra*, and *Upanishads*. Slowly, his mind was evolving towards the philosophy of *Karmayoga*, and in 1900, he achieved peace and stability at the philosophical level.[265]

It is important to understand whether Tilak's views changed over time or remained invariant. At the philosophical level, we can definitely say that his views remained invariant. He was a proud follower of Hindu *dharma* till his last breath. He believed in the superiority of Hindu philosophy over western philosophy. He held Bharatiya culture supreme. As he read and compared both philosophies, his original views became clear, and he finally attained stability in 1900.

Tilak read various commentaries on *Gita*. After rigorous intellectual analysis, he reached the conclusion that *Gita* teaches *Karmayoga*. He gave one lecture in Nagpur in January 1902 and the second lecture in front of *Shankaracharya* of *Karvir math* in August 1904. He also debated with his intellectual friends. He was imprisoned in 1908 and sent to Mandalay. Fortunately, the government granted permission to carry books and other things from Pune to Mandalay. He prepared the first

---

264 हिंदुत्व आणि सुधारणा (12/01/1904).
265 लो. टिळकांची धर्मविषयक मते पृ. क्र. 29.

draft of *Gitarahasya* in 1910-1911, which was improved upon from time to time, and finally published in June 1915. *Gitarahasya* completely describes the life and philosophy of Tilak. This was the fourth and final phase in Tilak's conception of *dharma*. He gave multiple lectures on *Gitarahasya* after 1915.

Tilak has defined *dharma* in different ways. The word *dharma* comes from the root *dhr*, i.e., to hold or uphold; hence it means that all human beings are upheld by *dharma*.[266] Interestingly Tilak also defined *dharma* as the path leading to the next world happiness. When we ask someone, 'What is your dharma?', we intend to ask him by which path he goes, whether Hindu, Christian, etc.[267] He further draws a distinction between two meanings of *dharma*. He calls the path towards next-world happiness[268] *mokshadharma* and *dharma* related to worldly life simply *dharma*.[269] He further says that Hindu scriptures use the word *dharma* which has the meaning of the numerous ethical duties which we perform in life; hence, according to Tilak, *Kartavyadharma* (duty), *niti* (ethics), and *nitidharna* (morality) are synonymous.[270] There is a definition of *dharma* given by Tilak in English. It is: "Religion in the true sense of the word means and includes the knowledge of the nature of the god and soul and the ways and means by which the human soul can attain salvation.[271] He has also cited and analysed other definitions of the *dharma* given by *Mimansaka* and *Mahabharata*.[272] But predominantly, he has used the word *dharma* to mean ethical duty.

---

266 Tilak, B. (1935). *Gita-Rahasya* (B. Sukthankar, Trans.). Tilak Brothers. (original work published 1915).p.90.

267 Ibid, p.88.

268 पारलौकिक सुखाचा मार्ग

269 Tilak, B. (1935). *Gita-Rahasya* (B. Sukthankar, Trans.). Tilak Brothers. (original work published 1915). p.88.

270 Ibid, pp.88-89.

271 लो. टिळकांची धर्मविषयक मते पृ. क्र. ३१

272 Tilak, B. (1935). *Gita-Rahasya* (B. Sukthankar, Trans.). Tilak Brothers. (original work published 1915). pp.94-99.

Dharma has two aspects. One is philosophical, and the other is behavioural.[273] In the philosophical part, the meaning of *moksha* is explained rationally after explaining the nature of *parameshwar* after properly considering the material body (*pinda*) and its relation to the cosmos (*bramhanda*). In the behavioural part, there is an explanation of how a man should live his life in this world to attain *moksha*.[274] Philosophical aspects can be further divided into spirituality, *paramartha*, *nitishastra*, psychology, etc.[275] Tilak has written extensively on these subjects in his magnum opus *Gitarahasya*. I will deal with it in a later part.

Behavioural aspects can be further divided into two parts, temporal and spiritual. Temporal behavioural aspects further degenerate into personal behaviour aspects and societal behavioural aspects. Hence, *dharmic* behavioural aspects are three, and for each aspect, there exists *sutragrantha*.[276] For the spiritual aspect, there is *shrautsutra*. The spiritual aspect deals with the method of worship like *dnyayoga*, *bhaktiyoga*, etc. For the personal behavioural aspect, there is *Gruhyasutra*. They govern the various events in domestic life, various *samskara*, etc.[277] For the description of the societal behavioural aspect, there is *dharmasutra*. *Dharmasutra* mostly deals with rules about the conduct of men as members of society.[278]

It is important to understand Tilak's views about *dharma*. His views are reflected in his editorials. He wrote an article in *Kesari* dated 23rd February 1892 titled 'Our *dharma*.' Below is the translation of the relevant extracts from the article:

---

273   लो. टिळकांची धर्मविषयक मते पृ. क्र. 118-119.

274   Tilak, B. (1935). *Gita-Rahasya* (B. Sukthankar, Trans.). Tilak Brothers. (original work published 1915). pp.18-19.

275   लो. टिळकांची धर्मविषयक मते पृ.क्र. 119.

276   उपरोक्त पृ.क्र. 123.

277   Kane, P. V. (1941). History of Dharmasastra-Vol I, Part I. p.11.

278   Ibid, p.11-12.

"Our empire, wealth, and freedom have gone. Hence, we think that our ancestors and we are fools. Our ancestors did not know politics, how to run the government and military, etc. Also, they did not know the *dharma* and *Ishwar*. It is obvious that people who are hopeless due to slavery are saying these things. Those who have power have prestige in the world, and their behaviour and thoughts are accepted and imitated by the people. Further, people believed that without replicating such prestigious men's behaviour, it was impossible to gain equal status with them. A similar situation has happened with *dharma*.

When western education was introduced, some people got blinded by their scientific knowledge and methods, and contempt was developed in their minds towards Bharatiya philosophy, and they quickly accepted western philosophy. Those people never contemplate the real nature of our *dharma*, the relation between *jiva* and *Ishwar* and texts of our *dharma* about it, the relation of this thought with external behaviour, etc. They established different sects which were influenced by modernism. They did not like the discussion of *dnyan*, *karma*, and *bhakti* in our texts. But the articles written by European authors who studied these texts opened the eyes of those people. Institutions like theosophy and articles written by authors like Max Muller brought back the glory of shining principles of Hindu *dharma*. The narrative that the thoughts of our *rishis* on *atman* and *anatman* and methods of *pranayama*, etc., of *yogis* are useless and futile began to change. It was discovered that some philosophical principles are out of the reach of materialistic sciences. Slowly, it got established that if texts of all religions were compared, then the philosophy of Hindu *dharma* would be the best. We understood the importance of the Hindu *dharma* when foreigners told us! If this trend continues, it will benefit the nation.

Professor Max Muller is giving lectures on *dharma* in England. It will be published in the form of a book. He said it is unfortunate that western people have not paid attention to philosophical texts, and Hindu people are facing slavery as they have not mastered the art of killing! There are very few Europeans who talk about Hindustan with such earnestness. It is not the subject of this article to discuss the causes of the slavery of Hindustan. Even if we suppose that the Bhartiya philosophy is partially responsible for our slavery, it does not downgrade the quality of our philosophical texts. When most of the nations in the world were living in the darkness of nescience and did not even know the *dharma*, the real nature of *dharma* was revealed in this country, and principles which are supposed to be discovered today were discerned and discovered by our *rishis*. *Vedanta* texts have excellent discussions on various questions like which *dharma* of *jiva* are in *Ishwar*, the relation of *bramhadnyan* with *achar*, the real nature of *dharma*, and the philosophy of external behaviour. Even though we have differences, we believe that *Vedantavichar* is the root of *dharma*. There are numerous religions (sects) in our *dharma*, but we believe they lead us to god just like all rivers end in the ocean. There is no other religion in the world which can exhibit such tolerance. In any religious text, there is a mixture of religion and ethics. Hindu *dharma* is the one and only one in the world that has discerned and contemplated the basic principles of *dharma*.

Today, as we are busy learning material science, we are bored with spirituality! That is why we neglected *dharma*. I hope modern people will welcome the thoughts of Professor Max Muller, who has studied our texts for a long time. Unfortunately, the people of this country are neglecting *dharma*. But at the least philosophical principles in this country are not dying but get an impetus, even from foreigners. Now at least, people should pay attention to our ancient spiritual texts."

Tilak wrote another article in which there is a reflection of his faith, devotion, and pride in *dharma*. It is an obituary article. It was written after the death of Swami Vivekanand. Tilak had much respect for Vivekananda. The article is also important to understand the influence of Swami Vivekananda on Bharatiya minds. It appeared in *Kesari* dated 8th July 1902, titled 'Swami Vivekananda attained *Samadhi*'. Below is the translation of the relevant extracts from the article:

"Thousands of Hindus who have solicitude towards Hindu *dharma* would feel sad after hearing the news that Swami Vivekananda attained *Samadhi* at *Belur* monastery. It is hard to find Hindus who have not heard the name Swami Vivekananda. He has explained the spiritual science practised in Hindustan for thousands of years and gained a reputation in the west and an acknowledgement from western people. This is not a small task. Theosophical society had begun the task of resisting the tide of materialistic science before Vivekananda. But Vivekananda brought '*Hindutva*' in those efforts. Today, education in our country is rational, due to which students start mockery of *Swadharma*. The nature of Swami Vivekananda in his childhood was such. He was originally from Bengal. His age was between 35 40 at the time of death. He received an education twenty years ago. One can guess the quality of education as the English schools of Kolkata, and the English schools of Mumbai and Pune are of the same nature. The name of *Swamiji* before *Sanyas* was Narendra Sen and was *Kshatriya*. He passed out from Kolkata university with a B.A. degree. He was fond of philosophy. In his youth, he leaned towards atheism. In debates with *dharmagurus*, he used to question whether they had actually seen the god. His thoughts changed when he met *Ramakrishna Paramhansa*. He became the *shishya* of *Ramakrishna* and then became a *sanyasi*. Max Muller has written a famous biography of *Ramakrishna Paramhansa*. He attained *samadhi* in 1886. His students took responsibility to spread his *Advaita* thoughts. Vivekananda introduced *Advaita Siddhanta* in front of the American people. Swami Vivekananda spent a few years travelling across the country and the *Himalayas* and meeting various *Siddha* people without revealing his identity. In this secret journey, he came to Pune in 1891-1892 and then went to *Mahabaleshwar*, and from there, he went to Belgaum, Dharwad, Madras, and Rameshwar.

The idea that Vivekananda should visit America first arose in Madras, and the people of Madras helped him to reach America. He went to the world religion conference arranged in Chicago. At the conference, he explained *Advaita Vedanta* of Hindu *dharma*. After the conference, he spread *Advaita Vedanta* in America. He established a monastery and gathered students. Today, America is home to all sciences. The task of explaining and spreading *Advaita Vedanta* in America in front of Christian missionaries was not possible for the common man. The opinion of *Swami Vivekananda* is as follows:

"The bond for Hindu people in Hindustan is Hindu *dharma*, and principles of Hindu *dharma* are supreme, and it is possible to spread these principles among the people of any country even at the end of the nineteenth century. Further, it is the primary duty of Hindu people to spread these principles."

He has repeatedly said, "The only remarkable thing which has remained in the hands of Hindu people is *dharma*. If they neglect *dharma*, then they will be mocked by the world. Learn principles of Hindu *dharma*, compare it with other sciences, and spread it worldwide." He believes that *Bhakti* is the principal symbol of *dharma*, but without the coupling of *Advaita Vedanta*, it becomes insignificant. He used to advise that *rajayoga*, *dnyayoga*, or *karma yoga* are paths of real *dharma* and thus have no conflict with any religion, and all should gain knowledge from it, and those who know these paths should spread it. He used to get disheartened after watching the contempt and neglect of Hindus towards *dharma*. He firmly believed that a nation's progress was impossible without the progress of *dharma*. He was making efforts for it.

After establishing a monastery in America and spreading *Advaita Vedanta*, he first came to *Srilanka* and then returned to Bharat. He arrived at Madras and then went to Kolkata and then to the *Himalayas*, where his monastery is at *Almora*. He has also established a monastery at Belur at the banks of *Hugaly* and the *samadhi* of *Ramkrishna Paramahansa*. In 1896-1897, during the famine, volunteers from *Ramakrishna* Mission went to *Rajputana* and stopped the conversion activities of Christian missionaries. His students are at Kolkata, *Almora*, *Ajmer*, Madras, etc. The mission has not yet spread all over Hindustan. In 1900, *Swami*

Vivekananda gave a lecture on *Vedanta* in Paris. Newspapers in France praised him.

He had heart problems for a year. That is why he could not visit Japan even if the Japanese had invited him. As per the telegram that has come to me, he completed his usual evening round and then called his students and told them that he was about to leave the world and attain *Samadhi*. It is unfortunate for the nation that *Swamiji* attain *samadhi* at such a young age. *Ramkrishna Paramhansa* was *bramhanistha* like *Swami Samarth* from *Akkalkot*. *Vivekananda* spread the *Advaita Vedanta* worldwide and increased the prestige of Hindu *dharma* and Hindus. He began the work of rejuvenation of *dharma* with his intellect, speech, and enthusiasm. All were hoping that *Vivekananda* would complete the work, but the hope was shattered due to *samadhi* taken by *Swamiji*. Before 1200, *Shankaracharya* did similar things at the end of the nineteenth century. But the work of *Vivekananda* is yet to be completed. I request his students (or other people) to continue work.

The only asset which has remained in our hands is our *dharma*. Our splendour and freedom have gone. But *dharma* has remained in our hands. We have also experienced the greatness of our *dharma* in a modern nation. At this stage, we should not neglect it. At the current time, if we have some valuable thing in our hands, then we should find its proper valuation in the competitive global markets. *Swami Vivekananda* performed the same task. To return his favour, we would have to follow his path. I hope that more and more people will take inspiration as a nation from *Swami Vivekananda*. In the future, one of our great rishi's decedents would unify all religions in *Advaita Vedanta*. Invitations were sent to *Swamiji* to conduct lectures in Pune. But it was unfortunate as the people of Pune missed his lectures as he was unwell or for any other reason."

This article is living proof of the devotion of Tilak towards Hindu *dharma*. We find another brilliant obituary article on the death of *Shridhar Ganesh Jinasiwale*, dated 25th August 1903, in which he elaborates on the contemptuous attitude of western-educated youth towards *dharma* and gives an example of *Jinasiwale* and his pride in *dharma*. Below is the translation of the relevant extracts from the article:

"I am sad that Professor *Shridhar Ganesh Jinasiwale* died on Tuesday in Mumbai. People of Maharashtra know him through his lectures and reports of lectures published in newspapers. His qualities of patriotism, solicitude, intellect, reading, etc., are well known. He was among very few intellectuals who passed out from our university in the past thirty to thirty-five years. Many graduates and postgraduates pass out from university. But people who continue their thirst for knowledge and reading in school, college, and after college are rare. In this way, it can be said that the death of *Jinasiwale* is a great loss to us.

Jinasiwale was originally from *Gwalior*. He was from an aristocratic family. His father had a property dispute with his relatives and left *Gwalior* by leaving his claim on the property. *Jinasiwale* was born in November 1852. His education began during his childhood. It continued even in its poverty. He completed his B.A. in 1872 and his M.A. in 1876. His favourite subjects were history, logic, economics, philosophy, and Sanskrit. He had a private collection of five to six thousand books. Graduates rarely spend such an amount of money on books! He was a school teacher at Pune high school for a few years and became a Sanskrit Professor at Wilson college of Mumbai. He remained in that position for 14 to 15 years. But due to the deceptive efforts of a few people, he was forced to resign from that post.

His views about the political condition of our country were shaped by his vast reading of the history of different nations. The government and its 'close friends' never liked his views! But he boldly stated his views as after the analysis of the history; he had reached a conclusion that one day, our country will get out of slavery. He considered it his principal duty. He used to make very eloquent speeches, especially on the condition of this country based on the history of various nations. He indeed lacked leadership qualities. But he had various qualities such as patriotism and love for the country, being free from all addictions (which are spreading in the educated class), total faith in *Swadharma*, etc.

Jinasiwale was a representative of the specific philosophical thought among the people who had received an English education. English education creates delusion in the minds of the person of ordinary intellect about Hindu *dharma*, traditions, and customs. It creates a schism in his thoughts and behaviour. Also, it creates a dilemma in his mind to follow Bharatiya traditions or western traditions, and most of the time, it results either in torpor or whimsical behaviour. The educated class thinks that their situation is obvious due to the struggle which is undergoing in between eastern and western reform movements. This opinion of the educated class is wrong, and *Jinasiwale* is a good example *Jinasiwale* was not less talented than other people with an M.A. degree; maybe he was even greater in intellect. He was first educated in his home and received *samskaras*; English education had no evil effect on his mind. He was of the opinion that as he was Hindu, his *dharma* was *Vaidik dharma*; there was no need to change the method of worship as decided by *dharma*. Further, he used to say that it was his responsibility to follow the *dharma* and that the nation's welfare lies in it. He believed that "I am Hindu. I will remain Hindu. I shall die as a Hindu, and I will achieve prosperity with the help of *Hindutva*". He proved all educated classes wrong as his views never changed and reflected in his behaviour. The young generation should take inspiration from his life. Those who go where the wind blows or lack the courage to maintain their independent identity without caring about mockery or persecution have mocked *Jinasiwale* and will mock in the future.

He was not against the reform but was against concepts like 'double life' coined by the educated class and the eccentric behaviour of the educated class. He used to protest against such behaviour with firm determination. Western education does not have any adverse effects on religious scholars of Christianity. This is evident from the life of

Gladstone. Hence, *Jianasiwale* used to think that the adverse effects of western education on Bharatiya people were due to the lack of *dharmic* education and education at home. That is why he was intolerant to concepts like double life or the dilemma explained above. To uphold the *dharmic* (and societal) behaviour, we need more people like *Jinasiwale*. That is why it was a significant loss to us due to his death. He was the one who could have guided the youth whose minds were fickle after watching the behaviour of their forefathers who were practising a 'double life'. There are intellectuals who have earned M.A. in Sanskrit or history, and there will be such people in the future as well. But the exceptional quality in *Jinasiwale* is becoming rare. It is true that qualities of firmness and resolution are partially hereditary. But by following role model and contemplating, one can earn these qualities."

Now I will explain the importance given by Tilak to *achar*, tradition, and *samskara*. He had immense respect for tradition, *achar*, and *samskara*. There is one Tilak speech in which he demonstrated his views. It is given below[279]:

"In any country, common people do religious duties with faith and belief. It is the duty of educated people to save and uphold *dharma* and to give new directions by preserving tradition. But our newly educated class is different. They do not like *dharma* and *samskara*. They also ridiculed the *bhaktipanth* practised by people who go to *Pandharpur* for pilgrimage. The first generation of the educated class became highly agnostic. After some time, they started believing in the existence of god, maybe because of *purvasamskara*, and also felt the need for a method of worship. But they were not ready to accept Hindu *dharma* towards which they had looked with contempt. They took good from each religion and made an amalgamation of all religions. But as they had broken the tradition and mocked it, the schism between the newly educated class and common people widened.

____

279 The speech was given in 1904 '*Ganapati Utsava*'. It is reported in: लो. टिळकांची धर्मविषयक मते पृ.क्र. 208-209.

People who got jobs with little education had no scope to receive *dharmic* education. The only religious education given was Christianity in missionary schools. Hence, this class became faithless and indifferent towards *dharma*. But farmers, traders, artisans, etc., preserved the tradition by having firm faith in the path followed by unselfish, austere ascetics and saints.

We all know the tactics used by missionaries for conversion, their activities, and their institutions. Due to the persistent efforts of missionaries and our neglect, *dharma* is in severe danger. It is the duty of educated people to understand the nature of the threat to *dharma*, *dharma* itself, find ways to tackle the challenges to *dharma* and to spread awareness about *dharma,* and make efforts to achieve the unity of educated people, traders, and farmers."

Tilak's behaviour in college and, overall, in life was *dharmic*. He never shied away from following *achar* prescribed by *dharmashastra*. He always respected tradition. He acknowledged that with the change in time, tradition also requires change, but it should be conserved to a possible extent, and we should have pride in it.[280] He thought that the *dharmic achar* was a kind of social bond and must not be broken unless a new bond is formed, and if broken prematurely, it would result in anarchy.[281] He thought educated people should follow social conventions if they were not immoral. Such social conventions show the distinctiveness and uniqueness of society.[282] He tried to define it based on *samskara*.[283] There is one article written by Tilak in *chitramatajagata* in January 1915 in which he expressed his views on separate Hindu identity. It is:

"To be a part of a particular religion, only a rational understanding of religion is not sufficient, but it also requires external *samskara*. Without external *samskara*, a person cannot fully become part of

---

280 लो. टिळकांची धर्मविषयक मते पृ.क्र.1-2.
281 उपरोक्त पृ.क्र.11.
282 उपरोक्त पृ.क्र.11-12.
283 उपरोक्त पृ.क्र.186.

religion. As such *achars* are to be done many times in life, a person following those becomes familiar with his religious identity, the goal of his religion also gets clear, and his faith in religion becomes stronger. The utility of *achar* is to increase faith in *Swadharma* and increase unity by bonding people together. When there is a talk about religion, a person automatically thinks about the specific and unique *samskara* of that religion. A person who does not follow conventions at the time of birth, death, or festivals or does not follow any daily religious duties should be declared neither Hindu nor *yavan*!"[284]

Now I will discuss the achievements of Tilak in the field of *dharma*. First is his push for *dharmic* education. He defined *dharmic* education as which increases faith and pride and makes students dutiful and truthful, and according to him, such education is necessary for the student's life.[285] He believed such education would increase respect for our ancient culture in the mind of students.[286] Tilak wrote one article in *Kesari* dated 19th January 1904 titled 'One-sidedness of Educated people' in which he explained the ill effects of contemporary education. Below is the translation of the relevant extracts from the article:

"In the last article, I have explained the meaning of doing reforms with the base of *Hindutva* (or by conserving Hindutva) by giving examples. If some people have understood that I endorse those examples, then it is absolutely wrong. I have used those examples to prove that different paths are available to achieve the same motive. Some will not like non-violence or the direction given to reform by *Arya Samaj*. But it does not reduce the importance of the parable.

Our society is ancient, and some rules regulate it. These rules did not exist simultaneously, but there were changes in them relative to changes in space and time. If the current form of rules is not favourable to present conditions, then it is necessary to make relevant changes,

---

284 उपरोक्त पृ.क्र.105.

285 लो. टिळकांची धर्मविषयक मते पृ.क्र. 80.

286 उपरोक्त पृ.क्र.80.

and there is no doubt that it will happen. The only question is whether to attempt to bring such change and in which direction.

Some people would say let the change happen automatically, without our interference. I do not agree with these people. The difference between people attempting the reform and me is in the direction. This difference in direction is extremely important, and I have given examples in the previous article to prove my views. My view is that if reform is based on *dharma,* then people would not oppose it. My reliance is on the direction and not on obstacles! That is why it is important to expose the mistakes of people attempting to change in the other direction.

It is the duty of educated people to carry out reforms of any kind, as sunrays strike peaks of mountains first and then valleys! Reforms in ancient times, in *dharma* and traditions, were brought by *Shankaracharya.* Recent examples of saints like *Dnyanadeva, Namadeva, Eknath,* and *Tukaram* are also perfect. These activators of *Bhagwat dharma* had knowledge, equanimity, *vairagya*, and faith in *dharma.* The irony is that even though we have excellent examples of how to bring out change, we do not understand the way to bring out a change in our traditions in current times. It is due to current education which has made us prejudiced. In the past, intelligent people used to study foreign sciences, but generally, they never abandoned their language, *dharma,* or tradition. Examples of people abandoning their *dharma* or tradition were rare. In Islamic rule, many people converted to Islam due to torture or other reasons. But those who remained Hindu were not sceptical about Hindu *dharma* like today.

As the religion of rulers is different, they have neglected *dharmic* education. Hence, our schools have become factories producing people with some practical capabilities. Such education is being imparted for three to four generations. People should have established independent institutions providing *dharmic* education. But nobody made such efforts. Hence, each educated generation is becoming more utilitarian, and the gulf between them and those who do not know English is being widened. This may be good for the state and missionaries but not for the nation.

In old times, there was a class of intellectual people. But they were not separated from society like that of current intellectuals. They used to think that to bring out reforms in society, it was necessary to advise them. The opinion of current reformers is radically different. The views of reformers about *dharma* are well known. They have never read (or understood) our ancient texts. They do not know the nature of *dharma* and its necessity in the development of the nation. These people obey some social conventions or *dharmic* traditions ostensibly. As there is a complete lack of faith in *dharma*, these people abandon these traditions if they hurt them in their way. If somebody confronts them, they are ready to debate with the help of Mill, Spencer, or Beckon. They even do not have the idea that to maintain our independent identity in the social or *dharmic* sphere, it is sometimes necessary to endure particular difficulties. It is one of the components in *dharmic* education to prepare people to endure such difficulties. Most social reformers of today belong to the same class.

They lack the courage which comes from *dharmic* education. They do not care for *dharma*. The example is in front of us. Missionaries are making huge efforts to convert Hindus to Christianity. Some missionaries have declared by words or some by activity that famine had been created in Bharat by their god to help them! This is a pathetic situation for Hindu *dharma*. Some reformers even say it would be good if the whole nation became Christian. If people are not paying attention to the cacophony of reformers, then it is not people's fault. That is why I say that if you want to carry out reforms, then do it based on *dharma*.

Hindus would not tolerate the discussion of social reforms by the current social reformers as Europeans would not tolerate the discussion of social reforms in European society by Hindus, or Hindus would never tolerate the discussion of reforms by European in Hindu society. These reformers are Hindus only by birth. But they converted to foreign religions through education and philosophy. This is the opinion of people. In such a situation, reforms in society are not possible and, if taken, would be detrimental.

It is wrong to say that there is no nationality to Hindu *dharma*, as three to four religions are present in Hindustan. If we look from the perspective of the population, Hindus are the majority. This huge majority is possible due to the bond of *Hindutva*. To destroy or neglect this bond and not uphold it means the neglect of two-thirds majority of the people of Hindustan. It is a misapprehension that breaking *Hindutva* would benefit the nation. We indeed need means other than *Hindutva* to unite thirty crore people. But we should understand that out of these thirty-crore people, bonds of Hindutva tie twenty crore people. It is important, necessary, and beneficial for the nation to uphold *Hindutva*. Hence, social reforms should be done by keeping in mind the (national) policy of *Hindutva*. But as English-educated people are prejudiced, the gulf between them and people is widening. We blame traditional scholars for their prejudice, but modern scholars are also prejudiced. Traditional scholars cannot comprehend the altered situation, and modern scholars do not have faith in *dharma*, lack the ability to work with people, and have no solicitude for *dharma*.

The situation will not become better unless there is a change in education policy. Faith in *dharma* includes the endurance of dangers and dying to protect the dharma if required. Missionaries have received English education. Still, they are ready to spread their religion by working with poor people. Is anyone from reformers doing such work? No, but they categorised people as lower class. Hence, they feel ashamed of having a conversation with these people. Such people cannot carry out any reforms or cannot do anything for the nation. This is a deficiency or prejudice of the educated class. Real solicitude towards people, willingness to make relentless and unselfish efforts for people by mixing with them, and faith in *Swadharam* are absent in English-educated people. The fault is indeed in education. Still, until their prejudice vanishes, they cannot carry out real reforms. These people blamed traditional scholars, but their direction was also prejudiced, just like traditional scholars. They have become blind, and the first reform is to make efforts to remove this blindness! Once it disappears, the educated class can lead society; otherwise, it will not. This is the opinion of Mrs. Annie Beasant and Professor *Rangacharya*. Moderates would not like it. But it is beneficial and favourable. I hope moderates would understand this. B.A. degree has lost its special status. As the number of people receiving English education has increased, questions are being raised about whether it is the highest accomplishment. This revolution in thoughts is due to discussions which are taking place on Hindu *dharma* and its texts for the past many years. Maybe, the previous generation lacks the *samskara* of this revolution. But it is foolish to neglect this revolution and not leave their method of social reforms. A person who has knowledge of English is not omniscient. The direction of people who received an English education had been lost. People are getting this fact, and if leaders who want to do something for the country, then they cannot neglect them."

In this article, Tilak has represented his views on the prejudices of the people who had received an English education. In 1904, Wrangler *Paranjape* wrote one article in the magazine 'East and West' and said that Hindu *dharma* is a collection of stupid beliefs, and *dharmic* education instead of benefiting would harm the nationality. Tilak wrote one article in *Kesari* dated 31ˢᵗ May 1904. Below is the translation of the relevant extracts from the article:

"Critics wrote articles in support of *Paranjape's* views after the publication of my article on the article written by principal *Paranjape* in 'East and West'. Some said that the attack of professor *Paranjape* was on stupid beliefs and not on the original principles of *dharma*, while some said that as there are students from all religions in school, it becomes impossible to give education of particular religion. The third critic called my criticism biased and had sprung from hatred and had not refuted even one point made by professor *Paranjape*. But critics have become confused as professor Selby also had deduced the meaning of the article similar to the meaning deduced by me. Selby also had given his opinion that the opinion of *Paranjape* is wrong and there is no wrong in teaching original principles of *dharma* in schools (which is in the agreement of late M G Ranade and Dr. Bhandarkar). Critics hesitate to support the true opinion of professor *Paranjape*. It is impossible for them.

I have read the article of principal *Paranjape* in 'East and West'. The principles written in the article can be stated in brief:

1. If *dharmic* education is given in Bharat, it would harm the nation and nationality.

2. *Dharma* is not the foundation of morality, but morality is (should be) the foundation of *dharma*.

3. Religious fanatism cannot be controlled.

4. *Dharma* is a collection of stupid beliefs that will not exist perpetually in front of new ideas.

5. Not just beliefs, traditions, or behaviour, but all principles of *dharma* are wrong. Hence, the nation's progress is impossible without annihilating these principles.

I think these principles are wrong and ill-considered. As there is a lack of *dharmic* education in our schools and colleges, young and intelligent graduates would have absurd views like that of principal *Paranjape*. Some graduate in the course of time, change their views, move towards *Vedanta*, *Yoga*, theosophy, etc., and finally develop complete faith in the *dharma*. The defect is not in youth but in the education they are receiving.

I would not have criticised him if he had not been the principal. I have seen and listened to the young graduates who recently passed out from college who habitually make such fatuous and cretinous statements. I have not written about these people apart from simply telling them that their opinion is wrong. If *Paranjape* had been just a wrangler, I would have adopted the same policy towards him. But when such statements are made by the principal of the private college, which was established based on public support, it was necessary to expose the perilousness of those statements. When *Paranjape* returned as a wrangler, *Kesari* congratulated him; now, as he has made a blunder, it is the duty of *Kesari* to point it out.

I do not think there is any reason other than atheism practised by *Paranjape,* due to which he developed the ridiculous idea that *dharmic* education is a threat to nationality. If the existence of numerous denominations of Christianity in England does not hurt the nationality of England (so are conditions in Japan and Russia), then why is there a problem with different *sampradayas* of Hindu *dharma*? All different sects, doctrines, etc., of Hindu *dharma* are united in *Vedanta*. This is historically proven. But it appears that *Paranjape* never thought about it. The other opinion of *Paranjape* is that the religious differences between Hindus, Muslims, Christians, Parsis, etc., will disappear if *dharmic* education would not be imparted in schools. This opinion is idiotic. There is no other religion which is as tolerant as Hindu *dharma*. It is the opinion of Hindu people that each person should live according to his religion. That is why it is the vacuous idea that the education of Hindu *dharma* in school would hurt nationality.

It is not clear from the writings of *Paranjape* whether he believes in the separate existence of *atman* from the body. But it appears from his previous article that he does not believe in an independent existence of an *atman* from the body. It is obvious that a person possessing such thoughts thinks that *dharma* is a collection of stupid beliefs. It is important and necessary to say that such thoughts are wrong and are a threat to the nation. If atheists are claiming that they have shown courage (by giving such statements) as the majority believes in god, then even blind people can make the same claim as the majority of people are not blind! Still, I would not have cared about atheistic thoughts of *Paranajape* as he is a frivolous atheist vis-à-vis *Charvak* and others! Hence, there was also no need of exposing their mistakes. But as he is the principal of a prominent private educational institution which has developed due to public support and made such statements, I was compelled to write this article.

In the texts of Hindu *dharma*, we find subtle and profound thoughts on the relationship between *jiva* and *parameshwara*. Such thoughts are not explained as profoundly as in Hindu texts in any other religion. Paranjape lacks the *samskara* of these *dharmic* principles, so he narrowly understands dharma as a collection of stupid beliefs. As his belief is firm, he has dared to blurt out absurd, puerile, and vacuous statements in front of the world. Suppose that his article had been kept for examination in front of the managing board of Fergusson college. In that case, I do not think the board or council would have agreed with his views and would not have granted permission to publish it. That is why such asinine and puerile behaviour of *Paranjape* is despicable and iniquitous, and it is my duty to protest against it vigorously. Suppose *Paranjape* had been the principal of Deccan college instead of Fergusson college. I do not think I would have used 'mild' language against him. In fact, I think as he is the principal of Fergusson college, I have not used strong words! One has no authority to interfere in *dharma* because he has become a wrangler. The *dharma* is an independent science, just like mathematics. Mathematics demands distinctive intellect, learning, understanding, and reading. Similarly, *dharma* requires a distinct mindset, learning, understanding, and reading texts (perhaps *dharma* requires more of the qualities mentioned above). *Paranjape* does not possess that ability. It is evident from his articles. He is not the first person who has attacked *dharma*. There were brilliant intellectuals, some even possessing greater intellect than *Paranjape*, who had attacked *dharma* in the past. Even after that, if profound principles of *dharma* have remained intact, then criticism of *Paranjape* would not damage it. Still, I have written this article to ensure that the views of *Paranjape* would not get unnecessary importance which it might get as he is the principal of the college."

In this article, Tilak developed and supported his views on *dharmic* education. His views on practical implementation in schools and the curriculum of such education are reflected in an article written in *Kesari* dated 3rd November 1904 titled 'Recent books on Hindu *dharma*'. Below is the translation of relevant extracts from the article:

"Officers in the education department are so intolerant towards Hindu *dharma* that they cannot even tolerate *shri ganeshaya namah* or *shri* at the beginning of the Marathi book. I do not know why officers in the school education department, especially the incumbent director, are disgruntled at Hindu *dharma*. The majority of students who are learning in school, in which standard textbooks prescribed by the school education department are in use, are Hindu. There is a rare possibility of Muslim students or native Christian students in the school. But to drop popular stories from *Mahabharat, Bhagwat,* or *shri ganeshaya namah* from the beginning of Marathi textbooks for minority students is idiocy. I would have termed it religious fanaticism, but the government of India usually stays away from such religious fanaticism. Hence, the education department officers' act should be called capricious, ludicrous, and impolitic. I have even heard the news that the director of the education department has passed an order to ban teaching songs of *Shiva, Vishnu, Rama,* etc. Hindu deities to girls in the female high school or training schools! If the news is true, then there is a conflict between the resolution of the government regarding reforms in the school education department and the conduct of the director of the government education department. Students should imbibe qualities such as patriotism, adherence to the truth, resoluteness, etc., to develop their character. If this is true, then I do not understand the occurrence of events mentioned above in government schools.

Dharmik education would not be imparted successfully, especially to the small children, by telling basic principles of different religions. Children or students of primary school are predominantly emotional than rational. They cannot grasp the religious values of those religions whose preachers, activators, etc., are unfamiliar to them (or those whose stories have not been listened to by children from their elders). Hence, *dharmic* education should be given to children based on their religion. If one agrees with this principle, then to impart *dharmic* education in government schools, respective texts on religions must be given for reading to students. The question is whether such books are being written by the government department of education.

There are numerous texts on the Hindu *dharma* in *Sanskrit* and *Prakrit*. But as there is not enough time to learn *Sanskrit* or the literary style of Sanskrit and *Prakrit* texts have become obsolete, these texts are not studied in government schools. Also, there is no room for studying such texts in the current curriculum. Hence, when a boy enters primary school and comes out from the factory called a university with M.A. or L.L.B. degree, he does not know anything about *dharma*. He can tell the story of 'grace darling' from his Marathi or English textbooks, but if he reads about the story of *Harishchandra,* he would be compelled to search in Sanskrit texts for this allusion. The education in college is of this type. Students memorise principles of logic, astronomy, mathematics, and economics. When such students start reading and thinking about *dharmic* literature, they develop a false line of thinking. This is the state of rational aspects; emotional aspects like love towards *dharma* have already been devasted. After graduation with twelve to fifteen years of study, these people become faithless and selfish. They do know the dictionary meaning of unselfishness but cannot practice it. They can only earn bread and butter and lack the capacity to work beyond that. They cannot work relentlessly in a particular field with full faith. They lack the patience and resolution to achieve something in life. The main goal of life is to achieve *moksha,* and *dharma* is the means to achieve it. But faith in *dharma* also benefits worldly affairs. Leaders of the nation require such faith. But in our country, such education is not being imparted, and officers in the education department have no desire to make provisions for such education.

Mrs. Annie Beasant has published three books on Hindu *dharma* for the Hindu college in Banaras. The first book is up to the fourth to the fifth standard. The second is up to the sixth to the seventh standard. The third is in college. They are in English. They can be used in other schools too. In this book, the nature of Hindu *dharma*, principal texts of Hindu *dharma*, different ways of reaching the god, concepts of ethics in Hindu *dharma*, etc., are explained in simple language. These books are not perfect. There is much scope for reform. But as such a book is written for the first time, Hindu students should read it. But when government support for the book was demanded, the director refused because books were written only for Hindu *dharma* and not for others![287] The director should have understood that books were written for Hindu people, and the education should give permission to teach these books to Hindus, not Christians. This was the request of Mrs. Beasant. Nobody asks to teach the Christian religion to Hindus or the Hindu religion to Christians. Is it not stupidity to refuse such books on Hindu *dharma*?

Let us put books written by Mrs. Beasant aside. What is the problem in accepting a book (titled *atmavidya*) by *Hari Narayan Godbole*, the principal of *Dhule* high school, for secondary or higher secondary students? It is the first book in Marathi in which there is a critical analysis of old and new texts on Hindu *dharma*. Ancient thoughts have been written in a new way in this book. The author of this book (in fact, his family) is highly intellectual. The school education department can ask him to prepare such books for children. There might be some issue with the book's philosophy, which is *Advaita Vedanta*. But it is not impossible to resolve. But who wants books on Hindu *dharma*? A committee is appointed to reform the existing textbooks. Thousands of rupees would be spent on this committee. This committee would eradicate the content of *dharma* and patriotism (which means seditious content, as per our officers!) and make our textbooks neutral. But if the determination of the director, which appears in 'reforming' over textbooks, is not present in the work of creating books for *dharmic* education. How reform would take place if the government is not ready to accept existing books or not prepared to create one. Private schools in Maharashtra should have paid attention to this issue, but they lack

---

287 Tilak has used the word 'एकदेशीय'. It means books written focused on just one religion.

the courage. The original aim behind establishing private educational institutions was to start an institution free from government education's defects. The original aim has been lost in a way. The government is not interested in giving *dharmic* education, and owners of private educational institutions have a fear of even conversing on the issue! In such a situation, there is only one way to give *dharmic* education to students. People of respective religions should establish independent institutions which would only impart education of *dharma*. The spirit of *dharma* should be kept alive in these institutions. If such attempts are not made, then the real nature of *dharma* would fade away."

These are views of Tilak on the necessity of *dharmic* education.

The second achievement of Tilak in the field of *dharma* is the awakening of *dharma*. Tilak wrote articles and gave speeches on *dharma*. He explained deep and difficult philosophical concepts in Hindu *dharma* to common people. It helped in the awakening of *dharma* and also preserving its roots. Unfortunately, as his principal field was politics, he could not spend full time on *dharma*. Still, he paid remarkable service to *dharma* in the limited scope available to him.

The third big achievement of Tilak is his resistance to Christian missionaries and radical reformers. This topic has been covered hitherto. The time of Tilak was dreadful for Hindu *dharma*. Missionaries and radical reformers were attacking the *dharma*. The educated people were faithless. They were attracted to western philosophy. They were looking towards Hindu *dharma* with contempt and neglect. On the other hand, some uneducated people had tremendous faith in *dharma*. Tilak ended this dichotomous world by creating a new faction of educated people having pride and faith in *dharma*. This was the biggest achievement of Tilak in the field of *dharma*. With his magnificent intellect and astounding organising abilities, Tilak led the resistance against the onslaught of missionaries and radical reformers. He battled hard for the existence of *Hindutva* among Hindus. In tough times, his faith and devotion remained unshackled. He was subjected to a torrent of abuse and barrage. He endured that abuse and launched a vigorous counterattack without crossing his limits. His fiery speeches and blazing articles busted the propaganda. Upcoming generations of Hindus will remember Tilak for his work.

The fourth achievement of Tilak is the beginning of two new national festivals. There are various manifestations of the national consciousness. It may take the form of the development of the mother tongue or the national language, the research history, the hero worship of historical personages, the songs inspiring patriotic feelings and so on. Sometimes these are the causes and consequences of the national consciousness. Two new national festivals started by Tilak were one of the manifestations of the national consciousness.[288]

Tilak did not start the *Ganesh* festival. It was being celebrated with splendour and enthusiasm; the ingenuity of Tilak resided not in originating the festival but in giving it a collective aspect and utilising it as the most efficacious means of creating national consciousness.[289] The development and the account of the origin of the festival are given in Tilak's biography given by Kelkar.[290] Fatuous and naïve objections were raised to the festival. Tilak silenced his critics in an article written in the year 1896. Below is the abstract of the article:

"I pity those hapless people who do not have any connection with *dharma* and cannot comprehend metaphysical principles. Those who would first level down the whole surface of the earth and then uprear ranges of mountains in suitable places and convenient shapes with streams and rivers running according to their plan would always meet with failure.[291] It is necessary to conserve existing national festivals (and if they do not exist, then to begin a new one) to preserve our nationality. I sincerely request educated people not to neglect it."[292]

---

288 Kelkar. (1928). *Life and Times of Lokmanya Tilak.* p.279.

289 Ibid, p.282.

290 केळकरकृत टिळक चरित्र खंड १ पृ. क्र.420-422.
      Kelkar. (1928). *Life and Times of Lokmanya Tilak.* p.282-283.

291 Kelkar. (1928). *Life and Times of Lokmanya Tilak.* p.284.

292 केळकरकृत टिळक चरित्र खंड १ पृ. क्र.424.

In articles written in *Kesari* dated 1st September and 8th September 1896, titled 'Necessity of national festivals' and 'What should educated people do in the time of national festivals?' respectively, there is a critical and historical analysis of national festivals. In the first article, he established the necessity of such national festivals by referring to similar institutions in Greece and Rome. The great unifying and rousing effect of the Olympian and Pythian festivals and also of the circus was emphasised with convincing force. He also highlighted ancient *Bhartiya* institutions like *yagna* and gigantic fares in honour of some deity which attracted people in huge masses and created in their minds a deep ferment of enthusiasm.[293] In the second article, he critically analysed the obsolescence of some old festivals. He asked the people to abandon them and substitute them with new festivals. He maintained that it was their duty to change the course of those festivals and give them a complexion of instruments for preparing the mind of the people for some kind of national work. He said that such festivals provided ample opportunities for the educated class to come into their very spirit, to understand their needs and grievances and to make them co-sharers in the benefits of education and all other new notions.[294]

Tilak also was instrumental at the beginning of the *Shivajayanti* festival. With his peculiar vision, he discovered the great potentialities of the idea of the *Shivjayanti* festival, developed it through the *Kesari* and, with the help of outside propaganda, gave it almost a lasting shape.[295] The account of this movement is given in Tilak's biography written by Kelkar.[296] Soon, it spread all over Maharashtra and further outside Maharashtra. Social reformers were furious at Tilak because he described *Chhatrapati Shivaji Maharaj* as an incarnation of god.

---

293 केळकरकृत टिळक चरित्र खंड १ पृ. क्र.424-425.
    Kelkar. (1928). *Life and Times of Lokmanya Tilak.* p.285.

294 केळकरकृत टिळक चरित्र खंड १ पृ. क्र.425.
    Kelkar. (1928). *Life and Times of Lokmanya Tilak.* p.285-286.

295 Kelkar. (1928). *Life and Times of Lokmanya Tilak.* p.286.

296 केळकरकृत टिळक चरित्र खंड १ पृ. क्र.426-438.
    Kelkar. (1928). *Life and Times of Lokmanya Tilak.* pp.287-293.

They said that Tilak had wasted his education![297] Tilak silenced those critics with an article in *Kesari* dated 19th May 1896. The title is 'Is it not schadenfreude?'. Below is the translation of the relevant extracts from the article:

"Social reformers have displayed their benightedness, immaturity, and puerility. Today, the movement related to is in full swing in Maharashtra *Chhatrapati Shivaji Maharaj*. Any sensible, sagacious, and noble-minded person would be delighted and feel pride. Unfortunately, many reformers are disgruntled about this festival. I have explained the cause and aim behind this festival. But reformers were dissatisfied. One reformer has sent me a letter advising me. To answer such ludicrous, asinine, and deranged fanatics means giving them importance. But as the topic is important, I have written this article.

Critics have said that if *Chhatrapati Shivaji Maharaj* is considered an incarnation of the god, the festival of *Shivajayanti* will become like that of *Ramanavami,* and it would not be effective as conceived by us. I have written before that this fear is baseless. What can be called an incarnation of the god? If we believe that a particular person is an incarnation of a god, then the question is whether people get motivated to imitate his behaviour. The answers given by social reformers are vacuous and senseless. If we accept that *Chhatrapati Shivaji Maharaj* was great, I do not find any difficulty accepting that he was an incarnation. One has to accept that the birth of a person with magnificent intellect, valour, fortitude and imagination in a country is not in the hands of humans. It is not necessary that brave people like Napoleon and Alexander were born in every generation, and we cannot predict how and when they were born. This is beyond our control.

It is the grace of god that a particular person possesses divine qualities in him. A person possessing divine qualities needs the assistance of some 'invisible' power to achieve big things. One calls

---

297 केळकरकृत टिळक चरित्र खंड १ पृ. क्र.438.
    Kelkar. (1928). *Life and Times of Lokmanya Tilak.* p.294.

that impossible thing 'time', 'luck', or 'grace of the god'. There are some incidents in the life of great men where it is impossible to say that they have won just because of their valour or intellect. It does not mean that they are incapable. In those situations, there is no use of ability, and success depends on things outside the purview of efforts. Men with similar qualities as *Shivaji Maharaj* might have been born before. Maybe they lacked the external conditions favourable to *Shivaji Maharaj*; today, people do not even know their names. The meaning of the saying that 'it needs favourable time' is this. Only those men can be categorised as great if they have succeeded. Part of their success is due to their efforts, and some are due to the grace of god.

Hence, we have to accept that *Shivaji Maharaj* was an incarnation of the god. I have not read the definition of the god's incarnation as one with a body similar to the *Ishwar* in our *shastras*! There is a small fraction of divine power in every person. Still, when the existence of a greater fraction of divinity than usual in someone is evident, then we call it an incarnation of the god, which applies perfectly to *Shivaji Maharaj*. Hence, there should not be any objection to calling *Shivaji Maharaj* an incarnation.

I do not know from where the idea that if a particular person is an incarnation of god, then people would not imitate him came from the mind of social reformers. Hindu *dharmashastra* does not support this idea. All texts of Hindu *dharma* explicitly ask to imitate the great men. Further, our *shastras* say that by contemplating about divine qualities of the god, one can imbibe good qualities in himself. If this rule is about the god, it applies to its fractions. There is no rule that the incarnation of the god happens only once.

We have learned since childhood that '*dharmasanthapanarthaya sambhavami yuge yuge*'. Hence, nobody should think that if we accept *Shivaji Maharaj* as a divine incarnation, there will be no incarnation in the future! Even though such men are not present today, nobody can say they will not appear in the next five to twenty-five years or fifty years. Such men became great only after achieving big in their life. That is why each person should read and understand biographies of great men. A person needs ability and luck (or divine grace) to do great things. Even though luck is not in our hands, in some sense, the ability is, and we should put all efforts according to our ability. The coordination of luck and efforts can be achieved in this way. Efforts alone or luck alone do not lead to success. Especially to achieve big things in life, effort and luck are needed. If reformers do not agree with this principle, they should be called immature."

Tilak himself had called the *Shivajayanti* festival a national festival. The title of his article in *Kesari* dated 28th April 1896 is 'The national festival of *Shivajayanti*'. He knew that hero worship is a feeling deeply implanted in human nature, and political aspirations need all the strength which the worship of a *Swadeshi* hero is likely to inspire our minds.[298] He never told people to copy every incident in the life of *Shivaji Maharaj*.[299] He said in his speech, "To turn to the *Shivaji* festival, the knowledge we have or the knowledge which we want to inculcate among the people in this connection, relates not to the actual use of identical measures which *Shivaji*, for instance, took, but a proper appreciation of the spirit in which he resorted to the measures suitable to his time. Festivals like these prove an incentive to the legitimate ambitions of people with a great historical past. They serve to impart courage. Such courage as an appreciation of heroes securing their salvation against all odds can give. They are an antidote to vague despair. They serve like manure to the seeds of enthusiasm and the spirit of nationality.[300]"

Tilak achieved Hindu unity through national festivals. He roused people from their political lethargy and stirred their minds with national

---

298 Tilak, B. G. (1919). *Bal Gangadhar Tilak: his writings and speeches*. Ganesh and Company, Madras. p.48.

299 Ibid, p.49.

300 Tilak, B. G. (1919). *Bal Gangadhar Tilak: his writings and speeches*. Ganesh and Company, Madras. p.70.
केळकरकृत टिळक चरित्र खंड 2 भाग 5 पृ. क्र. 53.

pride.[301] Kelkar quotes Sir Valentine Chirol in Tilak's biography, which perfectly sums up Tilak's achievement. It is given below:

"It is his contention that by means of these two festivals, one in the worship of the god and another in honour of a name full of great historic appeal, Tilak secured a necessary platform from which he could carry on with tremendous advantage, his campaign of political awakening. By the first, he gave a religious point to his political agitation, and by the second, he fleshed the sword of politics thus tempered on people's natural pride in their own history.[302]" Thus, through these two festivals, Tilak tried to achieve the revival of *dharma*, culture, and fighting spirit in people.

Tilak viewed *dharma* as an element of nationality. His view is evident in one speech he gave in *Bharat Dharma Mahamandala* in *Varanasi* on 3rd January 1906. Below are the relevant extracts from the speech. I request all readers to read the full speech, which is reported in the book, whose citation is provided below.[303]

"I am sorry I cannot address you in any other language except Marathi and English. English should be boycotted for religious purposes. But I cannot help and hope you will excuse me. I shall speak a few words on the importance of the Hindu religion, its present condition and the efforts that are being made to preserve it from decay. What is the Hindu religion? If you go to the different parts of India, you will find different views about the Hindu religion entertained by different people. Here, you are mostly *Vaishnavas* or followers of *Shrikrushna*. If you go the south, you will meet followers of *Ramanuja* and others. What is the Hindu religion? *Bharat Dharma Mahamandala* cannot be a *Mahamandala* unless it includes and coordinates these different sections and parts. Its name can only be significant if different sections of the Hindu religion are

---

301 Kelkar. (1928). *Life and Times of Lokmanya Tilak*. p.281.
302 Kelkar. (1928). *Life and Times of Lokmanya Tilak*. p.281.
       केळकरकृत टिळक चरित्र खंड १ पृ. क्र.419.
303 Tilak, B. G. (1919). *Bal Gangadhar Tilak: his writings and speeches*. Ganesh and Company, Madras. p.35-41.

united under its banner. All these different sects are so many branches of the *Vedic* religion. The term *Sanatana dharma* shows that our religion is very old, as old as the history of the human race itself. *Vedic* religion was the religion of *Aryans* from a very early time. But you all know no branch can stand by itself. Hindu religion as a whole is made up of different parts co-related to each other, so many sons and daughters of one great religion. If this idea is kept in view and if we try to unite the various sections, it will be consolidated in a mighty force. So long as you are divided amongst yourselves, so long as one section does not recognise its affinity with another, you cannot hope to rise as Hindus. Religion is an element of nationality. The word *dharma* means to tie and comes from the root *dhri* to bear or hold. What is there to hold together? To connect the soul with the god and a man with man. *Dharma* means our duties towards god and duty towards man. Hindu religion, as such, provides for a moral as well as a social tie. This being our definition, we must go back to the past and see how it worked out.

During *Vedic* times, India was a self-contained country. It was united as a great nation. The unity has disappeared, bringing on us great degradation, and it becomes the duty of the leaders to revive that union. A Hindu of this place is as much Hindu as the one from Madras or Bombay. You might put a different dress and speak a different language, but you should remember that the inner sentiments which move you all are the same. The study of the *Gita, Ramayana* and *Mahabharat* produces the same ideas throughout the country. Are not this common allegiance to the *Vedas*, the *Gita* and *Ramayana* our heritage? If we lay stress on it, forgetting all minor differences between different sects, then by the grace of providence, we shall ere long be able to consolidate all the different sects into a mighty Hindu nation. This ought to be the ambition of every Hindu. If you thus work to unite, you will find within a few years one feeling and one thought actuating and dominating all people throughout the country. This is the work we have to do. The present condition of our religion is not at all one that is desirable. We think of ourselves as separate, and the feeling of unity at the root of our advancement in the past is gone. It is certainly an unfortunate circumstance that we should have so many sections and sub-sections. It is the duty of an association like the *Bharata Dharma Mahamandala* to work to restore the lost and forgotten union. In the absence of unity, India cannot claim its place among the nations of the world."

This portion of the speech is explicitly showing the relation of *dharma* with the nation as envisaged by Tilak. In the same speech, he says:

"*Shrikrushna* says that the followers of other religions worship god though not in a proper form. *Shrikrushna* does not say that the followers of other religions would be doomed to eternal hell. I challenge anybody to point out to me a similar text from the scriptures of other religions. It cannot be found in any other religion because they are partial truth, while our Hindu religion is based on the whole, the *Sanatan* truth, and therefore it is bound to triumph in the end. Numerical strength is also a great strength. Can the religion which counts its followers by crores die? Never, unless the crores of our fellow followers are suddenly swept away, our religion will not die. All that is required for our glorious triumph and success is that we should unite all the different sects on a common platform and let the stream of Hindu religion flow through one channel with a mighty consolidated and concentrated force. This is the work which *Bharata Dharma Mahamandala* has to do and accomplish. Let us be all united. Because a particular man wears a particular dress, speaks a different tongue, and worships a particular *devta*, is that any reason for our withdrawing our hands of fellowships to our Hindu brother? The character of our Hindu religion is very comprehensive, as comprehensive as its literature itself: we have wonderful literature. Wisdom, as is concentrated in *Gita* and epitomised in about seven hundred verses, that wisdom, I am confident, cannot be defeated or overcome by any philosophy, be it western or any other."

In the next paragraph, he writes about the threat to Hindu *dharma*. In the concluding part, he says:

"You would be wanting in duty to yourself and your ancestors if you do not give up provincial prejudices and promote the unity that underlies all sects. We have been very idle. We have grown so stupid owing to our idleness that we are required to be told by foreigners that our treasures conceal gold and not iron. Modern science and education are prepared to help you if you take advantage of them, and the time will come when instead of Christians preaching Christianity here, we shall see our preachers preaching *Sanatana dharma* all over the world. Concentrate all your forces. The idea of a Hindu university where our old religion will be taught along with modern science is a very good one and should have the support of all. In conclusion, I would again draw your attention to bring about a harmonious union of all sects and rightly claim and obtain our rightful place among the nations of the world."

Tilak tried to define the characteristics of *dharma*.[304] He was trying to define *dharma* in such a way that Hindu *dharma* would be separated from all other religions. He defined three characteristics: 1. Faith in *Vedas* 2. Existence of multiple paths towards *moksha* 3. Existence of multiple deities to be worshipped.[305] This definition is a typical example of a definition according to *Nyaya shastra*. The first characteristic unites all existing *sampradaya* in Hindu *dharma*. The second and third characteristics show the distinctive character of Hindu *dharma* vis-à-vis Abrahamic religions. Tilak held *Vedas* in high esteem. He had an excellent understanding of philosophy. He wrote a commentary on *Gita*. *Gita* is considered part of *Prasthantrayi*, which contain *Bramhasutra*, *Upanishad* and *Gita*. *Upanishads* contain various kinds of thoughts, and some of them are mutually contradictory. *Badarayana Maharshi* has reconciled these inconsistencies and harmonised all *Upanishads* in

---

304 प्रामाण्यबुद्धिर्वेदेषु साधनानामनेकता । उपास्यानामनियमश्चैतद्धर्मस्य लक्षणम् ॥

305 This definition is cited in the supreme court judgement. The citation is given below:
Shastri Yagnapurushdasji and others v. Muldas Bhundardas Vaishya and another 1966 AIR 1119, 1966 SCR (3) 242.

Bramhasutra (also known as *Vedanta sutra* or *sharirak sutra*).[306] In *Gita*, there is an epitome of the philosophy of *Upanishad* and *Bramhasutra*. Together with *Gita*, *Bramhasutra* and *Upanishad* form *Prasthantrayi*. *Gita* is considered to be the ultimate authoritative text of Hindu *dharma*. It is the epitome of *Vedic* philosophy. Tilak wrote a commentary on *Gita* in which he explained the *pravruttimarg* as stated in *Gita*.

Gitarahasya is not just important for this reason. Tilak has given the English title to his original Marathi text as 'The Hindu Philosophy of Life, Ethics and Religion'. He derived ethics from *Gita*. This is an extremely important achievement of Tilak, which is often neglected. He always held philosophy in high esteem. He has defined *dharma* somewhat peculiarly, separating *moksha dharma* and *niti dharma*. But this difference is artificial. In Hindu *dharma*, one cannot separate philosophy from *dharma*. Tilak has commented on a change in the attitude of western people. He has said:

"But as a result of the growth of material sciences, this belief has now lost ground in western countries, and people have begun: 1. To consider whether morality, i.e., rule by which the world is maintained, can or cannot be based on something other than *moksha dharma* and 2. To base sociological or materialistic (visible or perceptible foundation).[307]" He compared the *Bharatiya nitishastra* and western ethics and concluded with the superiority of *Bharatiya nitishastra*. First, we shall see the importance of *nitishastra*.

A person who lives is bound to perform several duties. He has to take decisions. He has to decide what is good and wrong, moral and immoral. Sometimes he may find himself in a critical position in which he is caught between two mutually contradictory paths of duty and often become irresolute. *Arjuna* faced a similar situation at the beginning of the *Mahabharat* war. When he observed the opposite

---

306   Tilak, B. (1935). *Gita-Rahasya* (B. Sukthankar, Trans.). Tilak Brothers. (Original work published 1915). p16.

307   Tilak, B. (1935). *Gita-Rahasya* (B. Sukthankar, Trans.). Tilak Brothers. (Original work published 1915). p.707.

side, he saw familiar faces, his relatives, elders, *gurus*, et. He imagined horrors after killing them. It was the clash between two duties, one was the duty of *Kshatriya*, and the second was the collection of various duties towards elders, *gurus*, brothers, etc. He became doubtful and ambivalent about which duty he should perform. He was irresponsible to decide in between right and wrong. At such a delicate and crucial juncture, *Bhagwan Shrikrushna* cleared his doubts and cleared the path of duty which was appropriate for him. This dialogue between *Shrikrushna* and *Arjuna* is *Bhagwat Gita*.

Mahabharata is full of such examples where a person becomes irresolute. Tilak has cited various examples.[308] In fact, *Mahabharata* is a text which guides us about what should be done and what should not be done (*Karmakarma*) and what is wrong (*dharmadharma*). Such conflicts are common, and in such situations, general and common ethical principles are insufficient, which results in exceptions. Hence, any person with a common intellect naturally feels the desire to find a definite and perceptual framework for determining what should be done and what not (or what is one's duty and what is not).[309] Hence, the discernment between doable and not-doable becomes an independent science, and it is even more difficult, subtle, and abstruse than logic and grammar. Tilak says that, technically, in old *Sanskrit,* this science was named *dharmashastra* and the word *niti* used to be applied specifically to regal jurisprudence (*Rajaniti*). But he has called it *nitishastra* since the word '*niti*' includes both duty and good conduct.[310] In *Gita*, there is a scientific examination of all subtle and perplexing questions in which there is a conflict between two duties and the enunciation of universal principles underlying them. *Gita* is the most ancient text in *Sanskrit* literature, which discerns between the doable and non-doable based on *Vedanta*.[311]

---

308 Ibid, pp.41-68.
309 Ibid, p67.
310 Ibid, pp.67-68.
311 Ibid, pp.68-69.

This reliance on *Bharatiya* philosophy and *nitishastra* distinguishes Tilak from his contemporaries. Ethics decide our behaviour. They affect the beliefs, practices, customs, and traditions an individual and society follow. Ultimately, ethics affect the culture. Ethics followed by the great men become precedents for upcoming generations. In Bharat's case, a specific system of ethics was being followed all over the country. One important change occurred when the British colonised Bharat and began colonial education. Through colonial education, the British successfully bought an axiological shift in the people who received British education. The educated class mimicked western customs, traditions, philosophy, and ethics. Hence, the conception of good and bad in the minds of the educated class thoroughly changed. Most of the educated class was affected by colonial education because they lacked the intellect and faith in Bharatiya philosophy. Tilak was different. He had marvellous intellect, magnificent command over *Sanskrit* and staunch devotion towards *Vedanta*. Hence, he was able to escape from the trap set by colonialists. The coloniality disturbed the cultural fabric of this country. Tilak never blindly accepted western philosophy or ethics. He critically compared them with Bharatiya philosophy. Now I will briefly represent his comparison of western ethics with Bharatiya *nitishastra*.

Tilak defines *karma* as all the actions a man performs, for example, eating, drinking, playing, sitting, meditating, breathing, performing a sacrificial ritual, etc. Actions can be physical, vocal, or mental.[312] There are several processes (means) in which a particular action can be performed. The science which answers questions such as which is the best and purest way to perform a particular action; whether it can always be followed; if not, what are the exceptions to it, and how they arise; why is that path which we call good, really god; or that which we call bad, really bad and on the strength of what is this goodness or badness to be decided and who is to do so or what is the underlying

---

312 Tilak, B. (1935). *Gita-Rahasya* (B. Sukthankar, Trans.). Tilak Brothers. (Original work published 1915). p.75.

principle in it, etc. is known as *Karmayoga*.[313] There are different ways in which this science can be expounded. This difference is due to different conceptions about the formation of the universe. The subject matter of any science can be discussed in three different ways:

1. Materialistic[314]

In this method, the perception of an object is considered to be true as perceived by organs. This method rejects any existence beyond the material world (physical dimension). Tilak has given an excellent example. If you look upon the sun not as a deity but as a round mass of gross matter and analyse only its physical properties such as heat, light, weight, distance, etc., then it is called a physical interpretation. Modern sciences, like physics, chemistry, etc., use this interpretation. Further, materialistic people are often satisfied with the external examination of an object and think it is useless to examine it further.

2. Theological

Suppose we examine what there is at the root of the object in the material world and whether the activities of the object are due to only external properties or if there exists another principle behind those activities. In that case, we have to transcend the materialistic point of view. For example, if we assume that there exists a deity called 'sun' which regulates the activities of the material sun, which is a round mass of gross matter, then it is a theological point of view. According to this point of view, there are in the water, air, etc., innumerable deities, which are distinct from those objects and regulate those objects.

3. Spiritual

According to the spiritual point of view, there are no multiple independent deities, but there exists only one spiritual force imperceptible to organs which regulates all activities in the world,

---

313 Ibid, p.83.

314 A translator has used words like positive and materialistic. I have used the words materialistic and physical since it's better for understanding.

and this spiritual force (factor of consciousness) exists in the human body as *atman* and is responsible for an episteme of the world which occurs to the human. It believes that movements of the sun and moon or even of the leaves are inspired by the spiritual force, and mere is no distinctive and independent deities.[315]

These differences are onto-epistemological. Tilak has compared these methods with the methods used by sociologist August Comte to consider the constitution of the society. According to Tilak, Comte had not invented these methods, but he had fixed a new historical order for them, and the only discovery made by him is that of all the three, the materialistic (positive) system is best.[316] Now I will briefly represent the views of Tilak on the materialistic theory of happiness.

Physical sciences principally deal with tangible objects. Hence, those persons who have spent their lives studying the physical sciences or who attach much importance to the critical methods particular to these sciences get into the habit of always considering only the external effects of things; and their philosophical vision being, thereby, to a certain extent, narrowed. They do not, in discussing any particular thing, attach much importance to causes which are metaphysical, intangible, or invisible or which have reference to the next world.[317] Due to this reason, Tilak says western intellectuals have neglected metaphysics (spirituality) for the consideration of ethics. According to western ethics, the goodness or badness of action depends only on the external effects which are visible to us. The correct method of deciding ethical problems is to determine the moral value of all actions by weighing the greater or lesser possibilities of each action producing happiness or preventing happiness.[318] That's why Tilak gave the title materialistic theory of happiness. The division in materialistic

---

315 Tilak, B. (1935). *Gita-Rahasya* (B. Sukthankar, Trans.). Tilak Brothers. (Original work published 1915). pp. 83-86.

316 Ibid, pp. 85-86. See footnotes on both pages.

317 Ibid, pp. 102-103.

318 Ibid, p.103.

philosophers is based on problems such as whether external material happiness is one's happiness or the happiness of another person and whether of one person or several persons.[319]

The first class is those who are selfish and egoistic. They value only their self-interest, and the action which leads to their material happiness is just for them. Their definition of morality revolves around their self-interest. This is the lowest state reached by materialistic theory. It does not even deserve the name of ethics.[320]

The second class is of people who follow long-sighted selfishness. If one pursues pure selfishness, it is obvious that personal happiness would interfere with the happiness of others. Hence, in the real world, there is a need to place constraints on a person. These people make some sacrifices for other people to achieve their happiness in the long run. They are different in this aspect from first-class but have maintained the stand that the human being is a statue cast into the mould of selfish physical desires. Materialistic discussion of ethics begins in this class.[321]

The third class consists of people who follow enlightened self-interest. According to these people, the tendency of human nature is not just selfish but also altruistic. They do not regard benevolence as an act of long-sighted self-interest. They give equal importance to the happiness of individuals and other people. But their view is materialistic as their definition of happiness is constrained to materialism. Normally, there is no conflict between the interests of an individual and the interest of other people. Hence, actions performed by man are beneficial to society. But when there is a clash between the interests of an individual and that of society, there is very often a chance that a person would choose self-interest. Hence, this method of deciding the ultimate ethics is wrong.[322]

---

319   Ibid, p.105.

320   Ibid, pp. 105-107.

321   Tilak, B. (1935). *Gita-Rahasya* (B. Sukthankar, Trans.). Tilak Brothers. (Original work published 1915). pp.107-111.

322   Ibid, pp.111-114.

The next, possibly the best class, is virtuous[323] (benevolent) materialists. This class believes in the greatest good of the greatest number. According to them, a particular action cannot have good effects on all people. If it is bad for some people, it cannot be said that it is not beneficial to all. According to Tilak, this doctrine is acceptable to spiritual people, and according to him, it was first stated by the metaphysical school. He cites examples from the *Gita*, the *abhanga* of *Tukaram Maharaj* and *Mahabharata*.[324] But according to Tilak, there is a difference between using this doctrine of *sarvabhuhit* (welfare of all) specifically (and occasionally) in ethical problems and using this as a general and ultimate principle of ethics. Materialistic uses the general way.[325]

Tilak has not only objected to this principle but also supported his opposition with critical and intellectual arguments. There is a significant difference between the meaning of the words 'happiness' and 'benefit'. Tilak, however, supported that *sarvabhuthit* means the greatest good for the greater number. He then cites the example of *Arjuna*. Suppose instead of *Shrikrushna*, virtuous materialistic would have been answering questions of *Arjuna*. According to his doctrine, *Arjuna* should kill *Bhishma*, *Drona*, and others if the greatest number of people would become happy. But the *Pandava* army was seven *akshouhini,* and the *Kaurava* army was eleven *akshouhini.* Hence, the defeat of *Pandava* would have resulted in the happiness of eleven *akshouhini* people. So, according to majority doctrine, *Pandava's* side becomes unethical! Hence, it is wrong to decide questions of morality based on numbers. There is no connection between a number of people to morality or ethics.[326] Also, even if we accept the doctrine of the greatest good for greater people, one important question remains. The

---

323 Ibid, p.115.
324 Ibid, p.115.
325 Ibid, p.116.
326 Ibid, pp.116-117.

important question is who shall decide where the happiness of lakhs of people lies, and how shall it decide?

Also, some other objectives can be raised. It is not possible to always decide the morality of an action by examining its external effects. All saints strive for the betterment of the world. But a person who strives for the betterment of the world need not be a saint. We must see the mind of the person. This is the biggest difference between man and machine. Tilak has cited an example from America.[327] The external effects of doing charity without desire and for reputation are the same, but morally, the first act is considered superior. Thus, it is not possible to conclude the morality of an action by considering its external effects (i.e., whether the action will produce the greatest good of the greatest number or not). It is important to note that Tilak never considered the doctrine of the greatest god of the greatest people useless.[328] The big defect in this theory is that it does not take into consideration the intellect of the doer. This principle escapes from the scrutiny of motives. Hence, it is enough to check whether a law passed by the legislative body results in the greatest good for the greatest people as the legislative body is composed of many individuals, and it becomes unnecessary to scrutinise their objectives and motives.[329] Hence, it is important to give preference to the purity of the mind of the doer rather than the externally visible effects of his actions while deciding the morality of an action.

The difference between the fourth and third stages of the materialistic theory is that if there is a conflict between one's self-interest and other people's interest, then later must be pursued. A materialistic philosopher has given an interesting explanation for it. According to him, in as much as the quality of maintaining one's

---

327 Tilak, B. (1935). *Gita-Rahasya* (B. Sukthankar, Trans.). Tilak Brothers. (Original work published 1915). pp.118-119.

The example is taken from the book 'The Ethical Problem'.

328 Ibid, p.120.

329 Ibid, pp.119-120.

progeny or community just as one keeps oneself and helping one's fellows as much as possible without harming anyone is to be seen being gradually more and more developed from the stage of minute organisms to the human race, we must say that that is the principal feature of the mode of life of the living world. Tilak further gives examples from Sanskrit texts.[330] According to him, further, it rises to the higher stage of humanity and philanthropy. Still, according to him, this last stage of the materialistic theory of happiness is not perfect since it does not consider internal purity and internal happiness.[331] Even though it is true that the efforts of humans are directed towards obtaining happiness (or preventing unhappiness), materialistic theory cannot be held true until the question of whether perceptual and real happiness lies in the enjoyment of worldly pleasures or not is answered. Even materialist philosophers admit that mental happiness is better than physical happiness. Physical happiness is ephemeral. *Niti* (ethics) is not ephemeral. Non-violence, veracity, etc., *dharma* does not depend on external happiness and is invariant, hence applicable to all circumstances. Materialism cannot satisfactorily explain why moral principles have perpetual existence. As the nature of external happiness or external unhappiness is transient, the ethical principles based on such a transient foundation are tenuous and fragile. The invariance of ethical principles is not proved by the doctrine of the greatest good for the greatest people.[332][333]

After the analysis of materialistic theory, Tilak has analysed the intuitionist school. According to this school, when a man decides to do an action, he does not think about the profit that would be gained or about *atman* and *anatman*. A person is doing an action because of the

---

330   Ibid, pp.122-123.

331   Ibid, p.125.

332   Ibid, pp.126-127.

333   Tilak has written about the real nature of happiness and unhappiness. See: Tilak, B. (1935). *Gita-Rahasya* (B. Sukthankar, Trans.). Tilak Brothers. (Original work published 1915). pp.129-166.

virtuous and noble mental impetus, like pity, kindness, philanthropy, etc. These noble impulses of the mind are the foundations of ethics. They are inherent and, in a way, independent deities. A man knows the nature of these deities. But due to hate or jealousy (or other reason), he defies the inspiration of these deities. Sometimes there is a conflict between various mental impulses, and it becomes necessary to take the help of some other deity besides the deities of justice, kindness, etc. Even on this occasion, there is no need to think about *atman* or *anatman* or the calculation of happiness and unhappiness. According to the intuitionist school, one should consult a mental deity (*manodevata*), and it will resolve the conflict. Thus, they regard conscience as the ultimate deity. Here, conscience means the power to discriminate between good and bad.[334] According to Tilak, this is the view of the western intuitionist school, and Christian preachers principally promulgated it. Such views have been expressed in ancient Hindu texts. Tilak has given a few examples.[335] He has also explained how western materialistic philosophers have refuted the intuitionist theory.[336]

Ancient philosophers of Bharat also do not subscribe to this philosophy. They do not accept that the intellect, which decides between *dharma* and *adharma* and one which determines between black and white, are different. In ancient texts, we find a detailed and subtle examination of knowledge, how it is gained, and regulations of the mind and body. This epistemological exercise is called *Kshetrakshetradnya Vichar*. *Kshetra* means body, and *Kshetradnya* means *Atman*.[337]

The body of the man resembles a factory. The first means of acquiring knowledge are his organs. There are two types of organs. The organs of action are feet, hands, voice, anus, and generative organs. The organs of perception are the eyes, ears, tongue, skin, and

---

334 Tilak, B. (1935). *Gita-Rahasya* (B. Sukthankar, Trans.). Tilak Brothers. (Original work published 1915). pp.167-168.
335 Ibid, pp.169-170.
336 Ibid, pp.173-177.
337 Ibid, p.177.

nose. As in any factory, there are doors to take materials in and send them out; organs of perception are doors in the human body to take the material in, and organs of action are doors to send it out.[338] The 'material' comes into the body through doors of organs of perception to the clerk called the mind, and the mind examines this material. The way in which this examination takes place divides the mind into further sub-sections.[339]

The impressions created on the mind through organs of perception are first placed together in one place, and by comparing them with each other, discrimination in between good and bad and then the person becomes ready to perform a particular action.[340] It is intellect (or reason) that judges and determines. The mind is an organ that plans actions, realises, believes, understands, and desires without arriving at any decision. The mind is like a pleader or lawyer who places various ideas for decision before reason (intellect, which is the supreme judge). But the function of the mind does not end here. It executes the decision taken by reason from organs of action. In Sanskrit, this process is known as *vyakarana* (which means development or expansion). The mind does not discern his ideas. It is done by the intellect. The reason discerns, decides, and gives us knowledge of the object.[341] In Sanskrit, this process is called *vyasaya*. Hence, the intellect discriminates and arrives at a decision, and the mind executes the decision through the organs of the action.

The reason is like a sword. It is function is only to cut whatever comes before it. It has no other qualities or functions. Planning, desiring, wanting, memory, faith, enthusiasm, kindness, etc., are qualities of the mind. When such impulses are activated in response to the situation, man becomes ready to perform the action. For example, suppose that a man is highly intelligent and has complete knowledge of the pathetic

---

338 Ibid, p.178.
339 Ibid, p.179.
340 Ibid, pp.179-180.
341 Ibid, pp.181.

condition of poor people. But he would not even think to help those people if pity did not arise in his mind. A person will not fight a war even if he has the desire but not courage. As desire or courage are not qualities (*dharma*) of *buddhi*, it cannot execute the action. It can only forecast the good and bad effects of particular actions. On the other hand, though the mind can inspire organs to perform an action under the sway of anger, hate, etc., without the scrutiny of reason, it will not be necessarily pure. Without the help of intellect, mind impulses are blind. To perform a good action, there must be a combination of pure reason (one which will arrive at the correct decision) and the mind, which acts as per intellect (and organs). Hence, the reason becomes superior (judge), and the mind becomes its clerk.[342] (There are two other sections of mind, namely, *Chitta* and *Ahamkara*, but they are not discussed.)

It is impossible to gain knowledge about any object unless it is identified by pure reason (*vyasayatmka buddhi*), and without knowledge, there is no desire to acquire that object. Hence, as in practice, the mango tree and the mango fruit are called by the same name, 'mango'. Tilak has referred to later as 'practical reason'[343] (*vasantmaka buddhi*). According to Tilak, even Immanuel Kant also has differentiated reason into similar categories.[344] If the intellect is pure, unwanted desires never erupt in the mind. *Patanjala Yoga* is a way to make your intellect pure. It is the principle of *Gita* that the motive of the doer must be examined first rather than its external effects.[345]

Now according to Tilak, the (so-called) deity, which differentiates between good and bad, cannot be included in the mind and, as pure reason, has unique existence, we cannot give an independent place for *sadsadvivekbuddhi*. There may be numerous matters about which

342 Tilak, B. (1935). *Gita-Rahasya* (B. Sukthankar, Trans.). Tilak Brothers. (Original work published 1915). pp.182-183.
343 Ibid, pp.185-186.
344 Ibid, p.187. See the footnote.
345 Ibid, p.187.

one has to think and discriminate. But it does not mean that reason is variant. The discernment remains invariant in all circumstances.[346] Hence, it is impossible to accept the separate, distinctive, and independent existence of *sadsadvivekbuddhi*. Hence, even intuitionist school is ineffective for the discussion of ethical problems.

The only metaphysical method remains for ethical problems. The above negation of the intuitionist school is the base for the metaphysical school. Hindu texts have declared the reason those who do not have the knowledge of *Atman* is not pure. The question of *Atman* has two aspects:

1. *Sharirak* or *Kshetrakshetradnya vichar*: In this aspect, there is an examination of the body and the mind and its activities. Further, one has to explain how as a result of such examination, one has to admit the existence of *Atman*.

2. *Ksharaksharavichar* or *Vyaktavyaktavichar*: In this aspect, the question of whether the principle derived from the first aspect matches with the examination of the world or not is considered. The principle which is beyond the reach of the above two principles and is their root is called *Paramatma* or *Purushottam*, and the knowledge of this fundamental principle makes one's reason pure and equanimous. A person having such a stable, pure, equanimous intellect cannot perform any wrong act. This is because first, there is desire, and then action (to fulfil the desire) takes place. Hence, pure desire will lead to pure action.[347] The philosophy to which Tilak subscribed was the *Advaita Vedanta* of *Shankaracharya*.[348] Tilak has enlisted the fundamental principles of *Advaita Vedanta*. They are as follows:

---

346 Ibid, p.188.

347 Tilak, B. (1935). *Gita-Rahasya* (B. Sukthankar, Trans.). Tilak Brothers. (Original work published 1915). p.512.

348 Ibid, pp.324-325. To understand the *Advaita* philosophy in Gita, one should read the whole chapter of Adhyatma (The philosophy of absolute self).

1. The multiplicity of various objects in the world, such as 'I', 'You' or all the other things, is not true. There is in all of them single, pure, and eternal *Parambramha*, and various human organs experience a sense of multiplicity as a result of an illusion (*Maya*) of that *Parambramha*.

2. *Atman* of a man is the same that of *Parambramha*.

3. The knowledge of the unity of *Atman* and *Parambramha* (experience) only leads to *Moksha*.

This is called *Advaita* because, according to this philosophy, there is no other independent and real substance except one pure, self-enlightened, eternal and free *Paramatma*, and multiplicity visible to our eyes is due to illusion (*Maya*), and illusion is not distant, real or independent substance.[349] The final goal of human life is to realise that there is only one *Atman* in all created things. As the end goal is defined, it is easy to establish the basis on which one has to perform actions in this world. The actions should be performed in such a way that they would not be inconsistent with an equable frame of mind, which looks upon the *Brahman* as identical to the *Atman*. Further, the way chosen by Tilak towards *Moksha* is *Nishkam Karmayoga*. Hence, the principle of self-identification (*Atmoupamya*) is the root of ethics. The ultimate goal of ethics is *Moksha*.[350]

One of the important doctrines of Tilak is *Loksangraha* (public benefit). According to him, the public benefit does not mean gathering a large crowd. It means binding people together and protecting, maintaining, and regulating them in such a way that they might acquire that strength which results from mutual cooperation, thereby putting them on the path of acquiring merit while maintaining their good condition.[351][352]

---

349 Ibid, p.19.

350 Ibid, pp.688-689.

351 Ibid, p.456.

352 Tilak also quotes the *Manusmruti*, where the word *Rashtrasangraha* is used in the same sense.

In *Gitarahasya*, there is an analysis of nationalism and *Vishwabandhutva*. He begins his discussion with the doctrine of altruism. According to Tilak, materialistic theory cannot explain the doctrine of altruism. It can only tell us that it is the inherent quality which gradually evolves. But it does not establish the immutability of philanthropy. The principle can only explain that the *Atman* of the other man is the same as mine.[353] This principle of *Atmoupamya Buddhi* is also applicable to social interactions. Family is the first lesson in the process of self-identification. But instead of continuously engrossed in the family, the contours of the self-identification should be increased to relatives, friends, inhabitants of the village, community and ultimately, all human beings. It simply means: 'Udarcharitanan tu Vasudhaiva Kutumbakam' (the whole universe is the family of great persons).[354]

Tilak also cautions us about the blind application of the *Vasudhaiva Kutumbakam* doctrine. One can criticise this doctrine as it destroys virtuous qualities like pride in the nation, *dharma*, and family, which help in the advancement of the nation. Tilak cites various *dharmashastras* which answer this dilemma.[355] It is true that in ordinary circumstances, the rule of self-identification is that one should not cause harm to others by doing activities which, if done by oneself, would cause harm to oneself. But *Mahabharata* has given an exception to this rule that it should not be followed in a society where there do not exist persons who follow the other principle 'others should not cause harm to us'. According to Tilak, equality does not mean giving a man the grass (the food of a cow) and giving a man's food to a cow![356]

According to Tilak, the principle of *Karmayoga* accurately explains and justifies the pride of one's family, *dharma*, and country.[357,358]

---

353 Tilak, B. (1935). *Gita-Rahasya* (B. Sukthankar, Trans.). Tilak Brothers. (Original work published 1915). p.535.

354 Ibid, p.544.

355 Ibid, p.546-5447.

356 Ibid, pp.547-548.

357 Ibid, p.556.

358 Tilak calls *deshabhiman, Kulabhiman*, etc., as *Kartavyadharma*.

Ultimate *dharma* is one by which the welfare of all living beings can be achieved. But pride in one's family, *dharma* and country are ascending steps which lead to the highest step (which is the welfare of the universe) and hence they never become unnecessary. Just as the worship of qualified *Brahman* (*Saguna*) is necessary to realise qualityless *Brahman* (*Nirguna*), so is the ladder of pride of one's own family, community, religion, country, etc., necessary to acquire the feeling of *Vasudhaiva Kutumbakam*. Every generation climbs up this ladder. Hence, it is always necessary to keep this ladder intact. There is no doubt that the state of every human being in the world will improve gradually and reach the stage where everyone realises the identity of *Atman* in every created being. But so long as everyone has not reached this ultimate state, saints must preach the doctrine of pride in one's country, etc., by understanding the state of the society in their contemporary time. As after building higher floors of the building, it is not possible to deconstruct lower floors or as the necessity of pick-axe does not end because of the sword or as the necessity of fire does not vanish because of the sun, so also does the patriotism or even pride of one's own family do not become unnecessary although one has reached the uppermost level of the welfare of all human beings. This is because a specific function performed by the pride of one's family cannot be performed merely by patriotism, and a specific function performed by patriotism cannot be merely performed by *Vishwabandhutva*. Even in the highest state of society, there is a need for *dharma* like *deshabhiman, Kulabhiman,* etc., along with the equitability of the reason. But if national pride is considered the highest ideal, then the nation is prepared to cause harm to other nations. It is impossible if the benefit of all created beings is looked upon as one ideal. If there is a conflict between *deshabhiman, kulabhiman* and *Vasudhaiva Kutumbakam*, then ethically, the duties of the lower order should be sacrificed for the higher order. But also, as there is only one *Atman* in all created things, each individual has the natural right of being happy in the world. No individual or society has an ethical right to cause detriment to the other society and the individual just because they are majority or possess greater strength or more means to conquer others. Suppose someone seeks to justify the selfish conduct of a society which is bigger in numbers than other societies on the ground of the doctrine that the greatest good of the greatest number, then it must be looked upon as a demonical. Sometimes the highest *dharma* of self-defence is sacrificed by a few individuals in the interest of family, nation, or universe. This action is the epitome of morality.[359] Ultimately, the base of ethics is the highest ideal in the shape of the equitability of reason.[360] Tilak has also commented on the doctrine of religious tolerance.[361] He has also cited various examples from *shastras* and has also given an example of *Chhatrapati Shivaji Maharaj.*[362]

This was an exhaustive account of Tilak's writing on *dharma*. It will not be wrong to conclude that the nationalism of Tilak was based on the *dharma*. The philosophy of self-reliance stem from self-belief. The self-belief of Tilak stemmed from *dharma* which manifested itself in the form of national pride. Tilak has enlisted four pillars of nationality: *Swadharma*, patriotism, and historical consciousness.[363] He has also said that the growth of *Swabhasha*, faith in *Swadharma*, and analysis of history in our way are responsible for the development of the nation.[364] According to Tilak, Bharatiya people have maintained a particular nationality, and we should keep the pride of this nationality alive, and that nationality (*Rashtriyatva*) is *Hindutva.*[365]

The advocacy of *dharmic* education, opposition to Christian missionaries, etc., were manifestations of the pride in *swadharma*. The epitome is Tilak's comparative analysis of the ethics and doctrine of

---

359 Tilak, B. (1935). *Gita-Rahasya* (B. Sukthankar, Trans.). Tilak Brothers. (Original work published 1915). pp.557-559.

360 Ibid, p.564.

361 Ibid, pp.585-586.

362 Ibid, pp.588-591.

363 लो. टिळकांची धर्मविषयक मते पृ.क्र.22.

364 उपरोक्त पृ.क्र.22.

365 उपरोक्त पृ.क्र.75.

Vasudhaiva Kutumbkam. There was an entrenchment of coloniality in Bharatiya culture. Tilak resisted or held it as a necessary evil and kept free in spirit, and attained *Swaraj* in ideas![366] He holds a special place in the battle for self-reliance in the freedom movement. He was among a few philosophers like *Swami Vivekananda, Yogi Aravind, K C Bhattacharya, Gurudev Ranade* (R D Ranade), etc., who successfully defended Hindu *dharma* from the onslaught of western philosophy. His battle for *Swadharma* will be remembered by future generations.

---

366   *Swaraj* in Ideas by K C Bhattacharya.

Chapter 7

National Education

The public life of Tilak began with the New English School, founded on the principle of national education. The path followed by Tilak and his colleagues, the growth of educational institutions, and his resignation is described in the second chapter. To a significant extent, Tilak's views about education were identical to the views of *Chiplunkar*. He viewed education as one of the most important tools in nation-building. His approach toward education was nationalistic and patriotic. *Vaman Shivram Apte* first expounded the philosophy of national education in the evidence before the Hunter Commission, which is explained in the second chapter.

Tilak was a furious critic of the education system introduced by the British. He wrote on national education, the role of schools, private educational institutions, professional and military education, etc. There are two series of articles written in 1905 and 1906. These articles clearly illustrate his view on national education. He wrote one article in *Kesari* dated 25th February 1896 with the title 'True University'. Below is the translation of relevant extracts from his article:

"Ancient Bharat was famous as the centre of learning and arts. In this country, there was a time when intellectuals used to form an assembly and remained busy pursuing knowledge and spreading it. It leads to the flourishment of different sciences and literature. Students used to learn from such wise and learned people and used to spread the knowledge throughout the country. There were centres of learning, and different masters in their respective subjects used to test their knowledge at those centres. Such *'ashramas'* (in which knowledge was being worshipped) were abundant in our past. There were universities like *Nalanda* where hundreds of students used to reside, learn and return to their respective places. Even foreign students used to visit those ancient universities to pursue knowledge.

When various persons with experience in different fields reside at one particular place and due to their wisdom, people from different parts of the country (and world) visit such places to learn from them, then such a place can be called a university. This definition holds even in modern nations like Germany, England, France, and America. They have not established universities to churn out graduates. The establishment of a university is to study different branches of knowledge and achieve advanced breakthroughs in them. To achieve this objective, the university appoints intelligent people to boost the creation of knowledge and its spread (by paying them well). When such universities exist, the domain of knowledge expands and becomes perpetual.

Today, physics is being studied with great stress rather than psychology. The university must keep its laboratories updated to continue the study and its growth. Our benevolent government has also established universities so we will learn western sciences and would spread it in our country through Bharatiya languages. Macaulay's education system has spread in the form of different universities since its inception. In each province, universities were established and began an examination of students in various streams, and if a student clears the examination, he receives the degree. Up to this point, the system appears to be satisfactory. But after the experience of the past fifty years, it is clear that the western model of university education is replicated senselessly in our universities. Our traditional learning centres have died, and institutions that have replaced them are not ideal (strong) enough. Hence, our country does not produce people who pursue knowledge vigorously. It is not that Bharatiya people lack intellectual ability. This is a country of *Panini*, *Kanada*, *Bhaskaracharya*, and *Shankaracharya*. But today, we are unable to produce intellectuals who achieve breakthroughs. It is the duty of each person who wants to spread the knowledge to contemplate this fact and to identify the root cause of the decline of the intelligentsia in our country.

In any modern country, the administration of universities and colleges is in the hands of teachers and professors, which is obvious. These people devote their lives to learning and teaching. Hence, they know the problems faced by students and their strengths and weakness. This is true in the case of European universities. But in our country, the situation is drastically different.

The knowledge and character of the teacher affect the minds of students only when the teacher is genuinely pursuing the knowledge and is behaving properly with students. In our case, both students and teachers lack these qualities. Hence, intelligent people in our country top the examination, learn the law and earn a livelihood. Mumbai university was established in 1857. Even after forty years, not even one world-class scholar has been produced. Some people like *Telang*, Ranade, and Bhandarkar are graduates of Mumbai university. But they have wasted their intellect and wisdom as they have pursued different careers. Some say that the vacuum in science is compensated in the field of law. There is some degree of truth in this statement. But what is its use? We criticise those people who do not give justice to their capabilities. Our teachers and professors do not have a thirst for knowledge, and administration is in the hands of those who do not belong to the teaching class. University stamp B A and M A certificates and do not do any other work. From chancellors to syndicates, all are busy with their other professional duties. Such universities are not universities but registered companies!"

Tilak wrote one article in *Kesari* dated 19th August 1902 in which he indignantly criticised universities. The title of the article is 'Universities, aka Government Labour Manufacturers[367]'. Below is the translation of relevant extracts from the article:

---

367 हमालखाना

"Many people believed that we should thank the British for their reforms in education. They also further say that the British have shown the highest liberal sentiments by teaching us western sciences. I have heard these statements from many people. When the first generation who received British education graduated, they accelerated this propaganda. The people who received English education get higher posts in the government. Hence, the propaganda received a boost due to unfamiliarity with English education and the authority gained by few people who have received an English education. But now the myth is breaking.

Now, people are noticing that English education is monotonous and intends to instil qualities required for becoming a government servant. English education does not teach *dharma*, *Niti*, professional education, sciences, etc., disciplines necessary for the nation's progress. People who have received an English education remain ignorant of the above-mentioned branches of knowledge. Slowly, government jobs started shrinking, and hence the authority of Anglisied Indians was reduced, and their inefficiency and half-wittedness were exposed. Thirty to forty years have elapsed, and the experience has taught us. There is also another reason behind this realisation.

Almost fifty years have passed since the establishment of a university in Bharat. But it can be said that no (real) scholars are produced. But in Japan, a contrasting situation is observed just after thirty years of the inception of universities. We have attained a low state because we are not receiving real education from present institutions. Bharatiya students earn the first rank in Cambridge, but another Bharatiya student in Bharat is reduced to the lowest possible state. The only answer to this paradox is an inefficient education. In short, we need a complete restructuring of the education system in universities so that universities would start producing real scholars and become real centres of learning. I want universities with scholars who are experts in different branches, huge libraries, and laboratories. A person who knows the functioning of universities in Europe or England would definitely agree. Unfortunately, even after fifty years of the establishment of universities, the government is not willing to reform education. Recent recommendations of the university commission (even though it contains some of the abovementioned recommendations) are hopeless.

The government policy is not in our favour. I had this doubt in my mind when the university commission was appointed, and after reading the recommendations submitted by the commission, I am convinced that government do not wish to see us as their equal counterparts in scholarly disciplines, trade, or business. If Japan can reform itself in thirty years, then why cannot Bharat replicate it? The only reason is stated above. People think professional, technical and scholarly education should be imparted through educational institutions. But the government has another policy. England is a developed and advanced country. There is no political capital in carrying out reforms in Bharat. But to administer the country, the British government needs (at least at lower posts) an educated person, and to meet this need, the government sets up educational institutions. Some British diplomats have uttered liberal thoughts about reforms, but there exists dissonance between thoughts and government policy.

Some students began noticing discrepancies in the functioning of the British government after receiving an English education. The government knew that education gives courage and analytical power and makes a person observant. But as people with such abilities were few, the government ignored those people. The number of graduates has increased two times than employment opportunities. Hence, it is obvious that graduates began understanding the inefficient and hopeless education they had received and are discerning keenly about current government policy. This was a politically dangerous situation. Hence, the government started rethinking its education policy.

According to government policy, universities are government labour manufacturers who supply people who can perform lower-level government jobs. As the currency's value fell, the government tried to regulate the falling currency by introducing legislation.

Similarly, the university commission is trying to reduce the number of graduates graduating from the university. According to the university commission, the recommendations like raising college fees, shutting down colleges granting M.A. degrees, and limiting the number of law classes would serve this purpose. The university commission says that recommendations are made to reform the situation! If it is true, the commission should have at least recommended removing third-rate professors in government colleges and appointing real scholars as professors. But no such recommendation is found in the report. There is a recommendation for establishing libraries and laboratories. But unless the government spends significant money on such things, they will remain on paper. Up to this day, native people at least had minimum authority in the university's administration. But now, the administration is to be controlled by government policies and directives. The government wants to control universities which are government labour manufacturers (i.e., they churn out graduates), just like it controls the government mints. The aim is to reduce the number of unnecessary graduates and readjust the number with government job openings. This motive is clear from recommendations given by the university commission.

The motive of the policy adopted by the government may be right and suitable in the government's view. But it is not a sign of progress. It is a sign of deterioration. The sole aim behind imparting education is to create bureaucrats is wrong. Lord Curzon likes the policy. Hence, in his reign, education will never be reformed. There is no doubt that Curzon is intelligent and a man of action. But only intelligence or show-off do not guarantee the welfare of people. The viceroy also needs sympathy and sincerity, and Curzon is devoid of those qualities to this day and will remain as it is even in the future. The ultimate effect on the works, such as the university commission, police commission, and irrigation commission, would surely result in total disappointment. The people who wish to extend the stay of British people in Bharat will definitely praise Curzon's rule. But people who want to spread knowledge and education in Bharatiya people so that arts, sciences, trade, and business will flourish in Bharat and it would match the shoulders of western nations would believe that Curzon's decision is wrong. It would further accelerate the deterioration of Bharat.

If universities were to be reformed, such hyperactivity would not be needed. I do not think the quality of education reduces if some poor students pass out of university. Conversely, our state is such that if poor but intellectual students receive an impetus, it would further spread education. But the commission has not focused on this issue. The only question stressed by the commission were government control in university administration, how to reduce the number of graduates, how to maintain discipline in colleges (so students would not be left with self-respect!), and how to extend government control over private schools and colleges. The debate is centred on the government rather than people and would remain as it is till Curzon remains viceroy."

In these two articles, there are a number of references to Japan. Tilak wanted to highlight that Japan could transform itself in a few decades in the field of education, but such was not the case with Bharat. In one article in *Kesari* dated 6th December 1904 titled 'Japan and Hindustan', he discussed the reasons behind it. Below is the translation of the relevant extracts:

"In the Russia-Japan war, Japan has achieved splendid success. Japanese people have proved their military capability, courage, and bravery in this war. It has compelled Europeans to rethink their views about Asian people. I have already written about it in previous issues.

Hitherto, Europeans believed that even though Asians were strong and resilient, they lacked national consciousness. Hence, Asian nations needed the assistance of Europeans to match the level of modern European nations. Europeans, even intellectuals, believed that it was their duty to rule and colonise Asia, Africa, and America and to plunder the resources of native people by giving them a minimum share so that at least they could stay alive. If Europeans did not do that, god would punish them. Due to the Russia-Japanese war, this opinion is being revisited. This is the historical benefit of the Russia-Japanese war.

Suppose Asian people receive poor military education and have an adequate supply of arms, ammunition, and other things. In that case, they can strongly compete under the leadership of the Asian general against an excellent European army operating under the European general. In short, the qualitative difference between Asian and European is not natural but artificial. If Asian people get new arms, technology, and education, they can compete with modern European nations. Many people accept this fact. Different people from different nations indeed have different sets of capabilities. Even though the difference exists, it does not mean that Asian nations should stay under European forever. Japanese people have displayed this truth to the world through their actions.

I want to write on this issue and will write in future. Today's question is different. It is inspired by the speech given by Lord Bishop in Madras. Lord Bishop was amused with the paradox that if the Japanese nation had made remarkable progress in forty years due to western education, then even after hundred years of western education, the Bhartiya people underperformed even after their association with the British. This question was tickling in many people's minds, especially after watching the Japanese's bravery, unity, and success. Hindus are not physically or intellectually weak vis-a-vis Japanese. Hence, any intelligent person would like to discern that the same western education, if consumed by the Japanese, becomes nectar to them and, if consumed by the Bharatiya people, becomes poison. There are only two answers possible. First, Bhartiya people are not receiving similar education compared to the Japanese, i.e., as there is a difference in direction, policy, and nature of the education in Bharat and Japan, the same western education has affected both countries in different ways. The second answer is that education in both countries is the same, but its effect will be different on the Japanese than on the Bhartiya person. In conclusion, one party says that the difference is due to differences in the education system, and the second party says that the difference is due to different social conditions in Japan and Bharat. If the first party is true, then the government is responsible; if the second party is true, the responsibility lies with the people. In such a situation, it is evident that one class would try to inflict responsibility and would like to keep it on the shoulders of the people. *Madrasi* Bishop belongs to this class. The abstract of Bishop's speech is as follows:

"Due to defects in Hindu society, western education did not benefit Bhartiya people, and the most significant defects are in the social sphere. After receiving education, national consciousness emerged in the Japanese people, and they became ready to reform their social conditions. Bharatiya people do not have a *reformist* mindset. Also, the thirst for knowledge which is strongly evident in the case of the Japanese, is absent in educated Bharatiya people. They do not take strong positions, and their mind is confused about the old and new systems. As they lack decision-making capacity, there is no hope for them. This is not the case with the Japanese. After observing the progress and splendour of European nations, the Japanese have become completely western. If educated Bhartiya people get rid of the old prejudices by taking strong positions, they will also rise like Japanese people."

Bishop is politically correct. It is beneficial for the government if Bharatiya people start hating themselves (having doubts over their capabilities). But it is not true. The first mistake is to equate education in Bharat to the education system in Japan. Take the example of military education. Soldiers and subordinate officers receive military education, which makes them capable of understanding orders given by their senior officials and their execution. There is no military industry in Bharat that produces modern military equipment and no military educational institutions that train native soldiers. In such a situation, even though Bharatiya people with similar physical and intellectual capacities cannot match Japanese generals, a valid argument can be put forward that foreign rulers cannot impart military education like native rulers. So, let us keep the question of military education apart and analyse the situation of other disciplines. In the past thirty years, the Japanese government has sent many students on scholarships to foreign to learn chemistry, geology, business, arts, etc. Has the Bhartiya government performed such tasks? There are only two scholarships. But hundreds of students should have been sent before if the government wanted to lead the nation toward progress. Even Bishop accepted that it is impossible to govern a huge country like Bharat with the help of a few British officers; the government imparts education only to create subordinate officers who assist European officers in the administration. In such a situation, it is not surprising that our universities have not produced any original research scholars.

The difference between Bhartiya students and Japanese students is like the difference between ornamental trees (garden trees) and giant trees found in the forest. The government severely restricts the thinking power of Bhartiya minds and tries to install loyalist tendencies. The irony is that the same students are blamed for not being courageous or intellectuals if compared to their Japanese counterparts. This is the biggest mistake in Bishop's arguments. Rulers of Bharat do not wish to give education in Bharat, maybe because they are foreign or for some other reason.

Instead of focusing on the principal issue, an attempt to divert the topic to social problems is condemnable. It is not that Bishop is not able to understand this fact. But what can he do? If Bharat is not developed as Japan after education, then blame should be put on the government. But Bishop and the government are both British. Hence, he blamed the Bharatiya people. But I want to convey to Bishop that we would not fall to his tactics. If one wants the solution to the problem and the reason for Japan's success, it is the same: ' freedom'. Freedom does not necessarily mean complete freedom from the British empire, but at least Bharat should be able to manage its affairs like other colonies. Till such a state is not achieved, the responsibility is on the shoulders of the British government."

After this, we find three articles in *Kesari* in 1905 about the relationship between student and teacher and Bharatiya and European concepts of the teacher. In those articles, he compared Bharatiya and European philosophy and Bhartiya and European pedagogies. These articles also highlight the nature of the British education system in Bharat and also the quality of the education. The first article appeared in *Kesari* dated 17th October 1905. The title is: 'They are not *gurus*!'. Below is the translation of relevant extracts from that article:

"Hitherto, I have written articles on the *Swadeshi* movement. This week, however, I am going to write on another question of interrelation between students joining the *Swadeshi* movement and their teachers in government colleges or private colleges. The reason behind this article is the letter written by Mr. Selby, the principal of Deccan College, published in *Induprakash*. An old student of professor Selby sent an article regarding the above-mentioned subject (which was published in *Induprakash*) to his master (Professor Selby) and requested his comment. Professor Selby gave his response in the form of a letter. Further, he gave permission to his student to publish his letter. The remark of the student is that the views advocated by his master are extremely important, and he hopes that people should read them. I also agree with the student, but the only difference is that I think even though they are important, they are one-sided. I request people to read my views so that they would not get confused due to the propaganda of Professor Selby.

In the ancient Bharat, infusing values, morals, knowledge, modesty, and bravery into the young generation was assigned to those who were calm, wise, and possessed spotless character. They used to reside in the forest where students came to study. During such time, it was obvious that students used to look at the *guru* with respect and reverence, in such *ashrama*, contemplation and discernment on various topics such as *dharma*, *adharma*, social conditions, *niti*, *aniti*, duties of the king, duties of the people, what people should do if the king becomes tyrannical, etc. used to take place. The contemplation used to be equanimous.

Hence, students completing studies under such *gurus* used to be bright and dutiful. Further, students knew that if they asked questions to their *guru*, he would give only true answers without caring even about kings. There are many stories in *Puranas* where even kings came to such *gurus* to seek their advice in difficult times. In our *dharmashastra*, the *guru* is considered to be even above the father. The statement applies to only those gurus who used to be knowledgeable, serene, and devoid of desire. There is no other entity which is as holy as knowledge. If someone trades his knowledge (maybe to earn his livelihood or due to selfishness), then the attempt to give equal status to his knowledge with that of real and holy knowledge is like equating holy water from Ganga with water flowing through gutters!

Further, when there is foreign rule, rulers take universities into their hands and use them to strengthen their colonisation policies. This is the difference between universities in an independent nations like Germany, England, America, France, and Bhartiya universities. When a public movement starts in any independent nation, professors (read intelligentsia) start expressing their views openly about the movement. They discern the nature of the movement, decide which direction is right for the nation's future, and try to mould students' minds accordingly. This is evident in the Russian movement against Tsar. In that movement, there were many students and professors involved. The real duty of intelligentsia is to guide the young generation to work for national interests and to tell them what national interests are and who serves foreign for money (also whose intelligence becomes narrow due to foreign service) is not a real *guru*. Such a person should not be given the status of the *guru* as in Hindu *dharmashastra*.

Professor Selby has written one statement in one of his articles that students should not cross their limits when speaking with the principal of the government college. I can read between the lines from professor Selby's statement. *Saraswati Devi* has become a maidservant of political power in government-run colleges and universities, and this bond of slavery is extended to a lifetime status by Lord Curzon! It is impossible to freely, openly, and publicly discuss important issues in front of nations in government-run colleges and universities. Hence, it is also impossible to decide which policies are of national interest and which are not. Universities and colleges are lapdogs of the government. Further, the government is keen to give specific education to Bhartiya people so that they would happily remain in the state in which government wants them to live. The government is also censoring content which is nationalistic in nature in government-run schools, colleges and universities. This is the peak of oppression in Curzon's regime. It has resulted in a situation where government-run schools and colleges have become useless (damaging) in teaching national interests to Bhartiya students and embedding nationalistic values in them.

In the old days, there were some excellent English professors. But that time has gone. Current professors like Selby, Macmillan, etc., may be intelligent like their predecessors. Still, they do not dare to tell the government that students should get authority in their hands as per their capability. They are not professors but mere bureaucrats appointed by the government to implement policies adopted by the government. Their job is to prepare ideal government servants and not expose students to subjects of national interest. Recently, Livarnar has published a book which explains the limits to which students should delimit their political and national thinking. Anyone appointed as a college or high school principal is compelled to follow Livarnar's book. That is why the government appoint only British people to the posts of high authority in high schools and colleges.

The conclusion is that a tremendous difference exists between universities and colleges in independent nations and the same run by foreign rulers in a nation controlled by foreign rulers. In an independent nation, educational institutions become a fountainhead of nationalistic thoughts. In contrast, the same institution becomes the instrument through which the mindset of the slave is inculcated in the nation if they are in the hands of foreign rulers. Further, such foreign-controlled intelligentsia instils self-hate and a defeatist mindset to shake our leader's faith and make them intellectually impotent. Our colleges are machines created by the government to control intelligentsia and their thoughts and compel them to serve the government's interests. They are not functioning to enhance our knowledge or to inspire our students. There are some exceptional cases where people with such education show a critical attitude and free spirit. But they are exceptions (and not the rule). The government bears such an exception as it is impossible to eradicate it. 'Intelligent' officers like Curzon display their intelligence to keep the effects of such 'exceptional' cases to a minimum extent.

This long prelude aims to familiarise people with the nature of colleges and schools. We should remember that if we want to inculcate nationalistic values in young generations, it is impossible to achieve this in government-run educational institutions. Intelligent professors like Selby have not come here to serve the national interest of Bharat, but they are here to inculcate the political philosophy of the British government. They have the authority to teach plays of Shakespeare or Beckon's book or to publish books for students on Shakespeare and Beckon. We know their authority, and we 'pay' them through fees submitted to the government. But if someone thinks that such professors would serve Bharat's national interests and teach nationalistic values to their students with a fearless attitude and equanimity, then he is wrong. Such professors are helpful if we want to learn about Milton, Beckon and Shakespeare. But if the young generation wants to learn nationalistic values, they cannot learn them from such professors. They should learn it from the nationalist like *Surendranath Banerji*. Professor Selby, collector and Times of India are useless in this domain. Professor Selby has said explicitly in his letter that the political movement in Bharat must be anti-British. His statement is correct. But the inference drawn from it undermines the authority of Selby. Both sides agree that the political movement is against the government and college principal is the servant of the government. The only question is whether we who ask the political questions to the government servants are fools or such servants who express their opinions on such issues are fools. Hence, I have titled this article 'They are not our *gurus*'. What do these people want? Do they wish that their students strive for the betterment of their nation so that their nation would compete with other nations and that students should receive nationalistic inspiration from education? The answer is no. Then, why should we pay attention to their propaganda? If you have any questions about Shakespeare or Beacon, you can ask them. But we should not take their opinion seriously on nationalistic values, policies, politics, political movements, etc.; it is useless and destructive.

There is a difference between professors who teach Shakespeare and earn a livelihood through government money and *gurus* in ancient Bharat. Professor Selby says that the *Swadeshi* movement benefits the nation, but students should stay away from the political movement. Has Professor Selby shown any sympathy towards the *Swadeshi* movement by using *Swadeshi* clothes or advising students to use *Swadeshi* clothes (He should have done it as he draws a salary from our money!)? And he is advising students to stay away from the political movement! Did students in Oxford and Cambridge remain away from the political movement started by Chamberlain? If our education department would not under government control and if professors were naturally inclined with nationalistic thoughts would have been present in educational institutions, then such professors would have travelled the length and breadth of this country (like *Surendranath Banerji*), giving speeches and spreading awareness about the *Swadeshi* movement. But under government control, our professors are reduced to the lowest degree, and such professors are trying hard to reduce students to the lowest degree. Unfortunately, people who started colleges to give affordable national education have also shamelessly adopted similar views and are behaving as per government directives and cutting off their ties with the *Swadeshi* movement.

Now people should decide whether to call such people (who try to brainwash students to stay away from the *Swadeshi* movement) our *gurus.* Lord Curzon has degraded the education department to the extent that professors are brainwashing students by taking advantage of the relationship of *guru* and *shishya* (which was in the ancient Bharat). This is politically correct. But from the people's point of view, it is the biggest sin! They are not our *gurus*! They are servants appointed by the government to teach us ABCD, the English language, and clerical work. It is wrong to give them respect, as told by Hindu *dharmashastra.* These are contract labourers who teach us the English language and take their salary. In the last part of his letter, professor Selby has tried to display his sincerity and has (fearfully) written that if relations between students and teacher is not maintained at the proper level, then the government school teachers will become mere taskmasters. I want to convey to Selby that his fear is correct. I want to declare that a *guru* who does not see the national interest of his student is not a guru. In such cases, professors and principals in government (or even privately) run educational institutions are useless for embedding nationalistic ethos in students. Hence, to remain dependent on such people will be a huge mistake."

The second article appeared in *Kesari,* dated 24th October 1905, with the same title. Below is the translation of the relevant extracts from the article:

"In a previous article, I described the nature of professors in government colleges who are mere government servants. I firmly believe that justice and real knowledge become rare in a nation where judges and professors become government lapdogs. It is against human nature that conquerors would teach *rashtradharma* to those they have conquered. Hence, we should decide the degree to which we should take the opinions of professors in government colleges seriously in the case of national affairs.

There is a stark difference between professors in an independent nation and professors in a colonised nation appointed by colonisers. Such professors are useless and cannot do the work of imparting nationalistic values to students. Japanese people invited foreign professors to gain their knowledge, and they deported them back after learning. Brave people like *Togo* and *Ito,* who strived for Japanese interests, were students at foreign universities. But they had devotion towards Japan, and Japanese intellectuals, by various methods, accelerated it. The conclusion is the way in which *Shukracharya* became a *guru* of *kach* (as he wished to learn *Sanjivani vidya*); similarly, people like Selby are our teachers from whom we learn specific subjects like Shakespeare's plays or Beckon's teaching. But when the question of a nation and its relation to its citizens arises, our *gurus* are also different. *Hiranyakashyapu* had appointed various *gurus* to train his son *Prahalad* according to his views. But *Prahalad* was a staunch devotee of *Vishnu.* Hence, he rejected the authority of those *gurus.* Those *gurus* were useless for *Prahalad* in the field of devotion towards *Vishnu.* Similarly, professors in government-run colleges are useless in imparting national education to our younger generation. They are unfit to teach *rashtrabhati* to our young people. The difference between education from foreigners and our people is this.

Whatever might have been the government's real aim behind their decision to impart English education in Bharat, it is certain that the government's attempt, right from the beginning, was that students should not gain nationalistic values. When Lord Curzon realised that the aim had not been accomplished to a full extent, he imposed draconian censorship in the field of education. Directors of different verticals in the education department are well-trained in Curzon's policy. Professors like Selby are working under such directors. Hence, it is no surprise that such professors are running propaganda that students should stay away from public movements as it disturbs the discipline of the college and undermines the teacher's authority. These teachers are not here to teach us our duties towards the nation; it is not their job. The experience of Japanese people is similar. Only one person advised the Japanese to make progress without caring about the opinions of his countrymen, and the name of that person was Herbert Spencer! He had told them in his letter (and requested not to publish it until his death). *Dharmaraja* also had a blot on his character due to his stance in *dronavadha*. Similarly, a great, equanimous, intellectual person like Spencer also had problems advocating for Japanese people. There is no comparison between Spencer and Selby!

Even though Spencer had put the condition of not publishing the letter until his death, at least he had given strong, perfect, and unbiased advice. Professors like Selby even lack this capacity. Again, I want to make clear that I do not doubt the intellectual calibre of Selby and others. But I think such professors are useless in deciding the degree to which students can participate in public movements. Such professors can only dance to the tunes played by Lord Curzon! People should neglect the propaganda run by professors, just like how *Prahlada* rejected (ignored) the advice of *gurus* appointed by his father in the field of devotion. Otherwise, a situation would arise that Hindus would be born in slavery and die in slavery. Curzon and Selby wished to implement the following policy: "Students being a student of the school should stay away from the movement, government servants should stay away from the movement being government servants, and pensioners should away from the movement being pensioners!" After implementing such a policy, there would be few defaulters, but the majority would mutely surrender to the tyranny and become ideal slaves. When one generation would get trained in the attitude of slavery, the next generation would inherit the 'genes' of slavery. In this way tradition of the loyal government servant (with no devotion towards the nation) would get stable.

Nobody indeed forces students in schools to become government servants. But it is also true that almost 90% of educated people are in government service. So, in school, professors and principals forbid students from joining the public movement; in youth (and in the government service), senior government officials would curb them, and an old age government would control them as they are pensioners. The conclusion is that as someone dies without taking the name of the god, the government ensures that our educated(?) class should not even have a glimpse of a political movement, and it should continue for generations.

Unfortunately, our leaders have not recognised this fact. Our professors cannot be compared with Spencer. Still, as said by *Pandit Shayamji Krushna Verma,* even people like Hume and Cotton are absent professors or principle in government colleges. They are not our *gurus.* We should neglect such people and should contemplate the rejuvenation of the nation. I do not have any personal bias against Selby. I know his qualities. But if the question of the participation of students in political movements arises, then professors like Selby hold no authority (as he is British and a servant of the British government). The question is of authority and interests and not of wisdom and intellect.

It is not that only teachers in government schools have become unworthy. The same case is with people who have established private educational institutions with selfless motives. This has happened due to new grants-in-aid rules formulated and implemented by Lord Curzon to affect all stages of life, i.e., childhood, youth, and old age. Further, he curtailed the freedom granted to private educational institutions by Lord Rippon. Due to that, when a student of Fergusson College gave a speech at a student gathering organised to support the *Swadeshi* movement, he was expelled from the boarding, and the principal also imposed a ten-rupee fine. Fergusson college has gone one step further than government schools. Are authorities in Fergusson college holding the opinion that *Swadeshi* movements and gatherings organised by students to support such movements are illegal? If they agree, they would also be included with Mr. Selby (as unworthy).

If private institutions are unable to impart national education to students (if compared to government-run educational institutions), then an important question of whether to establish schools and colleges as a mere copy of government colleges and schools and whether to offer selfless service or not arises. Even after this, we would find someone who would provide selfless service, as this is a matter of personal inspiration and instinct. But the real question is why people should support private institutions that have become the copy of government colleges.

The *Swadeshi* movement is in full swing and has gained unprecedented momentum nationwide. In this situation, it is unfortunate that private colleges (which receive support) punish a student who participated in the *Swadeshi* movement. These people should have learned lessons from *Surendranath Banerji*. Mr. *Banerji* is the private school's principal, and through his behaviour and speeches, he is demonstrating the *Swadeshi* movement to students. In our region, a similar thing should have been repeated. But Mr. Gokhale is supporting *Swadeshi* and boycott in Manchester, and in his college, a student is fined because he participated in the *Swadeshi* movement. The conclusion is that even these are also not our *gurus*!

The reason of the disturbance of discipline is often cited to support the incident mentioned above. But nobody thoughtfully discusses the definition and nature of the discipline. Suppose tomorrow a senior person prohibits children from visiting the temple or punishes them because they visited it. Then are we going to call it discipline? If it is wrong to arrange a student gathering to support the *Swadeshi* movement, and if any student from boarding attends such a gathering, the institute can penalise him. But if it is not wrong and some student from boarding attends it, then to penalise such a student for not taking permission in the name of discipline is nonsense. Suppose a student had not taken permission. But if he is assured that he would not get permission for such a good act, why should he take permission? The nonsense behaviour of teachers is compelling students to break laws.

I know that the relations between students and teachers are extremely delicate. I do not want to disturb it without reason. If the *guru* is perfect, I would advise students to follow him. But suppose a teacher orders students because of slavery, selfishness, greed, cupidity, or delusion or punishes students. In that case, he is not a real *guru*, and in such a situation, if a student does not follow his orders, then it is not indiscipline. Such situations are discussed in *Mahabharata*. We send our children to schools to educate them so that their national consciousness will arise, and we do not send our children to prohibit them from joining a national movement. A tyranny is going on in the name of discipline. It is the duty of the citizen of this country to minimise it. Such teachers are 'task masters' (as written in the last paragraph of Selby's letter). Students should respect them in their respective fields. But if they start ordering authoritatively in the field outside of their authority, then it is foolish to obey their orders. Students should find their way into the issues that are nationally important. If we want to get away from delusions and get rid of propaganda, there is no other way. Unfortunately, relations between students and teachers have attained such a low position. But we have to find our way through it."

The third and the last article of the series appeared in *Kesari* dated 7th November 1905 with a similar title. Below is the translation of the relevant extracts from that article:

"I decided to end the topic with two articles. But there are two reasons why I am writing this third article. The first is to answer the criticism of my articles, and the second reason is the circular issued by the Bengal government through the collector and district magistrate. According to the circular, the schools receiving grants-in-aid from the government should expel students taking part in the *Swadeshi* movement or give another punishment. If schools do not follow government orders, then schools will get closed. I had predicted such a situation in the article written in 1898.

Twenty-five years ago, in Lord Rippon's tenure, an education commission was appointed that recommended the establishment of private schools. The government also supported assuming that the penetration of education as envisaged by the government was impossible without the help of private schools. The government knew that private schools were not mere copies of government schools. But they are established to impart the values (and ethos) absent in the teaching of government schools. Often, such schools were run by the selfless contribution of educated people. Even though the government knew all of this, it continued its policy of supporting private education. Further, the government even frankly acknowledged the autonomy of private schools in designing their curriculum. The effect was the establishment and progress of new schools and colleges in provinces like Madras, Punjab, Mumbai, Bengal, Punjab, etc. The founders of such institutions tried hard to improve their institutions (at least) in certain areas if compared to the government schools. Fergusson College of Pune, *Pachapa* college of Madras, Central Hindu college of Kashi, Dayanand Anglo-Vedic college of Punjab and Rippon college of Bengal were founded in the same period. The aim of the founders was not to copy government colleges. Those new institutions were established to provide an alternative to the government's political, religious, and social policies in education. The government did not monopolise the education sector. It was not ready to monopolise the decision of which movements are good or bad, which religion is good or bad, and which movements students should participate in. It accepted that the impact of national education was possible only by independent people in autonomous private schools.

The pendulum of the government policy went to other extreme and is evident in recent circulars. This process began in 1897-1898 with the storm of sedition, and just after that, the governorship of Lord Curzon began. It resulted in a complete overhaul of government policies. I had written the real motive education conference in Shimla, which took place in the regime of Curzon. The real motive was the restructuring of government policies with respect to private schools. Curzon is intelligent and a man of action. But he wasted his intelligence in formulating and implementing procedures to enslave the Bhartiya people. Gokhale has demonstrated the vicious nature of Curzon in Britain. Curzon's policies are in complete opposition to Lord Rippon's policies. When education was started, some people hoped that Bharatiya people would become cultured, and if they began to demand rights, it would be a great day. Lord Curzon did not like this policy. His policy was to dominate the Bharatiya people at any cost. Hence, he brought policies to establish a government monopoly in the education sector. The idea was to destroy the autonomy of private institutions and get them at par with government-run educational institutions, which would result in the passing out of students with the same discipline and values. The same intention was behind the new legislation of the university act.

Lord Curzon knew that the nationalistic thoughts which gain momentum in students due to education are extremely dangerous to the undisturbed continuation of the tyrannical rule of bureaucracy. If it had been possible to ban education completely, Curzon would have banned it. But it was not possible. Hence, Curzon decided to bring all schools under strict government control and to implement policies with such terror that not even one student should pass out with nationalistic values. Many people had predicted the policies which Curzon would adopt. Hence, they started taking preemptive measures. But finally, Curzon implemented his policies and restricted the education system for Bharatiya people in a similar way to which *Hiranyakashyapu* designed the education system for *Prahalad.*

It appears that the Bhartiya people have not understood the damage (and its extent) brought by Curzon's policies to the education sector. The government is acting like parents who decide on behalf of their children what they should eat. Like parents, now our government decides which books our children should read, what should be the content in books, how to tailor the content in books so that they would not disturb the bureaucratic rule and, how to censor the syllabus, how to implement those policies. The only difference between parents and government is that parents sincerely hope their son will become wise enough to take his decisions one day. But the wish of the present government is that the Bharatiya people should never demand equal rights. Due to this policy, the autonomy of private schools in political and social spheres has vanished. Their directors are reduced to such a low state that after sacrificing for the spread of national education, they are compelled to impart education as per standards prescribed by the government. The first college that succumbed to this policy was Fergusson college. It was arranged (diplomatically) through professor Selby. A few years ago, I had described this calamity in my article. Today, the circular in Bengal has exposed the true nature of the policy. If continued, these disastrous policies would, one day, definitely kill the education in this country.

Due to the above reasons, I think the policies formulated and implemented in schools to teach history, politics, nationalistic values, etc., are useless and disastrous if they are taught in the early stages of education. Foreign rulers, who are like *Hiranyakashyapu*, would never teach such principles in schools, and it is a highly foolish expectation from them. Is it possible that foreigners would impart education which would result in a decrease in trade for England or the loss of power for the British people? It is certainly not possible. Further, restrictions have been placed on students to take admissions in schools and colleges where such education is being imparted. According to the government, the student's duty is to learn and not to participate in national movements. Hence, the government has issued unofficial instructions to its officials to restrict students from entering such movements.

People who do not know the seriousness of the situation or lack the ability to understand the situation, or even after understanding, lack the ability to protest against it should keep quiet. In previous articles, I have written that teachers and principle in government or private schools and semi-government schools influenced by the government are not *gurus*. Now readers will understand the real meaning of this statement. If we want to learn Shakespeare, Milton or Beckon, these people are our teachers, and we should accept their authority in this field. I never denied this. Further, I fully acknowledged that students should intensely focus on their studies. In fact, I have been advising students to concentrate on their studies. But things which should be learnt in bachelor years by students also include *dharmic*, political and social teachings, and this teaching is absent in government and semi-government schools. It might be possible that some teachers in such schools sympathise with the public movements. But what is its use? They lack the freedom to proclaim their opinion openly. Hence, even such people do not have the authority to become our *gurus,* and if this is so, who are these people to decide whether students should participate in the public movement or not? Professor Selby has cited Ranade and *Telang* in support of his views. But from my personal experiences, it would not be wrong to infer that Selby had made a mistake. Ranade had openly expressed that the students should get acquainted with different movements during their study period. He echoed the same opinion in Congress sessions held in Mumbai and Pune. Many public movements like congress, industrial conference, *Shivjayanti*, and *Swadeshi* were initiated by our leaders. If students are not supposed to get acquainted with them in their school years, when will they receive such education? After receiving an education, he would become a servant; after service, he would become a pensioner and die eventually. That is why it is disastrous for the nation to prohibit students from entering public movements.

Nobody says that students should concentrate all of their time on such things. They must gain knowledge from all dimensions. In these dimensions, one dimension is the public movement. Students should participate in a public movement which aims to advance the nation on the path of progress. Students should discern the nature and future of such movements before the end of their academic phase. Teachers who oppose them from doing such work are not their *gurus* but are enemies. They are mere lapdogs. It is wrong if somebody says I deny their authority in other fields. Such people are deliberately deriving wrong conclusions after reading my articles. Some people have given references from *Mahabharat* and said that the values embedded in *Mahabharata* are to obey elders and *gurus.* Their favourite example is the relationship between *Yudhisthira* and *Bhim.* Hence, they are accusing me of teaching a wrong interpretation of *Mahabharata.* The problem with such people is that they have not read the complete *Mahabharata.* Not only *Mahabharata* but all *shastras* tell us to respect elders and *gurus.* I know this and fully accept it. But the meanings of elders and *gurus* are different. No *shastras* in the world obey an elder (father) who is not giving freedom to his son, who has become wise enough to take his own decisions and has greed for property or to respect a *guru* who limits the knowledge and capability of the student. Hence, such people are not our *gurus*. *Shlokas* are given at the beginning of the article, uttered by *Bhishma* when he battled with *Parashurama,* which confirms my opinion. Similarly, when guiding *Yudhishthira,* we find the specific comment of *Bhisma* about the nature of relations between elder and younger brother, which also agrees with my opinion.

There is no comparison between teachers (simar to teachers appointed by *Hiranyakashyapu*) who teach only suitable content approved by the government to their students and *guru* who always strive for the betterment of their students and can even fight with the king on behalf of their students. Both shares only a common noun. There is also no comparison between elders like *Bhishma,* who even suggested *Yudhishthira* a trick to knock him out of the battle (as *Yudhishthira* could not win the war with *Bhishma* on the battlefield) and current elders who hide their wealth from the future generations, even after losing in the legal battle! The conclusion is that those teachers and elders who want to gain respect, as described in *shastras* then they should strive for the betterment of students and the next generation respectively. They should not involve themselves in a situation where they must bend philosophy to support their behaviour. If such behaviour is not possible, teachers will get respect in specific areas.

Now readers would have understood my opinion about relations between teachers and students. This question is very similar to the question of the importance of the jury system. The importance of the jury system is often unrecognised in general court cases. But when important cases where there is a conflict between the king (read government) and its subjects arise, the importance of the jury gets marked. The same case is with the relations between students and teachers. In general affairs of government or private educational institutions, the analysis of relations between *guru* and *shishya* is not required. But when teachers become instruments in the hands of the government to run its propaganda due to greed, delusion, anger, etc. and start advising students against entering the public movement, then it becomes necessary to proclaim that 'They are not our *gurus*' and 'Our students are not their *shishyas*'."

Tilak again wrote a series of articles in the last months of 1906. In those articles, he explained his conception of national education and the responsibility of private schools. The first article appeared in *Kesari* dated 17th November 1906. The title was 'National education and responsibility of private schools. Below is the translation of the relevant extracts from the article:

"After the advent of the *Swadeshi* movement (in fact, after the introduction of the university bill by Curzon), the national education movement has again gained momentum. I have used the word 'again' because this is not a new issue. In the declaration of 1854 by the British parliament, the education department in Bharat received an official and permanent status. But even before that, the importance and usefulness of private education had already been established. At this stage, there is no need to define national education. The education imparted by the government of any independent country is always national, referred to as national education.

This is a time of fierce competition. At such time, the education department of this country should keep a keen watch on other countries, their policies, their advancement in different fields, and their policies to undermine our nation. With the help of such analysis, the education department should consistently update its policies. It is the duty of the education department to educate the young generation so that the young generation can conserve and expand the country's political, industrial, and social prospectus. If the government is indigenous, then such reforms take place accordingly. Otherwise, wise men, intellectuals, and editors advise the government to adopt appropriate policies and reforms in the field of education. Even in Russia and Germany, where the political power is not fully in the hands of people's representatives like in Britain, it is evident that the government in these countries have been imparting education to their people to compete with England, America, or France.

Education does not only mean the ability to read and write. Every person should possess the ability to read and write. But it is not sufficient. It is the duty of every reformist government to decide the future and scope of various trades and businesses and to impart professional education (and business education) updated with new technological advancements to the people so they can earn money through it. A nation where the government forget this duty is bound to become poor. The government's responsibility is not just to maintain internal law and order. The government should always strive for people's betterment and let them evolve into bright, self-respecting, and deterministic conditions. The government which ignores these duties is selfish.

Unfortunately, our present government is such. Germany and Japan have become modern in the past thirty to forty years. The British government is not less modern than these two governments. Even though the Russian Tsar was tyrannical or Prince Bismarck was hard on socialists, they strived to continuously increase the political and economic splendour of the nation so that their nation could compete with modern countries like England. The effects of such policies are visible from the history of Germany. Germany founded several professional schools (and training programs and apprenticeships), outperforming England in the trade. Was it not possible for British rulers to adopt similar policies in Bharat? Were they not aware of the importance of such policies? It is not so. The British government is clever, and it understands these things perfectly. But this government does not treat us as sons but gives treatment similar to the treatment given to the stepson (perhaps even lower than that). Our unfortunate state is because of such policies adopted by the British government. I condemn this *reformist* government.

In the present regime, even after hundred years of education, people were not educated about the manufacturing of matchsticks.

Even though our nation produces crores of sugarcane, the indigenous sugar business has declined, and imports of sugar are increased (whose value is in crores) from British-controlled Mauritius and even Germany. The textiles, oil and leather businesses were destroyed, and we became dependent on agriculture. Maybe the government would give an excuse that it was not the fault of the government since it maintained internal peace (law and order); hence it was the duty of the people to do all those things. This statement and the excuse given by the government are wrong. Governments in Japan, Russia or America did not give such excuses and ran away from their responsibility. They identified their responsibility and started giving appropriate education to their people. If the British government in Bharat do not support these principles, then they have some other motives, and I openly proclaim that they have different motives.

There is no need to discuss the motive of the government. The motive is to keep Bharat in slavery forever and to shift trade and manufacturing in Bharat to Britain; let Bharatiya people acquire education but take care that they do not acquire virtues like self-pride, self-reliance, etc. This is because if such virtues manifest in the Bharatiya people, the tyrannical British rule would not last long. The government needs people who can run the government and not intellectuals. It does not need (and does not even wish to have) engineers, historians, judges, physicists, warriors, or philosophers. These people would be borrowed from foreign, and we would be 'trained' to work under these people. This is the government policy, and the school education department works according to this policy. The government do not wish to impart an education which would produce people who would excel in sciences, trade, manufacturing, artwork, etc. They just want servants who would work under foreign officers, and thus they have started schools which impart 'appropriate' education.

Sometimes few from the educated class might start thinking more than the government wants them to. But this cannot be stopped. The government ignores such voices. But the government do not need to expand its education policy due to the reasons mentioned above, and it is also not in favour of the government as it is foreign.

The process can be compared to the training of horses in the cavalry. A separate department of horse training aims to train horses for cavalry in battle. This department works under European control. A horse which is needed in cavalry should be athletic and well-built. Also, it should be obedient as cavalry units perform in parades as well. Hence, the powerful, well-built, and athletic but obedient horse is being trained by this department. The school education department works exactly like that. The government wants bright and efficient people to run the government administration. But like horses in cavalry units, such people should obey their (foreign) masters. Right from Curzon to Selby, all are working with the same objective. These people think education can produce the required types of people by deciding and controlling the degree and nature of education. This policy is against the spirit of national progress. Such a policy would never impart real national education.

Some say that the government does not tell you to pursue government jobs, so if you join the government service, it is your fault. This is a childish and extremely foolish argument. The government have dozens of officials and 'labourers' to endorse its policies. It is not our job. We need people who specifically point out errors in government education and elaborate on the real nature of government education without submitting to the government's pressure. The government is angry and sad as people notice its ill-directed policies. But now, there is no need to cry foul. Such policies were not mistakenly brought for implementation but were deliberately implemented. Why should we please the government? The school education policy of the government is to keep people ignorant, dependent, timid, and lazy, and if this policy continues, the nation will collapse soon. At such times, wise, intelligent and workaholic people must tell the truth in the public domain and constantly work to annihilate the ill effects of such education. The spirit (philosophy) behind the views expressed by *Pandit Madan Mohan Malviya, Surendrababu, Chintamanrao Vaidya,* Professor *Vijapurkar,* Lala Lajpatrai and Dinshaw Wacha is the same. These people also have raised their voices on establishing a national university.

Current education policy is wrong, and the hope that private schools would annihilate the wrongs of the government policy is also diminished. Lord Curzon has directed the same path for private and government schools. Recently, the document behind Fuller's resignation has been out. In that document, Mr. Risley, who is a secretary to the government of India, has remarked that the provisions of the new university act are to be enacted to prohibit students from entering political movements and to do so, an authority should keep watch on students inside the campus as well as outside the campus and once such provisions are enacted there is no need of separate rules for the private schools. Even after reading this, if a person does not understand the real motive behind the new university act, he either has attained salvation or lacks comprehensive abilities like an animal! Now, as the government policy is being implemented and has become steel-framed, it is necessary to recalibrate the responsibility of private schools."

The second article appeared in *Kesari,* dated 4th December 1906, with the same title. Below is the translation of the relevant extracts from the article:

"In the previous article, we have commented on the pathetic quality of education in government schools. When the act about the importance of giving British education to the Bhartiya people was passed in the British parliament, those legislators were not narrow-minded and shallow in thinking like Lord Curzon. This fact is evident in their contemporary articles. English history, literature, sciences, and skills help to increase a nationalistic approach and are inspirational and increase enthusiasm. Ancient Bhartiya sciences like grammar are extremely useful for expanding the intellect. But they lack the discussion of nationalistic approach, policy, a wealth of nations and international relations. Western countries have developed these new sciences, which are helpful in the alleviation of the state of the nation. If one studies the history of the western nations, it is evident that they have focused on these sciences in their literature and curriculum (read education system). Hence, one who learns these sciences gets acquainted with nationalistic values and the progress of nations. Further, one whose intellect does not get a touch of these values has not achieved anything from education or cannot digest it. But such people are few. For thousands of years, people of this country have dealt with deep, philosophical questions, and with this, they have developed an extremely sharp intellect. It is impossible that such people cannot digest British education. One or two people can fail, but it is foolish to think that Bhartiya people could not grasp western sciences and their basic principles. Japanese people are not great intellectuals compared to the Bhartiya people. If they have digested western education, then it is baseless to argue that Bhartiya people would not be able to grasp western sciences.

People who enacted the education act were aware of this fact. There were two options in front of British politicians. One was to keep Bharatiya education as it is or to impart British education. Doubts were raised, such as if the Bharatiya people got acquainted with British history, literature, and sciences, then they would also get acquainted with ideas of freedom, independence, wealth, and nationalism, which would hurt the British empire. The fear was not wrong. This is because knowledge and power are two powers which, if acquired, can give enormous power. The student who is not inspired by ideas of freedom after reading the history of people fighting for independence is not a real student but can only be compared to an animal. One who worships the goddess of knowledge (*Saraswati*) definitely receives her blessings, and every student must worship the goddess and receive her blessings.

British statesmen who started British education in Bharat were aware of the risk that the Bhartiya people would begin demanding *Swarajya* after receiving an education. But those statemen fearlessly told that "Even if it is true that Bharatiya would begin demanding freedom, it is not right to keep them in the darkness. Maybe our control over India may get loosened. Britain will get the credit for reforming the backward country.". The earliest policies were liberal. Further, some British statesmen had told us that they were imparting education to teach us how to rule. Once the Bharatiya people acquire knowledge, the British will happily return to their nation. I admire the liberal policies of those statesmen, but unfortunately, those policies did not last long.[368]

Greed affects the discerning power of man. The root cause of sin is greed. English education gave new dimensions to the thinking of people. But with this, British control over Bharat became concrete. Bhartiya trade, wealth and capability declined. The trade and wealth of Britain expanded as the inflow of Bharatiya wealth began. It is easy to give philosophical sermons on philanthropy. But when there is a question of relinquishing profit (of crores in magnitude) for Bhartiya interests, then sermons on philanthropy become meaningless. This is human nature. British bureaucrats and politicians do not want to relinquish their control over the wealth of Bharat and trade. Hence, their officers (like Lord Curzon) are deliberately downgrading the existing education system. Statesmen who had no problem with the demand for freedom from the Bhartiya people have passed away, and their successors do not like such ('unwanted') effects of education. Sir Richard Temple has commented that it is good that educated Bhartiya becomes obedient servants of the government. This is the policy which is advocated by the education department. The British government spends crores of rupees on the military, border management, and security which could have been spent on the education of the Bhartiya people in the past hundred years. But the liberal policy advocated earlier has faded, and

---

368 The views expressed by Tilak in these paragraphs clearly indicate the shadow of coloniality. There should not be any surprise in this fact, as Tilak also received colonial education. These are isolated examples, and one should ignore them given the time in which he lived, the resources to which he had access and his fearless attempt to speak the truth to the despotic British government.

the education department and professors have become narrow-minded, just like Curzon.

This was not the situation 25-30 years ago. In Maharashtra, *Chiplunkar* and his associates established private schools. Officially, the government had not adopted such narrow-minded policies. Officials like Lord Ray and Sir James Fergusson supported the principle that it is necessary to keep education in the hands of people. This was the condition all over Bharat. This fact is evident from the education commission report in 1881-1882. High-ranked officials like the governor of the Bombay presidency had said that the government wanted to spread education, but there were fiscal constraints; hence if selfless educated Bhartiya people came forward to spread education, then the government would assist them or completely transfer the education department to the hands of such people. Those were not rumours. A basic draft was prepared between Mr. Chatfield and governor Lord Ray to completely transfer the control of Deccan college (the first English college in Maharashtra) to the Deccan Education Society. Lord ray was of the opinion that if high schools were transferred to private education institutions on a grant-in-aid basis, then saved funds could be used to open more professional training institutions like Victoria Technical Institute of Mumbai. But our leaders were not in favour of the opinion of complete transfer of education into the hands of people (i.e., private educational institutions). No doubts were raised about receiving grant-in-aid from governments from members of private educational institutions. This is because contemporary directors and governors had not been crazy with sedition. Hence, they were ready to fund private educational institutions without limiting their autonomy. But today, the situation has changed.

Education commission was set up in 1881-1882 in the governorship of Lord Rippon. After the governorship of Lord Rippon, regressive policies were adopted, and this practice reached its peak in the governorship of Lord Curzon. Due to this, private schools and colleges have become slaves of the government. Curzon has implemented this regressive policy to limit the flow of ideas of freedom in the minds of young educated Bharatiya people. Hence, he has put dozens of constraints and enacted laws accordingly.

But I am of the firm opinion that this policy will never succeed. It is impossible to crush the demand for freedom that flourished in the minds of the educated Bharatiya generation (due to British literature or education), which is also ready to fight for it. Government cannot dismiss it in the name of discipline. It is the duty of the government to understand the mind of the Bharatiya generation and help them to achieve their goal. Instead of such a mature response, the government is busy adopting oppressive and regressive policies in education.

In such tough times, the biggest question is in front of people who have started institutions selflessly and with their funds. They are facing a dilemma of which policies to be adopted in response to the (regressive) policy reversal by the government. We should (strictly) know that we are not paying taxes to the government to keep the young generation in slavery, and there is no need to support the government if it has reversed its old policy. If we understand that private institutions have changed in twenty-five years, then I do not think there would be any argument over the duties of private schools. Hence, in this article, I have summarised the education department's policies in the past 25-30years. No movement would succeed if we let the government enact such a draconian policy. There is a proverb in English that will find its way. Our political will is strong, and we must display this fact in front of our opponents. I hope that our political leaders will show it to the whole world. There is no other way.[369]"

The third article in the series appeared in *Kesari* dated 29th January 1907. The translation of the relevant extracts from the article is given below:

"In the past two articles, I have described the pathetic condition of education in government schools and colleges. The policy of the

---

369 नान्यः पन्था विद्यतेऽयनाय।

government is to downgrade education. British officers and their loyal servants are working hard in its implementation. I had abstained from writing on this issue because it was to be discussed in the Congress session. As expected, Congress has accepted the loopholes in the existing government education system. The resolution of national education is passed by Congress. According to it, new schools providing national education should be established to provide an appropriate education to the next generation. This resolution is completely different from the previous one. Previous resolutions concerning national education were advisory in nature. That is, Congress used to adopt resolutions that suggested the policies the government should adopt with respect to primary, secondary, or professional education. In the 1906 resolution, Congress advised the people rather than the government. Congress is a public institution. Hence, it is the duty of Congress to implement the resolution. I hope that Congress will take the issue of national education into its hands and spread it all over the country by establishing new and independent educational institutions providing national education.

The subject of this article is not about the duties of Congress. We cannot neglect the systematic degradation of education in government schools and colleges. In a previous article, I described the policies adopted by the government 25-30 years ago. Due to such policies, it was possible for private educational institutions like Fergusson College to maintain their autonomy even after receiving grant-in-aid from the government. This policy has reversed. The government and bureaucrats now wish to impose constraints on the autonomy of private educational institutions. They want to downgrade the level of education in private schools. This will put private schools and government schools at one level.

The government thinks that as it puts money in private schools as a grant-in-aid system, it has all moral rights to control the policies of these institutions. The government also wants to take over private education through the grant-in-aid system. Government textbooks have been downgraded further, and their prices have increased. If private institutions shy away from government policy, the government will cut the funds allocated to these institutions. Additionally, if it is a university, then according to the recently amended university act, students of such universities would not be allowed to sit for the university examinations. So, if you want to learn, you do not have any other option other than the government framework, and if you take a different path, then the government would not let you appear for the examination and would not give you a job. This is oppression.

I am deliberately using the word 'oppression' because I think mental oppression is more severe than physical oppression. In *Panchatantra*, there is a description of the technique which says that if one wants to win over the enemy, then it is always good to confuse the enemy's intellect in the clouding of judgements rather than demilitarisation. The British government is following the advice of *Panchatantra*. Bureaucrats, British or Indian, do not favour students thinking independently (especially students thinking about freedom and pursuing different paths to achieve it). They want to put iron curtains over this independent thinking. Indian bureaucrats know these things. But these shameless people are licking the boots of foreigners to continue their service.

The only way to continue out of this pathetic situation is to establish new private educational institutions. A number of private schools have been established in regions like Pune, Nagar, Ratnagiri, Satara, Dharwad, Surat, and Ahmedabad. Even though their financial condition is not strong, they are at par with government schools in terms of quality. Twenty-five years ago, the government was ready to hand government-run schools to such private institutions. So, there is no need to raise a finger at the ability of private institutions to provide proper education. The only question is whether private schools have autonomy in providing appropriate and coherent education to Bharatiya people or have to follow government policies. This question is not limited to Maharashtra but is valid in Bengal, Madras, Punjab, the northwestern province, and the central province. Bengal province is two steps ahead due to the *Swadeshi* movement.

Congress has approved the policy of national education. Hence, all other provinces should also adopt the policy of national education. This is not a time when private schools should run behind government schools. Private schools indeed receive grant-in-aid from the government. But these institutions also use public funds and are established and being run by selfless individuals. Private schools were not established to adopt the impotent education policy of the government. The individuals who established and ran these institutions selflessly were not motivated by government policy. If the government is not ready to adopt the reformist policy, private schools should divorce themselves from the government. The days of government crushing the spirit of the people of this country have passed away. We do not want government education. This is because the government has deliberately and consciously transformed its education policy into a barren one. Also, the government is deliberately silent over the question of technical and professional education. If such education is continued to be served to the young generation, then a national rejuvenation is impossible. Managers and the chairmen of private educational institutions should think about this problem and solutions to the problem. Indeed, these people have selflessly run these institutions, but this selflessness has become useless due to changes in government policy.

It is unfortunate and horrible that people of this country are being trained under the government policy, and there is no one to show a different way. We do not want Longman or Macmillan's style of education. Private schools should show the direction of change in the policy, and if they do not have the courage to do this job, then people should stop supporting them and establish new private educational institutions. Efforts made by the government to 'reform' education are enough. People have the liberty to send their children to government schools. But those who are fed up with this pathetic education system should start working towards establishing new educational institutions. I congratulate Professor *Vijapurkar's* '*Samarth Vidyalaya*'. I want to ask the directors of current private schools why they should not adopt these new methods.

It is not impossible to raise public funds comparable to the government grant-in-aid system. If we do not get comparable funds in the beginning, private school directors should adjust as the issue is extremely important. It is true that if new schools are established that do not follow government policy, the government will not allow them to sit for university examinations. That is why fewer number students would get admitted to these schools. But we should not fear after watching the experience from Bengal.

In the previous year (1906), the national council for education was established. In its purview, one autonomous college and eight high schools in Kolkata, Dhaka, *Rangpur*, *Mymensingh*, *Komila*, *Dinajpur*, *Kishorganj* and *Chandpur* were established, and three are proposed. The structure of this council is similar to the university. It has its president, vice president, council, and secretary. They have raised ten to twelve lakh rupees in one year. Sir Gurudas Banerji was the president for the year 1906, Dr. Rash Behari Bose is the current president, Aravind Ghosh (from the national college) is the principal, and young and brilliant graduates from Kolkata university have cane forward to work as a professor with a meagre salary. This council has no official affiliation with the government-run university. They have full autonomy in their syllabus and examinations. In the last year, 720 candidates appear for the examination. Exams are due in June. National College and eight high schools of the national council of education have two thousand students. These two thousand students are receiving national education as per policy. They do not care about government exams or government services. Annual earnings of the national council of education have reached fifty thousand rupees. These earnings are used to run one college and one high school in Kolkata, and a grant-in-aid is provided to run the remaining schools in Kolkata. The National Education Council has further stated its plan to establish a business school. The library and laboratory are under construction. The work will be completed soon. East Bengal is ahead in this work than west Bengal. The work is in full swing under the guidance of wise and experienced people like Sir Gurudas Banerji. In Kolkata, people are so devoted that solicitors or barristers like Babu Hirendranath Datta give monthly donations of 200 to 300 rupees from their earnings to the National Council of Education. Babu Surendranath Banerji has agreed to affiliate his college with the National Council of Education, but it is said that, in practice, he has not done it yet. *Pandit Madan Mohan Malviya* raised his voice for the establishment of a Hindu university in December 1905. But there is no progress in that direction. The people of Kolkata (or east Bengal) are one step ahead and have started imparting national education. The fear that students would not join nationalistic schools, as they want to appear for government exams, is vanished. Another problem is the lack of public support for such institutions. People of east Bengal have found a satisfactory answer to this problem. There are two problems with government education. One is it is impotent, and the second is useless (it means it does not address current issues and needs)! Bengali intellectuals have found solutions to these two problems and have started independent syllabi and exams without depending on government support. On average, one year's experience is satisfactory, and these efforts have borne fruit. Suppose such an experiment and its success are in front of us. In that case, the important question is whether people from other provinces should continue to work as per government policy or should reform their syllabus (and also other things). The nation is awakening. If private schools and colleges are not ready to help in national rejuvenation, they are not worthy of public support. I have written three articles on this issue with the hope that this issue receives enough attention and contemplation."

Tilak wrote an article in *Kesari* dated 30th July 1907. The title is 'Slavery for quartern loaf". Below are relevant extracts from the article:

"My readers must have read articles in *Kesari* on the issue of 'National education and the responsibility of private schools'. Those articles were written before the last congress session. I had planned to write the last article after the adoption of the resolution of national education in schools and further contemplation at our provincial conference. But in a provincial conference held at *Surat*, the resolution was referred to the committee. That's why I have to wait for such a long time. The committee gathered in Sir Firoz shah Mehta's room last Friday and passed the resolution that public education should remain in the hands of the people. As the government keeps a keen watch on government and private schools, people need to establish nationalistic schools. It would have been better if the resolution had passed in the provincial council. But as the health of Mehta was not good, it took so much time for the resolution to get passed in Bombay province. Alas, we are fortunate that the provincial council and congress are finally in agreement. Hence, today I am writing the last article on this issue. But one incident has compelled me to think in another direction.

The incident is about the circular published by the government of India regarding students and its forceful implementation by police officers. Most Bengali students have revolted against these circulars, and directors of private schools have registered their protest to the government. The government has ordered the university to punish students involved in the *Rajahmundry* controversy. It is also planning to give universities extra power and set new rules and regulations. But the condition in Mumbai province is quite whimsical. The news about the fake news created and spread by police regarding Tilak's jubilee and the 'attentive' memo given by the school education department to the government and semi-government schools have already been published. Now the news has appeared that some students (who were on vacation) in *Umbergaon* (Thane district) read a few paragraphs from the novel *Ushakal* and sang a few songs with permission from their parents in the month of May at the *Shivjayanti* festival. Police officers reported this event and sent that report to a higher authority. The report was finally submitted to the director. One student was in Mumbai. He was suspended for this 'crime' of participating in a festival that government did not like. The school education department has sent a notice to the directors of *Nutan Marathi Vidyalaya* and 'New English School' in Pune. New English School has sent a letter of dissent to the government. But the final verdict has not come yet. Bombay provincial government is imposing its policies towards students in private schools which receive grants-in-aid. Intellectuals like Selby and his associates are helping the government. If we let this draconian policy imposition continue in private schools, our children will be sold as slaves, and the responsibility of slavery will be on our shoulders.

The first question is, why should we mutely tolerate such tyrannical behaviour of the government? Parents are the ultimate authority in the life of their children. Is it a crime for parents to send their children to a government school to learn English for five hours? Parents send their children for five hours to the government school. However, this does not mean they have surrendered their authority over twenty-four hours over their children to the government. The money spent on the government is taxpayer's money. Hence, this circular cannot be justified and is oppressive and tyrannical.

Parents send their children to government schools for education. It does not mean that they have sold their children to the government. The government should understand this. It is impossible to take away parental rights over their children. Even the government agrees with this statement, and the same government is trying hard to establish that parents do not have any right to control the behaviour of students outside school as they are taking education in government or private schools! If something is unpleasant for the government, it does not mean it is always illegal, seditious, and immoral. It is foolish to expect that students should hear and watch things that sound pleasant to the government's ears. As we have not sold our children to the government, it is extremely oppressive action by the government to pass such draconian order. The government is brutally crushing the rights of parents. Obedient servants like Selby or any other person should follow government orders. But if parents or directors of private schools, which do not depend on government support, begin following such despotic order, it is an insult to the truth, justice, freedom, and self-respect. Nobody wants indiscipline, and also, none is against students receiving education and becoming intelligent. But suppose, in the name of discipline, the government is trying to accomplish its hidden motives and starts imposing severe and harsh restrictions on our children; in that case, extreme anger develops in people's minds due to such unnecessary intervention by the government in the education sector.

What is discipline? In simple words, it means that children should obey the orders of teachers when they are in school and when outside, they should follow their parents' orders. Then, if children go to any conference (or rally) with their parent's permission, it cannot be called indiscipline. Today, the government dislikes *Shivjayanti*, tomorrow, it can dislike *Ganeshjayanti* or *Ramnavami*, and the government can even hate *dharmic* speeches. So tomorrow, we should not send our children to festivals, lectures, or *kirtan*. On what moral grounds is the government giving such orders? Why does the government involve its police department? Government can bring legislation to declare all forms of agitation illegal and can declare agitation as a criminal offence. But such straightforward action is not possible. So, the government is using school education departments to crush the parental rights of their children. It is a highly immoral, despotic, tyrannical, and impotent act.

In previous articles, I have expressed the hidden motives of the government behind such acts. The government is not happy with political agitation. But it lacks the courage to declare all forms of agitation illegal, but it is not possible due to the structure of British polity. As it is impossible to ban agitation completely, the government uses secret and indirect methods to deny it. Students should not get involved in political agitation, adults (government servants) should not take part in the government agitation because they are in the government service, and aged people should stay away because they are pensioners. In this way, the government uses dictatorial methods in the name of discipline in education and service. Professor Selby would have revolted against such an order if it had been issued in the west.

But today, the same Professor Selby has become an obedient servant of the government and is ready to brutally crush the authority of private school directors. When I wrote against professor Selby in the article 'they are not *gurus*' and exposed his real face, few people became angry due to views expressed in the article, but how events are occurring has made my prediction true.

The present circular is extremely oppressive. School teachers have received the authority to dismiss any student who goes to a rally with their parents. The tone of the language used in the circular is so arrogant that it sounds as if the government have given away child adoption to parents, and parents have to 'only' provide basic necessities like food to children (of course, at their own expense!).

The conclusion is that we send our children to the government for a few hours to receive an education and not to keep watch (and control) our children's behaviour. Parents should perform the role and have the right to provide direction to the young generation. The government has no right to unnecessarily interfere in this field if parents are not provoking their children to perform illegal activities. If the government had been bearing all students' expenses or if parents had transferred their authority and rights to the government, such behaviour could have been supported. Unless such events occur, it is definitely tyrannical and oppressive to crush parental rights with the help of Risley circular.

It is the duty of nationalist people and organisations to fight against the injustice and tyranny of the government. The government do not always act justly. The government or its officials do have seasons of tyranny! In such cases, it is our duty to protest and fight against such tyrannical behaviour. Forget about government servants who depend entirely on the government for bread and butter. But if institutions which are being run mostly on public support also start following dictatorial orders of the government, then they lose their independence for quartern loaf. Such institutions misuse public support. If private schools follow the policies of the government schools (the policy can be fair or unfair, useful or useless), then we do not want such private schools, and people should not support such private schools. Further, there is a misuse of public money in helping such schools. Private schools are established because people do not like the education given in government schools. Hence, the education given in private schools, *niti* and *dharmic* education given in these schools and discipline cannot be similar to the education given in government schools. At least in our province, selfless individuals with public support run private schools. If self-sacrifice and public support become a tool in the government's hands to complete its hidden motives, then the word 'self-sacrifice' would transform into suicide.

Private schools are not established to complete the government's motive to make the young generation coward. Directors of private schools should remember that many intellectuals are working on meagre salaries and schools depend on public support for their survival. They are not working hard (or people are not supporting) to dance to the tunes played by the government, police officers or education officers. Nobody is against discipline. But its contours should not be unnecessarily stretched. The discipline in our schools should have the same degree as that of schools in the western and other modern nations. If the government is stretching the contours of discipline without any reason, then it is the duty of private schools to fight against the government for the rights of private schools and parents.

Two thousand students are learning in one college and eight high schools which offer national education without showing concern about the government exam. The government is anxious to make the young generation of Bharat politically impotent. It is ready to impose harsh restrictions on private schools which run on public money to accomplish its evil motives. In such a situation, private schools and colleges should come together and fight against this injustice. Intellectuals who have earned the title of Wrangler are teaching in private educational institutions. If such people firmly tell the government that we are not ready to dance to tunes played by you just for quartern loaf (read grant-in-aid), then the government would be obliged to review its policies.

If the government continues its path, such people should follow their independent path. We do not want wranglers selflessly working for those schools that copy government schools or government labour manufacturers established to produce obedient servants. If you want slavery of the government, then become a 'complete' slave, why do you take quartern loaf? Take the whole! If you do not want to engage in slavery, then remember that those who have given the remaining three-quarters of loaf (read public support) are not incapable of providing the remaining quarter.

The government's policy is indeed evil. If the government gets angry, it can stop the grant-in-aid and disallow students from private schools to appear for university examinations. But why should we fear now? All provinces should follow the direction shown by Bengal. Deccan Education Society is considered to be the epitome of private educational institutions. We would be compelled to say that it has wasted public money on which it thrived if it does not come forward. The degree to which the direction of education should be changed for the sake of national interests is a very important question. It can be put aside for a moment. But we should specify a degree to which private schools should suffer from slavery for the grant-in-aid. If we do not specify at this moment, then I do not doubt that directors of private schools would become slaves of the government."

This was an exhaustive account of the writings of Tilak on national education. He viewed education as an instrument of national rejuvenation, awakening and transformation. He knew the government was educating people to produce 'loyal' and 'obedient' servants. He coined the term 'labour manufacturers' for universities. He was highly critical of the government education system, syllabus, and textbooks. It was killing the young generation's fighting spirit, self-pride, and entrepreneurship. Hence, Tilak criticised it. But he was not cynical or armchair critic or pessimist. He also elaborated and contemplated the meaning of philosophy and practical aspects of national education. According to Tilak, education policy in the nation should be framed in such a way that it should guide the nation on the path of progress. He says:

"Education given by the government is not for salvation. It is for the betterment of the people. It should be designed so that people's industrial and professional knowledge should be increased so they can earn their livelihood. Also, *niti* and patriotism should rise, people should live independently, and appropriate political and social narratives should prevail. Such education helps people to better their conditions and prosper further. Another important benefit of education is that it induces faith and devotion to *Swadharma* and *Swadesha*. In conclusion, real education motivates people to strive for the nation's political, social, *dharmic* and industrial prospectus."[370] This captures the essence of the conception of Tilak about education. He criticised the education system due to the degradation of Bharatiya languages, lack of *dharmic* and *niti* education, and no professional education. He stressed that it was education which was inducing slavery. According to him, education was responsible for the selfishness and hopelessness of the Bharatiya people. He was also aware of the importance of science and research. He believed the government should allocate adequate funds to education.[371] According to him, education had become a business of getting a job to earn bread, and it was not education but a form of labour. According to him, such a condition does not alleviate the nation's condition but further degrades it.[372]

Tilak further stressed the importance of industrial, technical, professional, business, and agricultural education. He connected *Swadeshi* with the above streams of education. He also suggested various ideas of industrialisation, like establishing sugar factories in the Pune area, as sugarcane's sugar level was comparable with Mauritius's.[373] He dreamed of spreading professional, business, and technical institutes

---

370　टिळक विचार पृ.क्र. 77-78.

371　उपरोक्त पृ. क्र. 78-80.

372　टिळक विचार पृ.क्र. 82-84.

373　उपरोक्त पृ. क्र. 85.

throughout Bharat. He also stressed the importance of manufacturing and also highlighted small and medium-scale enterprises. He criticised the government for not undertaking the task of surveying the industrial status of Bharat.[374] Another rarely discussed aspect of Tilak's views about education in agricultural education. Below is the translation of the relevant portion:

"Majority revenue of the government comes from the agriculture sector. Hence, it is the duty of the government to consider the problems farmers face. The real problem is that about 80% of people depend on farming to earn their livelihood. It was not a natural condition but was created by force. It is the duty of the government to rescue people through the crisis. Professional, business and agricultural education are intimately related. Agricultural education aims to teach farmers to take the maximum crop and magnify earnings from the available land. The basic aim of professional and business education is to increase trade and industry in the nation and discourage people from joining the agricultural sector. Agricultural, business, and professional education are for the lower middle class."[375]

Tilak delivered a speech on the subject of women and national affairs. It was arranged by *Hindu Mahila Samaj*. *Avantika Gokhale* has given an abstract of his speech. In that speech, Tilak focused on the following three points:

1. Tilak said, "The first duty of women towards the nation is to develop the patriotic and nationalistic generation."

2. Tilak says that women are teachers of the nation. Children are in close relationships with their mothers, grandmothers, and others. Hence, children develop as per the education they receive in childhood. Education to be received at such an age is not just academic. According to Tilak, the principal duty of the mother is to impart education to her children, which can

---

374 उपरोक्त पृ. क्र. 86-87.
375 टिळक विचार पृ. क्र. 88-89.

develop their character and make them selfless and workaholics and motivate them to work relentlessly for the nation without having any desire. In the same speech, Tilak also said that in *Vedic* times, women used to teach *Kavya* to their children, and even a few decades ago, women were proficient in Sanskrit and spoke fluently in Sanskrit at their home. Tilak has said that he had himself witnessed this fact. He further states that from this example, it appears that the status of women in education and knowledge was much higher.

3. Tilak says that women are guardians of the nation. He further states that historical analysis reveals that the nation was rescued from various dangers by brave women. According to him, Bharat has remained alive as a nation due to great and patriotic women.[376]

His critics criticised him for national education being about emotional fervour and lacking progressive thinking and scientific aptitude. It was not true. Tilak decluttered those myths. He was well aware of the importance of science and its advances in the west. He fully supported the teaching of science in schools.[377] He also stressed the importance of *dharma* and asked the government to include principles of *dharma* in the curriculum.[378] He also emphasised the importance of education in the mother tongue.[379]

Tilak used the concept of national education to annihilate the ill effects of the colonial education system. He viewed national education as the first step in attaining self-reliance. Education helps to identify the consciousness. In conclusion, national education is one which helps us to identify our identity, which gives an account of the state of people and nation, which helps to meet our needs and guides future generations.

376　बापटकृत लोकमान्य टिळक यांच्या आठवणी व आख्यायिका, खंड क्र. १ पृ. क्र. 252-253.

377　टिळक विचार पृ. क्र. 106.

378　उपरोक्त पृ. क्र.107-108. This topic is covered in detail in 'Swadharma'.

379　This topic is covered in detail in 'Swabhasha'.

Chapter 8

Towards Peaceful Revolution

Battle, shock and struggle themselves are no vain destruction; they are a violent cover for Time's great interchanges.[380] The last days of the Maratha empire were a period of great interchange. The defeat of the Maratha empire reduced Bharat to the status of a colony of Britain. British had arrived in Bharat as traders, slowly increased their political activity and became the political master of Bharat in the nineteenth century.

The primary aim of the British was the destruction of wealth and the exploitation of resources. Hence, the British created the government machinery to achieve these sinister aims. British were a minority and governed the huge land and population, so they needed native people to administer the government for the British interest. Hence, they created an education system and started 'educating' and 'civilising' the Bharatiya people, which produced obedient civil servants. It was easy for the British to govern the country with English as the official language; hence, it became the official language and medium of instruction in Bharat.

To achieve the vicious motives, it was necessary to kill the self-pride in the Bharatiya people so that they would become docile and obedient servants of the British empire. British achieved this aim through the education system. They systematically spread hate towards Hindu *dharma* and culture. Also, through the colonial education system, whose medium of instruction was the English language, western culture metastasised in the minds of educated

---

380 Aurobindo, S. (2016). *The renaissance in India.* Sri Aurobindo Ashram (1920). p.78.

people. It changed the worldview of educated people. They started looking towards the west with sincere devotion and became consumers of western ideas, philosophy, and culture. This internal alteration reflected in their outer behaviour, and they started looking towards Hindu *dharma* and culture with contempt and neglect. As colonial education granted the government service, it was natural that people got attracted to it and the cancer of coloniality entrenched further.

British colonisation of Bharat was a textbook example of colonisation. Coloniality was omnipresent in Bharat. It manifested in the political, economic, linguistic, cultural, and educational spheres. There was a need for a strategic response to coloniality. Exasperated people revolted in 1857. But it resulted in failure. The strategic resistance to coloniality was provided by four individuals, namely Bal Gangadhar Tilak, Lala Lajpatrai, Bipin Chandra Pal, and Yogi Aravind. It was the renascence of Bharatiya nationalism.

In previous chapters, I have already described the counter-response given by Tilak to coloniality. In *Swarajya*, there is a description of the fight given by Tilak for political freedom. In *Swadeshi*, I have described the battle of Tilak against economic oppression. In *Swabhasha*, there is a description of Tilak's advocacy of Bharatiya languages. In *Swadharma*, there is a description of the views of Tilak on *dharma* and Tilak's comparative analysis of western and Bharatiya philosophies. I have named the chapter *Swadharma* because it is impossible to separate *dharma* and culture in Bharat. Hence, *Swadharma* also highlights Tilak's fight against the cultural subjugation of Bharat by the British. The chapter on 'National Education' describes the faults in the British education system in Bharat, as captured by Tilak and his conceptualisation of national education.

Tilak had firm faith in Hindu *dharma* and culture. He was fully conscious of the glorious ancient past of Bharat. Hence, he never suffered from an inferiority complex. Faith in *dharma* and culture was the base of self-belief, which is the root of self-reliance. This self-reliance manifested itself in names and forms suitable at that time, but the spirit remained the same. An integrated view of Tilak's thoughts provides a clear picture of an edifice of self-reliance. Hence, Lokmanya Tilak is the architect of *Aatmanirbhara Bharat*.

Ten decades have passed since Tilak's death. The present time is starkly different from the time in which Tilak lived. But in this present, all that was in Bharat's past is still dormant; it is not destroyed; it is waiting there to take new forms.[381]

The colonial period was a period of decline for Bharat. The decline was the ebb-movement of a creative spirit which can only be understood by seeing it in the full tide of greatness; the renascence is the return of that great tide, and it is the same spirit that is likely to animate it, although the forms it takes may be quite new.[382] *Aatmanirbhara Bharat* is a framework which will facilitate the renascence of Bharat.

It is important to understand that the principle behind self-reliance remains invariant, even though its forms are variant vis-à-vis time and conditions. A reshaping of the forms of the spirit of self-reliance will have to take place, but it is the spirit behind past forms that we have to disengage and preserve and to give to it new and powerful thought-significances, culture – values and new instrumentation, greater figures.[383] The concept of *Aatmanirbhara Bharat* is a theoretical continuum of the Tilak school of thought.

A nation is a set of people with a common cultural ethos. The culture of a people may be roughly described as the expansion of a consciousness of life which formulates itself in three aspects. The first aspect is philosophy; the second is creative self-expression and appreciative aesthesis, intelligence, and imagination; and the third is practical and outward formulation.[384] Culture and nation are interdependent. A nation without culture is not a nation but just a state!

---

381 Aurobindo, S. (2016). *The renaissance in India*. Sri Aurobindo Ashram (1920). p.12. Aurobindo has not used the word 'self-reliance'.
382 Ibid, p.12.
383 Ibid, p.89.
384 Ibid, p.106.

Bharat is an ancient living civilisation. Today, it is necessary and important to recognise the gulf between what we are and what we may and ought to strive to be.[385] Bharat is a land of *dharma*. *Dharma* is an inner truth and law of each human or cosmic activity. This *dharma* is cast into elaborate form and detailed law of arrangement; its application in fact and rule of life.[386] This elaboration is artistic, spiritual, intellectual, and ethical. This abstract elaboration acquires different names and forms in the physical world, such as philosophy, literature, arts, music, logic, grammar, science, politics, etc. All of this form the core of the Bharatiya civilisation.

Bharatiya civilisation pursued opposite extremes of *Pravrutti* and *Nivrutti*. Yet it is noticeable that this pursuit of the most opposite extremes never resulted in disorder, and its most hedonistic period offers nothing at all that resembles the unbridled corruption which a similar tendency has more than once produced in Europe. Bharatiya mind is not only spiritual and ethical but intellectual and artistic, and both the rule of the intellect and the rhythm of beauty are hostile to the spirit of chaos.[387] This is the essence of Bharatiya consciousness. It is also the fundamental and defining characteristic of Hindus (i.e., *Hindutva*).

Ancient Bharat was the land of peace and wealth due to the absence of chaos. The era of invasion broke the peace and plundered the wealth. The spirit of chaos prevailed in Bharat. It resulted in the furious battle fought by our brave and valorous ancestors to maintain the distinctive Bharatiya identity. The *Vijayanagar* and the Maratha empires (*Hindavi Swarajya*) are the two most successful examples that preserved Bharat's distinctive identity. British snatched the political power from the Maratha empire and started their project of the destruction of the Bharatiya civilisation. The present is only a

---

385 Ibid, p.89.

386 Ibid, p.9.

387 Aurobindo, S. (2016). *The renaissance in India.* Sri Aurobindo Ashram (1920). p.12.

last deposit of the past at a time of ebb.[388] If one insists only on this period, it results in an inaccurate, incomplete, and false description of history. But it is important to understand the causes and nature of the decline. This is because, even in failure, there is a preparation for success: our nights carry in them the secret of a greater dawn.[389]

The greatness of the ideals of the past promises greater ideals in the future. A continual expansion of what stood behind the last endeavour and capacity is the one abiding justification of living culture.[390] Unfortunately, the spirit of self-reliance remained dormant for seven decades of independent Bharat. This dormancy is due to vestiges of coloniality which dominated the public discourse and influenced policymaking. It is extremely important to get rid of this coloniality. Even after seven decades of independence, a strategic and constructive response to coloniality is needed! *Aatmanirbhara Bharat* is a framework for multidimensional reforms that seek to offer a constructive and strategic response to multidimensional coloniality and reshape Bharatiya cultural forms to express more powerfully, intimately, and perfectly its ancient ideal.[391] It leads towards two approaches: the decolonial approach and the civilisational approach. Both approaches depend on each other. The decolonial approach involves the assessment of the origin, history, nature, and current status of coloniality, and the assessment must be based on the Bharatiya civilisational perspective. The civilisational approach involves the study of the origin, history, evolution, nature, and spirit of Bharatiya civilisation. Hence, both approaches are interdependent.

The decolonial approach precisely identifies coloniality which is camouflaged in our institutions. The further objective is eradicating

---

388   Ibid, p.12.
389   Ibid, p.81.
390   Ibid, p.85.
391   The cultural approach is inspired by the following:
      Aurobindo, S. (2016). *The renaissance in India*. Sri Aurobindo Ashram (1920). p.66.

coloniality and recalibrating institutions according to Bharatiya culture. The process of recalibration is called reform. Reforms involve the recalibration of roles played by stakeholders in respective institutions. Reforms are multi-dimensional. They include reforms in the government, economic reforms, reforms regarding languages, cultural reforms, and educational reforms.

Government reforms mean the recalibration of roles of the legislative body, judicial body, and executive body. They also include political, fiscal, military, and judicial reforms. Economic reforms include the recalibration of roles played by the government and the market.[392] Reforms regarding languages include all the reforms which would facilitate the growth of Bharatiya languages. This includes the increasing use of Bharatiya languages in government business, translating or creating content that is not available in Bharatiya languages, promoting education in the mother tongue, etc. Cultural reforms are subtle and profound. They make a base for all other reforms. Cultural reforms involve reshaping Bharatiya cultural forms to express its ancient ideal more powerfully, intimately, and perfectly.[393] Educational reforms involve redefining the roles of stakeholders in the education system. Educational reforms are the backbone of *Aatmanirbhara Bharat*. They aim to infuse self-belief and Bharatiya values in students. Special attention must be given to the teaching of history. This is just a brief description of the reforms. A comprehensive discussion of reforms is out of the scope of this book.

The framework of *Aatmanirbhara Bharat* envisages a complete change in the philosophy governing our institutions. It aims to bring out an absolute change in jurisprudence and political, economic, pedagogical philosophy, etc. It removes unnecessary constraints put on the creative spirit by colonial institutions (which continued even in independent Bharat). Once these constraints are removed, and the

---

392   I have already discussed this issue in the first chapter.
393   Aurobindo, S. (2016). *The renaissance in India*. Sri Aurobindo Ashram (1920). p.66.

spirit of self-belief is infused in the minds of the Bharatiya people, the creative spirit in the Bharatiya people will manifest itself in all possible forms and reach an epitome.

The vision of *Aatmanirbhara Bharat* is not limited to decoloniality. It aims to build a strong, influential, mighty, and vibrant Bharat who would be a contributor in the global arena. It further states that the growth of Bharat should be culture-led growth. It further aims to expand the sphere of influence of Bharat by creating a greater Bharat (*Brihat Bharat*). *Brihat Bharat* is to be achieved by spreading Bharatiya culture in our distant neighbourhood. The epitome of the vision behind the framework of *Aatmanirbhara Bharat* is to become *Vishwaguru*.

Aatmanirbhara Bharat is about regaining what was lost. It includes territory, status, wealth, power, prestige, etc. It requires effort from all possible directions. It cannot be left just in the hands of the government. It demands efforts from individuals, families, and society. This is a reawakening, resurgence, and renascence of a great civilisation.

I firmly believe that, among all possible paths, the path of self-reliance is the only one that brings about the material, moral and cultural renascence of a dormant nation and raises it to the greatest level by peaceful revolution.

www.ingramcontent.com/pod-product-compliance
Lightning Source LLC
Chambersburg PA
CBHW071425130726
47996CB00011B/91